101 Key Terms in Philosophy and Their Importance for Theology

101 Key Terms in Philosophy and Their Importance for Theology

Kelly James Clark
Richard Lints
James K. A. Smith

Westminster John Knox Press
LOUISVILLE • LONDON

Book design by Sharon Adams
Cover design by Eric Walljasper, Minneapolis, MN

First edition
Published by Westminster John Knox Press
Louisville, Kentucky

This book is printed on acid-free paper that meets the American National Standards Institute Z39.48 standard. ♾

PRINTED IN THE UNITED STATES OF AMERICA

04 05 06 07 08 09 10 11 12 13 — 10 9 8 7 6 5 4 3 2 1

Library of Congress Cataloging-in-Publication Data

Clark, Kelly James, 1956–
    101 key terms in philosophy and their importance for theology /
Kelly James Clark, Richard Lints, James K. A. Smith.—1st ed.
        p. cm.
    ISBN 0-664-22524-1 (alk. paper)
    1. Christianity—Philosophy—Terminology.   I. Title: One hundred one key
terms in philosophy and their importance for theology.   II. Title: One hundred
and one key terms in philosophy and their importance for theology.
III. Lints, Richard.   IV. Smith, James K. A., 1970–   V. Title.

BR100.C5415   2004
103—dc22   2003064507

Contents

Introduction:
A Reader's Guide

GENESIS AND TELOS

About two years ago Donald McKim, editor of Westminster John Knox Press, approached Kelly James Clark with the idea of writing a philosophical dictionary for theologians. Ever the competitor, Kelly was excited by the offer because one of his colleagues had just written a philosophical dictionary replete with about 300 terms. He was hoping to write 301 terms to beat his colleague, and secretly dreamed of defining 325 terms to make the victory decisive! But Don said he wanted a mere 101 terms, and that is what we agreed to do.

Although Kelly specializes in philosophical theology, he confesses to being a rank amateur at theology *simpliciter*. So he enlisted his old friend Richard Lints, who was trained in both philosophy and theology and teaches at Gordon-Conwell Theological Seminary. When it became obvious to them that neither Richard nor Kelly was competent to write on continental philosophy, Kelly recruited his colleague and friend Jamie Smith to fill in the gaps; Jamie ended up contributing a number of noncontinental entries as well.

The dictionary is aimed at anyone interested in theology and students of theology, as well as pastors and other practitioners. As such, we have tried to assume little philosophical knowledge and have aimed at maximizing accessibility. We have also attempted to determine the philosophical terms, concepts, and names that the theology student is likely to encounter in his or her study of theology.

SELECTION OF TERMS

This small dictionary makes no pretensions of being exhaustive, though we do hope it is both representative and comprehensive. Being limited to 101 terms required that we be selective, so a word about the criteria for such selection is in order. First, the dictionary tries to address both classical philosophical and theological questions as well as contemporary concerns. This dictionary has a specific context; if we were writing such a book in 1950, its shape would undoubtedly be quite different—even in the way that we engage classical figures and problems. We have tried to provide a resource for theologians at the advent of the twenty-first century who are grappling with phenomena such as "postmodernism" and "deconstruction," but our contemporary location also means that the questions we bring to Augustine and Aquinas have a unique shape and concern. In trying to craft timely explanations, however, we have tried to avoid discussions that are merely trendy. Nonetheless, the book is deeply rooted in history; the most cited terms are Plato, Augustine, Aquinas, and the Enlightenment. Thus, we hope the book will find a long life of usefulness.

Second, it must be kept in mind that this is a collection of *philosophical* terms and figures as they relate to theology and does not attempt to be a "theological dictionary." Readers will not find any entries on "soteriology" or "perichoresis," "Karl Barth" or "Paul Tillich." These would be entries in standard theological dictionaries. (Where we do discuss classical theologians such as Augustine or Aquinas, we have tried to focus especially on their philosophical contributions.) Instead, we have chosen to discuss philosophical terms and figures as they bear constructively on theology. Nonetheless we have discussed a few theological terms—*hell*, for example—which have inspired rich philosophical reflection. Two provisos should be noted on this score: on the one hand, there are many philosophical questions and figures not included here (e.g., discussions of W. V. O. Quine or philosophy of mathematics). This is because many philosophical themes have not had much bearing on theological discussions. On the other hand, there are theological loci that do not receive much attention here (e.g., eschatology) because there has not been much infiltration of philosophical language into these theological discussions. Overall, we urge the reader to keep in mind our boundaries of 101 terms and the necessary selectivity such a boundary entails.

Third, we have offered a balance between discussion of historical figures and philosophical concepts. Undoubtedly, with the constraints of selection in mind, this means that we inevitably end up with a kind of "implied canon," to which can be posed all kinds of questions: Why Scotus but not Bonaventure? Why Pseudo-Dionysius and not Teresa of Avila? Why feminism but not critical race theory? While all such questions are legitimate, we plead innocence on the basis of limitations. Moreover, our account of historical figures could not do justice to more nuanced interpretations and critical scholarship. Instead, our presentations of historical figures are representative of a "received" tradition, taking into consideration what Gadamer describes as the "history of effect." So, for example, the picture of Plato or the Stoics offered here is a common, received understanding of Plato or the Stoics as they have been appropriated in Western philosophical and theological traditions. More critical discussions will be found in works listed in the bibliography. With space for 101 terms, we needed to make some hard decisions, crafting a dictionary that would have the broadest possible utility. We concede that this inevitably entails silence in some areas and blind spots in others, but we hope that the result is a dictionary that remains comprehensive.

A USER'S GUIDE

This book can be put to use in several different ways. Sometimes the reader or student will come across a term such as "nihilism" or a name such as "Martin Heidegger" and will be able to turn directly to the alphabetically listed entry here. However, the coverage and comprehensiveness of the dictionary are not fully indicated by the list of terms itself. Under the rubric of these 101 terms, we have also addressed a number of other key issues and figures. For instance, a student may in her reading come across the name "Jacques Derrida" and wonder just who he is and what he is about. While she will not find an entry on Derrida here, if she turns to the comprehensive cross-reference index at the back of the book, she will find that there is an extensive discussion of Derrida in the entry on "Deconstruction." Or if someone wonders what "empiricism" is, in the index he could find that a discussion of empiricism and rationalism is included in the entry on "Epistemology." So while the list of terms is a first point of reference, the cross-reference index should prove invaluable for mining the resources of this dictionary. In addition, asterisks mark terms for which there are complete entries.

A second way to utilize this book would be to follow several of the references in the *See also* section at the end of each entry. These sections point the reader to related topics, figures, or movements where some of the ideas might be discussed more thoroughly. One could then proceed to the *See also* section at the end of that entry and follow the path of thought. Such a "chain reference" kind of study would give a comprehensive picture of the issues.

Finally, the book could be utilized as a bibliography of valuable books on the various topics. At the end of each entry is a bibliography. Most of the items in the bibliography are philosophical, but we have also tried to include philosophically informed theological texts. We have tried to list the items in each bibliography from the most reader-friendly to the most difficult.

ACKNOWLEDGMENTS

Kelly James Clark spearheaded this project, first conceiving it and enlisting the aid of Richard Lints and Jamie Smith, then shepherding it through to its completion. Rick and Jamie would like to thank Kelly for his leadership in the project. Kelly would like to thank Donald McKim for the invitation and Calvin College for supporting his sabbatical, which enabled him to finish the project. Special thanks is given to Angela Scheff, Kelly's former student, for her kind assistance in editing the volume. Thanks also to Michael Murry for his help with Leibniz, and Lee Hardy for his insights on Kant and Reid.

Aesthetics   The field of philosophy that investigates the nature of art. The term is coined from the Greek *aesthesis,* which refers to perception by the senses. Art, then, is primarily a sensuous phenomenon, engaging the senses of sight, hearing, smell, and so forth. However, precisely because of this, art and the aesthetic has been an object of reproach since *Plato. In the final book of the *Republic,* Plato launched an attack on art as deceptive and dissimulating, utilizing sensible pleasure to draw the soul away from reflection on the real, intelligible, and immaterial forms. Thus, because "*truth" was identified with rational, cognitive knowledge (such as the abstract knowledge of the Pythagorean theorem or the idea of *justice), followers of Plato have tended to disparage art because of its sensuous materiality. Art, in short, is not a medium of *truth;* in fact, because of its intimate link to the senses, it is considered deceptive. This *epistemological critique of art was coupled with an *ontological criticism of matter and materiality as "less real" than immaterial reality.

This Platonic devaluing of art spilled over into the early church, which tended to adopt a Platonic philosophical framework, inducing a suspicion about the aesthetic. This crystallized in a major eighth-century debate regarding *icons,* images used as aids in worship of the triune God (carefully distinguished from *idols,* which were treated as objects of worship). The iconoclasts rejected icons as inherently idolatrous, based on the Platonic critique of art coupled with an appeal to the Second Commandment. But in *On Divine Images,* John of Damascus articulated a careful defense of the use of images in orthodox worship, and thus justified the aesthetic as such, appealing to the central Christian doctrines of Creation (materiality is affirmed as good) and Incarnation (Christ is described as the "image *[eikon]* of God" [Colossians 1:15]). While John's primary concern was sacred or liturgical art, his arguments have been echoed as a justification of art *simpliciter.*

While strands of Christian, especially Protestant, theology have adopted the more rationalistic stance of Plato, throughout history many theologians have affirmed the aesthetics as a central medium of both revelation and truth, particularly Neoplatonic theologians such as Bonaventure. This emphasis on the aesthetics has received renewed interest in contemporary theology due to the work of Hans Urs von Balthasar, Jean-Luc Marion, and Jeremy Begbie. At the core of these theological aesthetics (or aesthetic theologies) is a rejection of the *rationalist axiom,* which assumes that truth is communicated only in cognitive propositions. Rather, there is a mode of truth telling that is unique to the aesthetic or "affective," that cannot be reduced to cognitive propositions. Appeal is often made to the liturgy itself as an example of this, particularly the rich eucharistic liturgies of Orthodox and Catholic traditions, where all of the senses are engaged in order to communicate the truth of grace. Theological aesthetics has entailed a double development: both a renewed interest in the arts and a retooling of theology in response to aesthetic reality.
See also Epistemology, Plato.

Bibliography. Jeremy Begbie, *Voicing Creation's Praise;* idem, *Beholding the Glory;* Hilary Brand and Adrienne Chaplin, *Art and Soul;* Hans Urs von Balthasar, *The Glory of the Lord;* Nicholas Wolterstorff, *Art in Action.*

Analytic/Continental Philosophy

Two schools or camps within contemporary *philosophy. *Analytic philosophy* is often called "Anglo-American" philosophy because of its provenance in the British Isles and the United States. Stemming from the work of Gottlob Frege and the early writings of Edmund Husserl, classic representatives include Ludwig *Wittgenstein, Bertrand Russell, the *logical *positivists, W. V. O. Quine, Donald Davidson, Saul Kripke, and Alvin Plantinga. *Continental philosophy* originates from continental Europe, particularly Germany and France. Tracing its lineage to Immanuel *Kant and Georg Wilhelm Friedrich *Hegel, representative figures in continental philosophy include Martin *Heidegger, Jean-Paul Sartre, Emmanuel Levinas, Jacques Derrida, and Michel Foucault. There has traditionally been a great deal of hostility between these two schools, but this is largely based on caricatures: analytic philosophy is caricatured as synonymous with logical positivism and as obsessed with fine but ultimately meaningless distinctions; continental philosophy is caricatured as *nihilistic and disdainful of logical argument. Any real distinction between the two should be understood as heuristic, and the two schools are certainly not mutually exclusive. Nevertheless, we can define some broad differences.

In analytic philosophy, priority is placed on distilling the essential propositions and arguments from texts in order to evaluate their cogency. In other words, the goal of philosophy is to tackle problems by clearly defining terms of a debate and then constructing arguments whereby true conclusions can be ascertained (or false conclusions unmasked). Propositions are taken to be eternal or timeless and so are not significantly conditioned by sociohistorical context. Thus, once someone distills a proposition, say, from *Aquinas's *Summa Theologica*, it really matters little who said it, or when it was said, or the influences on the philosopher who said it. What matters is the statement itself and the role it plays in an argument. As expected, in this school of thought the history of philosophy often has little or no role to play except as a source of arguments. Thus, in graduate programs in the analytic tradition, there are sometimes no requirements in the history of philosophy but instead rigorous requirements in logic.

In continental philosophy, emphasis is placed on the history of philosophy, with the consequence of sometimes devaluing logic (many continental graduate programs do not have requirements in logic). This grows out of basic convictions, for in the continental school there is a greater appreciation for the inescapability of *tradition* and for the *existential* (rather than logical) aspect of philosophical questioning. There is a deep sense of the historical nature of philosophy itself and significance is placed on the fact that a claim or argument is made by a particular philosopher, at a particular time, in a particular place, within a particular context of debate, and so forth.

Both traditions have provided resources for theological thought, and recent generations of philosophers and theologians seem to be coming to appreciate the complementarity of these two traditions.

See also Deconstruction, Epistemology, Essence/Essentialism, Logic, Metaphysics/Ontology, Mind, Necessity, Ontotheology, Phenomenology, Philosophy, Positivism, Postmodernism, Realism/Anti-Realism, Truth, Underdetermination, Wittgenstein.

Bibliography. Simon Critchley, *Continental Philosophy*; W. T. Jones and Robert Fogelin, *A History of Western Philosophy*; C. G. Prado, *A House Divided*.

Anselm   Saint Anselm (1033–1109) was born in Italy and entered a monastery in Normandy where he eventually served as abbot and later became archbishop of Canterbury. Sometimes referred to as "the Second *Augustine," Anselm affirmed the Augustinian priority of *faith to *reason and the Augustinian synthesis of Christianity and *Neoplatonic *metaphysics. Contemporary interest in Anselm's work centers on the explication of his philosophical method, *fides quarens intellectum* (faith seeking understanding), and the elaboration of the ontological argument for *God's existence. Anselm's theological reputation rests on his defense of the substitutionary theory of the atonement.

As with his intellectual forefather Augustine, the greatness of God plays a significant role in Anselm's thought. Anselm attractively defines God as "that being than which none greater can be conceived." According to this definition, God has every great-making property and has it infinitely. So, for example, since power, intellect, and goodness are great-making properties, God has these properties and has them infinitely: God is *omnipotent, *omniscient, and perfectly *good. If God were to lack a great-making property, we could conceive of a being greater than God, namely, the one with all of God's properties plus the great-making property that God lacks. And if God failed to infinitely possess a great-making power, we could conceive of a being greater than God, namely, one with more power or intelligence or whatever property God lacked. A brief way of putting the ontological argument is as follows:

1. God has every great-making property.
2. Existence is a great-making property ("it is greater to exist in reality than to exist in the mind alone").
3. Therefore, God exists.

This simple yet beguiling argument has been variously described as charming or cruel. It has earned the privilege of being one of the most universally attacked arguments in all of *philosophy.

Anselm's sharpest critic, a fellow monk by the name of Gaunilo, offered a counterargument in which he "proved" the existence of the most perfect island. But no such island could be "proven" to exist by mere intellectual reflection, anymore than God's existence could be so proved. Anselm replied that though Guanilo's reasoning may apply to things like islands, it did not apply to God for the very reason that the concept of maximal greatness applies to God alone. In medieval terms, God's existence and God's *essence are one and the same. Later critics such as *Kant contended

that existence is not a predicate and so existence is not a great-making property. In spite of vehement criticism, the beguiling ontological argument has been revived in the late twentieth century by Charles Hartshorne and Alvin Plantinga in versions unsusceptible to the traditional criticisms.

Anselm also defends a modified cosmological argument for the existence of God in his work *Monologion*. He argues simply that the fact of goodness begs for an origin: if there are good things then there must be an ultimate Good. Here Anselm follows the method of "faith seeking understanding." Believing that God is ultimately good, Anselm supposes that God must be the One that makes sense of all else that is good. Therefore, in reverse, if there are good things, there must be a final Good.

In his treatise *Cur Deus Homo (Why God Became Man)*, Anselm argues for the intrinsic rationality of the atonement without appeal to the biblical evidence (which he nonetheless supposed to be authoritative). Writing in the social context of feudalism, Anselm borrows the metaphor of "honor" and applies it to the redemptive story of the gospel. Redemption is rooted in the satisfaction rendered to God for the dishonor done to God by human sinfulness. Anselm dispenses with the older notion that Christ came to pay a ransom to the devil, reasoning that God could never be under debt to anyone, including the devil. Rather, Christ pays the debt of honor that humans owe God. In this sense, the atonement is substitutionary.

Anselm believes that the greatness of God is the center around which the entire philosophical and theological edifice is built. Anselm captures the Augustinian tendency to define God as the greatest possible being. This Anselmian intuition has influenced the development of what we now refer to as classical theism, the notion that God has a set of properties that *logic demands to be regarded as infinite and maximally perfect.

Bibliography. G. R. Evans, *Anselm;* idem, *Anselm and Talking About God;* Thomas Morris, *Anselmian Explorations;* idem, *Our Idea of God;* R. W. Southern, *Saint Anselm.*

Anthropomorphic Language In the Bible *God is called Father, sovereign, love, patient, *good, and friend. In addition, God is described as having eyes, ears, hands, feet, and a body. In what sense do these terms apply to God? We understand the term *father,* for example, in reference to our biological male progenitors. Our conception of sovereignty is bound up in our understanding of earthly monarchies. We understand these terms as they apply to humans. In what sense do human terms apply to God? The problem of anthropomorphic language (ascribing human attributes to nonhuman things) in describing God is a function of *transcendence. If God is transcendent, then God vastly exceeds human cognition and language. If God wishes to communicate to human beings, God must accommodate to human understanding. Does human language enable, limit, distort, or deceive human beliefs about God?

Attributions of body parts to God have almost universally been rejected as mere anthropomorphism. But beyond these terms, how do we decide which ones do apply to God? The Judeo-Christian-Muslim tradition claim that humans are created in the image of God implies that humans share properties with God. Perhaps we, like God, are knowers, moral agents, and capable of having dominion and entering into significant relationships with other people. But we also have feelings. Does God have feelings? In addition, although we know things, we rely on others to teach us and forget a great deal. Is God depen-

dent on others for God's knowledge, and does God forget? Humans also sin as well as change. Is God likewise morally imperfect and mutable (changeable)?

There is no simple, rule-governed means of determining which anthropomorphic terms are mere anthropomorphisms and which roughly (analogically) describe God's nature. The dominant tradition in Christian thought asserts that most anthropomorphic language—the vast array of biblical texts that ascribe human characteristics to God—should not be understood literally.

The issue of anthropomorphism arises not only in theological contexts, but also in contexts where people try to refute the existence of God. Consider the Christian's understanding of God's goodness in terms of paternal care. If our heavenly Father cares for his spiritual children as an earthly father cares for his biological children, then God the Father must be good to his children as earthly fathers are to their children. God, therefore, has an obligation to prevent the same harms that an earthly parent would be obliged to prevent. But such harms have not been prevented. Countless harms have occurred that an earthly parent, if present and able, would have been obliged to prevent. Hence, God the Father does not exist.

The Christian might respond that God's fatherhood is not like any earthly parent or that God is good but not in a sense that humans can grasp. But this would entail that we really have no idea what we mean when we say "God is Father" or "God is good." If we are too anthropomorphic, God is just a big human being; if we are insufficiently anthropomorphic, God becomes utter mystery. The need for a golden mean between the excesses and deficiencies of anthropomorphic language is clear. The doctrine of *analogy* affirms this golden mean by suggesting that our language for God does tell us something *true about, for instance, God's goodness, but that there is also an eminent difference between our goodness and God's.

See also Aquinas, Augustine, Eternal/ Everlasting, Hermeneutics, Ontotheology, Religious Language, Theodicy.

Bibliography. Walter Brueggemann, William C. Placher, and Brian K. Blount, *Struggling with Scripture.*

Anti-Realism   *See* Realism/ Anti-Realism

Apologetics   From the Greek word *apologia* ("to provide a defense," as in 1 Peter 3:15), apologetics is the art of defending a claim against objections. As applied to Christian belief, it involves a defense of the central truths of Christianity (e.g., existence of *God, the deity of Jesus, the reliability of the Bible, the resurrection). In the patristic era, apologetics was primarily defensive, responding to specific objections against Christianity. Two of the common objections to Christianity in the earliest period of church history were that members of the church were cannibalistic (John 6:53, "Jesus said, 'I tell you the truth, unless you eat the flesh of the Son of Man and drink his blood, you have no life in you'") and sexually promiscuous (John 13:34, "A new command I give you: love one another. As I have loved you, so you must love one another"). Apologetics in this period was concerned with clarifying misunderstandings.

With the advent of the Christian empire in the early medieval period, apologetics became much more expansive. The project of defending the *faith became one of providing the grounds that establish the Christian faith as the only reasonable conviction. It ceased being defensive and sought rather to demonstrate from commonly accepted beliefs or principles of *reason that Christian belief met all the necessary rational criteria. Such apologetics was based on the assumption of a universal rationality common to all human beings, which could be employed as an objective criterion for demonstrating the truth of the Christian faith. Such a project is modeled in *Aquinas's *Summa Contra Gentiles.* Aquinas, in his *Summa Theologica,* also developed proofs for *God's existence from philosophical notions of contingency, *causality, *necessity, and morality. Augustine, in his *City of God,* attempted to answer radical objections to the very foundations of Christian faith and to manifest the intellectual superiority of the Christian faith to all other rival religions.

During the Enlightenment era apologists offered new sorts of arguments in defense of increasing attacks on God in general and Christianity in particular. The rise of science seemed to indicate a world that functioned independently of God and some thought that natural laws precluded the miraculous. John Locke (1632–1704) defended the reasonableness of Christianity within the Enlightenment strictures on reason. *Kant attempted to demonstrate the moral necessity of belief in God and to understand as much of Christian doctrine as possible within the sphere of reason (and in so doing dramatically reinterpreted the doctrines). As astronomical phenomena seemed less and less in need of God as an adequate explanation, apologists began to exploit the biological realm as singularly in need of a creator. In the late 18th century William Paley would defend God's existence based on the apparent design of, for example, the camel's hump and human eye. In the early 19th century leading Christian scientists in England developed the multi-volume *Bridgewater Treatises* which offered a host of scientific evidences to prove "the Power, Wisdom, and Goodness of God as manifested in the Creation." Darwin's *Origin of Species* was a sustained attack on the belief in design exemplified in Paley and the *Bridgewater Treatises.*

The twentieth century saw major challenges to both medieval and Enlightenment notions of a natural rationality common to all of humanity. In the wake of these challenges came significant rethinking about the nature and purposes of Christian apologetics, resulting in the development of different apologetic "schools." There are some holdouts for the medieval view of reason: asserting their commitment to the notion of a neutral, autonomous rationality common to all, the evidentialist school (sometimes called "classical apologetics") holds that Christian theism can be demonstrated as true on the basis of evidence which is available to everyone. One motivation for holding this view is that it seems to make nonbelievers strongly responsible for their unbelief because God has made God's existence evident to everyone. Some apologists, aware of the problems with the neutral, autonomous reason, offer "proofs" for God's existence that are non-coercive: that is, they offer what they take to be true or reasonable premises in support of God's existence or in support of Christian beliefs, recognizing that one could reasonably accept the premises but is not obligated to do so. Non-evidentialist schools (such as "presuppositionalist apologetics" or "Reformed *epistemology") argue that everyone has assumptions that condition what counts as "rational" and thus influence the assessment of evidence. In other words, there is no neutral "reason"; instead, what is "rational" is conditioned by *pre*-rational beliefs and assumptions. As such, there can be no appeal to a neutral reason as arbiter. Moreover, as emphasized in Reformed epistemology, the Christian is rational to *begin from* her Christian beliefs.

Bibliography. Avery Dulles, *A History of Apologetics*; William Lane Craig, *Reasonable Faith*; Steven Cowan, ed., *Five Views on Apologetics*; Michael Murray, ed., *Reason for the Hope Within*; Peter Kreeft and Ronald Tacelli, *Handbook of Christian Apologetics*.

Aquinas, Thomas (1225–1274)   The most influential philosopher-theologian of the medieval era. Aquinas was born, raised, and educated in Italy. He entered the Dominican order as a young man against his parents' wishes and remained a teacher at Paris and Naples in that order for the remainder of his life. He was a prodigious author whose works run the gamut of theological and philosophical topics. His most influential works are the *Summa Theologica (Summary of Theology)* and *Summa Contra Gentiles (Against the Gentiles)*, which offer a remarkable synthesis of the two great philosophical traditions of the ancient world, Aristotleanism and *Neoplatonism, in defense of the Christian *faith. His life was brought to a close shortly after a mystical vision of *God at the age of forty-eight.

The greater part of Aquinas's corpus is directly theological, though he has many strictly philosophical works as well (in particular, his commentaries on *Aristotle). He distinguished the two disciplines (theology and *philosophy) according to two distinct methods. Theology begins with belief in God and reasons on the basis of divine revelation to the implications for the created order. Philosophy begins with the created order and attempts to display—on the basis of pure natural *reason—the knowledge of God both as the creative *cause of all that is and the end toward which everything is directed. There can be no final conflict between the *truths discovered by one method as against the other, for God is the author of all that is. Philosophy may prove certain truths of theology (e.g., the existence of God), may illuminate other truths it cannot prove (e.g., the Trinity), and may answer objections to Christian belief lodged against it by detractors (e.g., the problem of *evil). Aquinas thus made a distinction between the "preambles of the faith" (such as the existence of one God), which could be known and demonstrated by reason alone, and the "articles of faith" (such as the Trinity), which could be known only by divine revelation. Salvific knowledge, therefore, requires revelation: grace *completes* nature.

Since the philosopher is limited to reason as his or her *source of knowledge, God can be studied by the philosopher only as the cause of finite beings. Our knowledge of these finite beings is found in our sensory experience of them. This knowledge is guided by first principles that are self-evident (e.g., the laws of *logic and mathematics and *metaphysical principles). The wise person always reasons in accord with those first principles and looks for order in the universe as a result. Aquinas believed that things happen for a reason and ultimately those things make sense. It is the task of the wise person to make this manifest.

The "five ways" of Aquinas offer five different kinds of evidence that can be accounted for only on the basis of God's existence. The evidences marshaled in the five arguments include change, motion, contingency, cause, and morality/goodness. These natural phenomena force one to conclude that there must be a Creator of all that is but that is not itself created. Echoes of Aristotle's unmoved Mover are strong. Each of the five ways argues from facts about the created order to the Creator. Aquinas assumed that all rational creatures would accept these arguments if they were in fact acting rationally. He also assumed that the link between the created order and the Creator is not a point of great doubt. The rise of *modern science would question this linkage. And Aquinas failed to anticipate contemporary doubts about a universal standard of rationality to which all persons must submit. Aquinas lived in an age of belief and his arguments belong in that context.

For Aquinas, God is known by analogy with the creation. Claims to possess univocal knowledge (terms applying identically) of God are always false according to Aquinas, since our knowledge of God is always limited, finite, and mediated through the natural order. God may only be seen in the reflection of the creation. Humans may use words about themselves (e.g., good) and try then to apply them to God, but they must not forget the radical differences between themselves and God. The difference between the goodness of humans and the goodness of God is the difference between the finite and the infinite. This does not render our knowledge of God null and void. It merely reminds us that the creature and the Creator are vastly different even if they are also similar in some respects.

Aquinas's ethics have also made a significant impact on theology. Drawing on a tradition of both natural law and virtue ethics (following Aristotle), Aquinas's distinctly Christian ordering of the virtues made charity (love) that to which all others were ordered. In other words, love was the condition of possibility for authentic virtue. He also distinguished between "natural" virtues and "theological" virtues: natural or moral virtues (such as courage and temperance) are possible for all human beings and are aimed at human *happiness (*eudaimonia*); "theological" virtues (such as faith, hope, and love) are infused by God and have God as their object. As such, they are possible only for those who are part of the body of Christ. By focusing on virtue, Aquinas emphasized that "being good" is a matter not of external rules but internal character formation. His *ethical thought has been important for the contemporary revival of virtue ethics.

See also Anselm; Anthropomorphic Language; Aristotle; Augustine; Being and Goodness; Eternal/Everlasting; Free Will; God, Nature of; Happiness; Hell; Metaphysics/Ontology; Natural Theology; Ontotheology; Pseudo-Dionysius; Reason and Belief in God; Religious Language; Scholasticism; Theistic Arguments; Transcendence.

Bibliography. Ralph McInerny, *St. Thomas Aquinas*; Brian Davies, *The Thought of Thomas Aquinas*; Nicholas Healy, *Thomas Aquinas*; Etienne Gilson, *The Christian Philosophy of St. Thomas Aquinas*; Jaroslav Pelikan, *The Christian Tradition*; Eleonore Stump, *Aquinas*.

Aristotle (384–322 B.C.E.)   One of the two fountainheads (along with *Plato) of *philosophy in the West. Aristotle was born in Stagira, Greece, to Nichomacus, the court physician. Coming to Athens as a teenager to study at Plato's academy, Aristotle remained there for nearly twenty years. After Plato's death, Aristotle embarked on a series of travels, resulting in a wealth of biological and zoological discoveries. In 342 he became tutor to Alexander, son of King Philip of Macedon, who later became Alexander the Great. Aristotle returned to Athens in 335 and founded the school Lyceum. During this period most of Aristotle's writings took shape, largely as lecture notes written either by him or by his students. Following Alexander's death in 323, and no longer in possession of the king's favor, Aristotle voluntarily went into exile, "lest Athens sin twice against philosophy" (they sinned first when they sentenced Socrates to death).

Aristotle's relationship to his mentor, Plato, remains a source of great debate and controversy. Aristotle is usually considered the prototypical empiricist and Plato the prototypical rationalist. But we ought to be cautious of the traditional (and sometimes simplistic) contrast between Plato's otherwordly and abstract orientation in opposition to Aristotle's concern for concrete observation both of nature and of human thought.

Aristotle believed that all knowledge begins with sense experience: there is nothing in the *mind, he said, that is not first in the senses. There is a genuine order to be found in nature, and it can be known, if imperfectly, through careful observation. Aristotle was also convinced that the human mind is so constructed as to operate according to fixed principles of rationality mirroring the fixed patterns of nature. These patterns of thinking are organized under the traditional (i.e., Aristotelian) concepts of *logic.

Everything in nature is a combination of form and matter. The form of an object is its end or purpose. Its matter is the physical stuff of which a thing is made. These sorts of things can be explained in terms of the four causes—material, efficient, formal, and final—which act on things. The *material cause* includes the stuff from which an object is created. The *efficient cause* is the means by which it is created (the means by which the stuff is given form). The *formal cause* is the essence of what an object is. And the *final cause* is the goal or purpose of it. Consider Michelangelo's sculpture *David* (since sculptures are artifacts and not natural objects this is a bad but useful example). Its material cause is the marble of which it is made. Its efficient cause is the sculptor who forms the marble into shape. The formal cause is Michelangelo's idea of the completed statue. And the final cause is what motivated Michelangelo to sculpt the *David*—for beauty, for example, or profit. Formal and final causes are the most important as they provide the best explanation of an object. The final cause (purpose or goal) of a thing is the object in the fully realized perfection of itself (it is an objective property of objects, not imposed on the object by humans, as it is in the *David* example).

In his *Metaphysics*, Aristotle offered a version of the cosmological argument for the existence of God based on the motion of things, concluding that there must be a first and unmoved Mover. Based on his views of the good life as contemplation of the highest things (namely, *God), the Prime Mover sits in his heavenly realm and thinks only of himself. Aristotle's God "reigns but doesn't rule." God is a being that possesses everlasting life and perfect bliss, engaged in contemplation of the highest good, namely, God's self.

Aristotle's moral vision, especially in his *Nicomachean Ethics*, begins with the observation that all human actions are goal-directed and that the ultimate goal of all human action is *happiness (*eudaimonia*). Happiness is the highest *good (*summum bonum*) that orders our lives. Happiness is found in the life of virtue, particularly in the contemplation of the

Divine. Virtues are character traits that regulate our desires and are discoverable through the doctrine of the mean. The doctrine of the mean finds the virtue in the mean between the excessive or deficient expression of our desires. For example, courage is the virtue, the mean between the excess of foolhardiness and the deficiency of cowardice. Aristotelian virtues include courage, generosity, civility, wittiness, modesty, and high-mindedness (often translated "pride" but means something like a healthy self-respect). In addition, Aristotle thought that the happy life required external conditions of happiness, such as friends, good looks, and sufficient money to provide for the leisure that contemplation requires. Unlike "rules-based" theories, his account of ethics stresses the need for internal transformation and "character development" in ways consistent with the Pauline vision of the work and fruits of the Holy Spirit (Galatians 5).

Aristotle's metaphysics, including God, and conception of the good life would have an influence on Christianity, especially the Roman branch, after it was appropriated by Thomas *Aquinas. Despite Martin Luther's vigorous condemnation of Aristotle, his logical categories, as well as the analysis of different kinds of causality (efficient, formal, material, and final causes) would be employed by post-Reformation theologians in order to think about a diversity of topics such as the decrees of *God, human freedom, and the doctrine of creation.

See also Aquinas; Cause/Causality; Cosmology; Epistemology; Ethics; God, Nature of; Happiness; Immutability and Impassibility; Natural Theology; Plato and Platonism; Realism/Anti-Realism; Teleology; Truth; Universals.

Bibliography. Jonathan Barnes, *Aristotle: A Very Short Introduction*; Jonathan Barnes, ed., *The Cambridge Companion to Aristotle*; David Furley, *From Aristotle to Augustine*; Mark Jordan, *On Aquinas' Alleged Aristotelianism*.

Atheism   The denial of the existence of a *god or gods. Atheism is assumed in a variety of worldviews including secular humanism, materialism, and *naturalism. Adherents attempt to develop their nontheistic commitments into a complete philosophical system. What sort of *metaphysical, natural, and *ethical systems are possible if one begins with a denial of the existence of God?

The atheistic worldview holds that matter and/or energy (i.e., something nondivine) have existed *eternally, that everything is matter/energy (materialism) in various configurations governed by natural laws. If materialism is true, then *mind is matter or brain. If everything is governed by natural law (naturalism), then the universe, according to the atheist, is closed off to *miracles or perhaps even to *free will.

There are two primary, evidential, reasons alleged in favor of atheism: lack of evidence and the problem of *evil. Since God is intangible, there must be some means of rational access to the Divine. Historically, theistic arguments were offered to bridge this gap, but atheists and many theists consider these arguments unsuccessful. Bertrand Russell was once asked what he would say if he were to come before God. Russell replied, "Not enough evidence, God. Not enough evidence." The problem of human suffering is a powerful reason for atheism. For example, many Jews who lived through a death camp found it impossible to believe in God after their experience. Nonevidentialist atheisms—such as found in Sigmund *Freud and Karl *Marx—do not appeal to evidence, but rather reexplain theism in terms of "wish fulfillment" or "illusion."

Theists often believe that if they were to give up their religious beliefs, they would lose their sense of morality. On this point Dostoevsky is often quoted: "If God does not exist, everything is permitted." However, there are morally good atheists and atheists who have developed nontheistic foundations of morality. Social contract theorists, inspired by the work of Thomas Hobbes, offer one such account. According to this view, right and wrong are what rationally self-interested individuals would agree to in order to live in peace with one another. Social contract theories of morality require only human agreement and human punishments to enforce the agreement. Whether this is an adequate account of morality is a subject of much contemporary debate.

Humanism, in its secular form, is an antitheistic *philosophy that centers on humans. Humanism asserts the profound value of human beings, is committed to the natural world of which humans are natural products, and seeks a just social system in which humans can flourish in the here and now.

See also Apologetics; Dualism/Monism; Enlightenment; Evil, Problem of; Existentialism; Feuerbach; Freud; Hume; Kant; Marx; Modernity/Modernism; Naturalism; Nihilism; Positivism; Postmodernism; Reason and Belief in God; Theistic Arguments.

Bibliography. Stan Wallace, ed., *Does God Exist?*; Michael Buckley, *At the Origins of Modern Atheism*; Bertrand Russell, *Why I Am Not a Christian*; Robin Le Poidevin, *Arguing for Atheism*; Merold Westphal, *Suspicion and Faith.*

Augustine (354–430) Perhaps the greatest influence on Christian theology, Augustine was born in North Africa and was later appointed bishop of Hippo. His theology, as found in *Confessions, The City of God,* and *The Trinity* (among his over one hundred books), is a distinct combination of Scripture, *Neoplatonism, and *Stoicism, generating special tensions in his thought. His most famous quotation, "You have made us for yourself and our hearts are restless until they rest in you," captures his own personal journey from rebellion to peace with *God by *reason and grace. The false and seductive paths that carried him away

from God could not satisfy him because we are, after all, made for God.

Augustine's biblical theology of grace (he is referred to as the *doctor gratia*) begins with the doctrine of original sin as rooted in his understanding of the fall of Adam. Because the fall of Adam was due to his exercise of *free will, God is not blameworthy for the *evil in the world. This undergirds Augustine's account of evil as "privation" or lack. Since all that exists only exists because of God's creative work, and because God is perfectly *good, nothing that "exists" can be properly evil. Instead, we must understand evil as a *lack* of existence—a parasitic corrosion of good existing things. This is why Augustine will affirm that even Satan, insofar as he *exists,* cannot be absolutely evil. This corruption of a good creation is a result of the (free) sin of Adam (or ultimately, Satan). Because one of the effects of the Fall was the loss of such freedom, and because all of Adam's children are born with a tendency toward evil (original sin) and with Adam's guilt (original guilt), they are incapable of saving themselves. Hence, the need for grace.

Augustine's account of sin and morality is rooted in two important concepts: the distinction between "use" (*uti*) and "enjoyment" (*frui*), coupled with the notion of the *ordo amoris* ("right order of love"). According to Augustine (especially in *On Christian Doctrine*), because we are created by and for God, our ultimate *enjoyment* or *happiness should be found in the proper object of our *love,* namely, the triune God. As such, all of creation can be received as a gift to be *used* insofar as it directs us ultimately to enjoy God. There is, then, a "right order" to our loves: we must ultimately love God, and so order our "love" of everything else in relation to that ultimate end. Thus Augustine's view of immorality is best understood as a problem of misplaced loves. The disordered soul of the unrighteous person is inordinately attracted to things like power, fame, honor, wealth, and sex—this person becomes absorbed by the created order and *enjoys* what should only be *used*. In other words, the unrighteous person substitutes the creation for the Creator (cf. Romans 1:18–31). But satisfying these desires leaves us empty and self-destructed. Why are transient things sure to disappoint us? Here Augustine's reliance on Neoplatonism seems most clear: unchanging goods are better than changing goods. The soul seeks rest in the objects of its love, but it cannot find rest in things that lack permanence. Transient things are intended to move us to God in whom our souls can rest. Our only hope for the consistent and deep satisfaction of our desires is if our love is properly attached to God, who is unchanging, permanent, *eternal. Herein lie the seeds of the doctrines of classical theism.

Augustine's general skepticism and doubts about God—due largely to concerns about the problem of evil—were resolved through reading the books of the Neoplatonists, which helped him to resolve philosophical difficulties about God's nature as immaterial and grapple with the problem of evil (*Confessions*, VII). The Neoplatonists affirmed an intelligible, immutable, and noncorporeal God. In order to see unchanging *truths, we must look within. Thus in *On the Teacher*, Augustine emphasized the Platonic doctrine of "recollection" but translated this into a theory of knowledge as "illumination" in which Christ is the "inner teacher" who illumines the soul to knowledge.

By arguing that knowledge is possible only on the basis of illumination by Christ the inner teacher, Augustine understood himself to be explicating the principle that "I believe in order to understand." Even knowledge, for Augustine, is a kind of gift of grace. The correlate of this emphasis on grace is found in his account of our moral formation. Like *Aristotle, Augustine believed that adult character hardens like cement into stone: it cannot be retrained in new habits (*Confessions*, V). But unlike Aristotle, Augustine believed

in and experienced divine grace, a grace sufficient to soften one's heart and reorient one's will, a grace sufficient to free one from the bondage of sin. Augustine's most enduring contribution to Christian theology is the centrality of grace—and it is this centrality of grace that would be a principal influence in the later theologies of Martin Luther (a priest in the Order of Saint Augustine) and John Calvin.

See also Anselm; Anthropomorphic Language; Aquinas; Being and Goodness; Descartes; Dualism/Monism; Epistemology; Eternal/Everlasting; Ethics; Ethics, Biblical; Faith and Reason; God, Nature of; Happiness; Immutability and Impassibility; Neoplatonism; Omniscience and Foreknowledge; Plato and Platonism; Stoicism; Theodicy.

Bibliography. John Hick, *Evil and the God of Love*; Peter Brown, *Augustine of Hippo*; Eleonore Stump and Norman Kretzmann, eds., *The Cambridge Companion to Augustine*; Jaroslav Pelikan, *The Christian Tradition*; Brian Stock, *Augustine the Reader*.

Being and Goodness The thesis that being and goodness are synonymous. Drawing on a *Neoplatonic framework, medieval philosophers and theologians such as *Augustine, Bonaventure, and *Aquinas equated being with *goodness. Aquinas contended that being and goodness are interchangeable. To exist is good, so everything that exists is good. *God is the most real existent, so God is the highest good. God is good, according to this view, because God exists and is fully perfected. God is not the sole possessor of this sort of goodness. Every being qua being is good. Lesser existents such as rocks, squids, and persons share in the divine goodness by participating in the highest good, namely, God. That everything is good led Augustine to develop and Aquinas to affirm the doctrine of *evil as the privation of the good*—it is the absence of good, not the presence of something. It is like a shadow (the absence of light) that does not really exist. So God could not be responsible for creating evil because evil has no being.

Not everything is equally good in this *ontological sense. There is more goodness in a thing the more it is like God, the highest reality. So sentient creatures are more valuable than nonsentient creatures, cognitive creatures more valuable than merely sentient creatures, and so forth. Indeed, an entire scale of existents can be ranked according to the possession of progressively more valuable properties from the lowliest of existents up through human beings and finally to God. This has been called *the great chain of being.*

Are things good simply by virtue of existing (being and goodness are identical) or are things good when they attain their end or perfection—to function properly as a fully actualized thing of their kind? Aquinas explicitly endorses both senses of goodness: something is good simply by virtue of existence, and something is good insofar as it fully becomes a member of its kind. The latter sort of goodness obtains when a being moves from potentiality to actuality in the fulfillment of its proper nature. So, for example, human beings gain more actuality, and hence goodness, as they increasingly manifest their natural capacity to *reason (and, by extension, to be virtuous).

These two sorts of goodness are manifested in God's relationship with God's creatures. God is good to God's creatures if God brings them into existence and if God facilitates the fulfillment of their proper natures. So God is good to human beings by creating them and parenting them in such a manner as to facilitate the development of reason and virtue in them (brings them to full actuality).

See also Aquinas; Augustine; Evil, Problem of; Goodness; Metaphysics/Ontology; Neoplatonism; Plato and Platonism.

Bibliography. Etienne Gilson, *Being and Some Philosophers;* Scott McDonald, *Being and Goodness.*

Belief in God   *See* Reason and Belief in God.

Cause/Causality   The power or act of bringing about an effect; the ability of a prior event (or object) to bring about a second event (or object). The term can be broadened to include the explanation of why an event comes to pass. Ancient thinkers such as *Aristotle and *Plato offered frameworks in which the primary cause of an event is a purpose or goal. Many Christian thinkers, seeing all of history as goal-directed, would find this notion of causality congenial.

The Christian doctrine of Creation is the prime example of divine causation. *God is the cause of the world in two senses: God originally caused the world to come into existence and God sustains (continually causes) the world in existence. *Augustine supposed that God did not fashion the world out of any preexisting material (contrary to Aristotle) but created the world ex nihilo (out of nothing). Christians also believe that God providentially orders (i.e., causes) the events of salvation-history to occur. Difficult questions are attached to divine causality and human freedom. How do human and divine causality fit together? How can God providentially order (i.e., cause) these events without violating human freedom? Does God merely react to human choices? Does human freedom limit God's sovereignty?

The controversy surrounding divine and human causation is further compounded when the origin of *evil is considered. What or who is the cause of evil? If God is the cause of all that exists, then where does evil come from if not from God? Historically, Christians believed evil was introduced by the free choice of Adam and Eve. The concept of human freedom provided the "conceptual space" for the emergence of evil and thereby relieved God of the responsibility for being the author of evil.

Discussions of *free will have given rise to theories of agent causation, viz., the notion that human agents are the final and ultimate causes of their actions. In other words, there is no causal chain beyond people themselves (such as environmental forces or genetic makeup, things over which agents have no control) to explain the reasons for their actions.

David *Hume was skeptical of accounts of causation since we are not able to perceive the causal relations between objects. We can perceive the constant conjunction (repetition), spatial contiguity (nearness), and temporal succession of particular events (say, a moving billiard ball striking a stationary billiard ball) to other events (the first ball coming to a stop and the second ball careening off), but we cannot see any causal *necessity between events.

New controversies over causation have arisen with the advent of quantum physics and relativity theory. What is the relationship of causality on a microphysical level (things we cannot see such as subatomic particles) and on the macrolevel (things we can see)? In addition, how can human action arise from brain waves yet be a free conscious choice?

See also Aristotle; Cosmology; Dualism/Monism; Evil, Problem of; Free Will; God, Nature of; Hume; Kant; Leibniz; Mind/Soul/Spirit; Teleology.

Bibliography. Mario Bunge, *Causality and Modern Science*; D. H. Mellor, *The Facts of Causation*; Robert Koons, *Realism Regained*; Timothy O'Connor, *Persons and Causes*; Alvin Plantinga, *God, Freedom, and Evil*.

Common Sense Philosophy
This tradition of *philosophy dates to the eighteenth century and begins with the work of the Scottish philosopher

Thomas Reid (1710–1796). In its initial phase, the work of Reid was primarily a reaction to the empirical and skeptical philosophy of *Hume. Common Sense philosophy was the dominant tradition within American circles throughout the nineteenth century until it was replaced by *pragmatism and *positivism in the twentieth century. Twentieth-century philosophers influenced by this tradition include G. E. Moore, W. P. Alston, Alvin Plantinga, and Nicholas Wolterstorff. Common Sense philosophy was also important for early Princeton theologians such as B. B. Warfield and Charles Hodge, particularly in their accounts of the nature of *apologetics.

Reid's philosophical work was motivated by the conviction that Hume's skepticism arose from a flawed notion of the human *mind and unrealistic standards for human knowledge. Hume believed that people only had immediate access to sensory experiences that imprinted themselves on their mind. The resulting set of impressions provided a picture or representation of the world. Hume claimed that these pictures could never provide certainty with respect to claims about the external world, about *God, or about the *self because these beliefs extend beyond the world of sensory appearances and so cannot be justified by them. On the contrary, Reid believed that the mind does not merely possess representations of the world, but actually knows the world itself. There is no mediating "picture" between the mind and the world; rather, the mind has immediate access to the world. Though we rarely achieve certainty in our beliefs, Reid argued that knowledge of the external world is nonetheless possible. He thus rejected Hume's skeptical conclusions. Common sense is to be trusted, though it is not infallible. As a result, Reid's thought is sometimes called "common sense *realism."

Common sense *epistemology is often optimistic about the capacity of the individual to know the world. Its defenders tend to see sin as affecting the will with little or no impact on the intellect. Thus an individual could have fairly direct epistemic access to the facts of nature even if one's moral beliefs are affected by bias or prejudice. This epistemological optimism is criticized for its apparent failure to account for the influence of sin, history, and culture on knowledge claims.

See also Apologetics, Enlightenment, Epistemology, Hume, Kant, Realism/ Anti-Realism, Reason/Rationality, Reason and Belief in God.

Bibliography. Terence Cuneo and René van Woudenberg, *The Cambridge Companion to Thomas Reid*; Philip De Bary, *Thomas Reid and Scepticism*; Keith Lehrer, *Thomas Reid*; Peimin Ni, *Thomas Reid*; Mark Noll, *The Princeton Theology*; Nicholas Wolterstorff, *Thomas Reid and the Story of Epistemology.*

Cosmology   In its broadest meaning, cosmology refers to a worldview. In its more narrow usage, cosmology refers to a theory about the origins and nature of the universe. In this regard it is sometimes thought to belong to the branch of *philosophy known as *metaphysics. Typically, cosmology concerns questions about how the world came into being and how it continues in being. The advent of relativity theory in the early twentieth century raised anew the relationship between the origins of the universe and the nature of time and space.

In ancient Greek thought, the origin of the universe was explained by reference to a series of seen and unseen *causes. For example, Thales thought the world came from water, *Plato spoke of a demiurge (a god of sorts), and *Aristotle spoke of the unmoved Mover. In addition, Aristotle crystallized a tradition of empirical observation about planetary motion that placed the earth at the center of the cosmos with *God as the ultimate cause of all planetary motion. The Ptolemaic model of the cosmos, which was endorsed for a millennium, incorporated Aristotelian physics with mathematical rigor. Early Christian cosmological reflection was sympathetic to Aristotelian cosmology and the Ptolemaic model because it held that God is scientifically necessary for the continual sustenance of the cosmos.

In the sixteenth and seventeenth centuries, cosmological reflection was aided by the Christian belief that the Creator leaves "clues" of God's creative acts in the nature and structure of the world itself. "Natural revelation" claimed that information about the Creator can be empirically derived from creation. However, this would lead to a rejection of the Aristotelian worldview and Ptolemaic model and occasioned a tremendous debate within the church about the nature of authority—what if the Bible and nature conflict? As natural laws came to the fore (such as the principle of inertia and laws of motion), the explanatory role of God diminished. Although cosmologists such as Kepler, Galileo, and Newton believed that God played an essential role in the continual governance of the cosmos, God's routine activity as the mover or pusher of the planets gradually receded in the minds of most scientists. By the end of the eighteenth century, Laplace, the leading mathematical astronomer of his day, declared that God was no longer mathematically necessary to explain the motion of the planets.

Since Einstein, evidence is gathering that the universe is undergoing expansion from the big bang of an initial singularity, that is, an immensely dense and unstable "point" that contained all of the matter of the universe. Big bang cosmology has revived two older issues: whether the universe needs a Creator prior to the singularity, and second, whether the universe's unique nature, particularly as it allows for the astronomically improbable existence of life, evidences design and purpose. In both of these areas, theoretical physics and philosophical cosmology have virtually merged as disciplines in our time and become theologically suggestive.

See also Aquinas, Aristotle, Cause/ Causality, Hume, Kant, Leibniz, Metaphysics/Ontology, Natural Theology, Theistic Arguments.

Bibliography. Peter Coles, *Cosmology*; Paul T. Brockelman, *Cosmology and Creation*; Jeffrey Sobosan, *Romancing the Universe*; Arthur Peacocke, *Creation and the World of Science*; William Lane Craig and Quentin Smith, *Theism, Atheism, and Big Bang Cosmology*.

Deconstruction   A strategy of philosophical critique often linked with *postmodernism and primarily associated with the French philosopher Jacques Derrida (1930–). The term was introduced by Derrida in 1967 to describe his approach to the history of *philosophy. Unfortunately, the term is now employed in a very loose fashion in contemporary culture as a general term for a negative critique or dismantling of something. For Derrida, however, the term has a fundamentally *positive* meaning.

Deconstruction attends to the competing trajectories within a text or corpus of writings, showing the way in which a text often "undoes" itself because of this internal intention. It is for this reason that Derrida asserts that deconstruction is not a "method" or something that we "do" to texts; rather, texts deconstruct themselves. According to Derrida, this occurs when texts attempt to exclude what they assume. In other words, texts often feed off of that which they exclude. For instance, in his reading of *Plato's understanding of writing in the *Phaedrus* ("Plato's Pharmacy"), Derrida observes that Plato values speech over writing by construing speech as a realm of immediate presence, whereas writing is characterized by absence, since the author does not usually attend the text. But Derrida then goes on to show that the same "absence" also characterizes speech. So the binary oppositions that Plato wants to make (presence/absence, speech/ writing, soul/body) cannot be so distinguished and dispatched. But for Derrida, once we discover this, the result is not a loss but rather the production of a new understanding. This is why those who construe deconstruction as primarily negative or destructive have misunderstood Derrida's project.

Derrida's philosophical framework derives from *phenomenology, and at root his work is a claim about language. Famously, Derrida concludes that "there is nothing outside of the text"; however, this has often been misunderstood. Derrida does not mean to deny that texts have *referents*, and thus deconstruction should not be understood as a kind of linguistic *idealism. Derrida later clarified that by this claim he meant to say "there is nothing outside of context." In other words, our access to the world beyond texts is always mediated by "textuality," which, for Derrida, refers broadly to the system of signs and interpretation by which we navigate our existence in the world. Because these "signs" are subject to a diverse array of interpretations, deconstruction suggests that there is a certain "play" to texts and their meanings that cannot be pinned down by a simplistic appeal to authorial intent (though Derrida does not deny a limited role for authorial intent). While deconstruction is often understood as an "anything-goes" approach to interpretation, Derrida himself explicitly rejects such a notion; however, some of his American heirs tend to foster this notion by their practice.

Derrida's work since the 1990s has focused on the more positive aspect of deconstruction by explicitly turning to questions of politics, *justice, and religion. Here he shows his debt to Jewish philosopher Emmanuel Levinas by emphasizing deconstruction as ultimately an account of justice, where justice is understood as obligation to the

Other. And while deconstruction has long been associated with "negative theology," in his later work Derrida presents deconstruction as a more "prophetic" tradition concerned with justice for "the widow, the orphan, and the stranger."

Deconstruction has had a significant impact on theology: a first wave can be found in the "a/theology" of Mark C. Taylor, who construed Derrida's work in the primarily *Nietzschean terms of "the death of *God." A second, more positive appropriation of deconstruction for religion is found in the work of John D. Caputo. However, this deconstructive "religion" is evacuated of any determinate content and thus does not, properly speaking, have a "theology." A third approach is beginning to emerge that sees deconstruction as helpfully describing the conditions of finitude, and thus able to be incorporated into a theology of creation and incarnation.

See also Hermeneutics, Ontotheology, Phenomenology, Postmodernism, Semiotics.

Bibliography. John D. Caputo, *Deconstruction in a Nutshell*; idem, *The Prayers and Tears of Jacques Derrida*; Jacques Derrida, *Acts of Religion*; idem, "Letter to a Japanese Friend"; idem, "Circumfession"; Kevin Hart, *The Trespass of the Sign*; Stephen Moore, *Poststructuralism and the New Testament*; James K. A. Smith, *The Fall of Interpretation*; idem, *Speech and Theology*; Mark C. Taylor, *Erring*; Kevin Vanhoozer, *Is There a Meaning in This Text?*

Descartes, René (1596–1650) French mathematician, scientist, and philosopher, often referred to as the father of *modernity because of his revolutionary account of knowledge. Because the scientific revolution called into question the entire Aristotelian approach to science, Descartes sought a new foundation for secure and lasting knowledge. In his *Discourse on Method* and *Meditations on First Philosophy*, Descartes set out to address doubts that had given birth to a personal skepticism. "If I could have been so certain about something," he asked himself, "and yet later discover I was wrong, how can I know anything for certain? What if things that seem certain to me today are proven false tomorrow? Can I find any basis for *certainty?*" This quest for certainty and a sure foundation for knowledge, which came to be called "foundationalism," would become the dominant project of modernity.

Descartes' method was one of "methodological doubt." He resolved to reject as false anything that could possibly be doubted, until he could discover something for which there were no possible doubts. Then he would have discovered something certain, and thus a sure foundation on which to build science (Descartes often employed the metaphor of a house and its foundation to describe his beliefs and the basis for those beliefs). For instance, when Descartes considered his sensory beliefs (seeing, hearing, etc.), he realized that sometimes his senses deceived him. Therefore, there is a reason to doubt his senses; as such, his senses could not be a source of certainty.

Descartes continued this process of doubt until he hit upon something that could not be doubted. Imagine a worst case scenario (from Descartes' *Meditations*): I am the plaything of some evil demon, who is trying to deceive me about everything—even deceiving me about the fact that $2 + 3 = 5$. What if this evil demon has deceived me about everything? Descartes concludes that even if this evil demon has deceived me about everything, it must be the case that I exist in order to be deceived. Therefore, the one thing that must be certain is that I exist. In the earlier *Discourse on Method*, Descartes famously proclaims, "I think, therefore I am" (*Cogito, ergo sum*). In the later *Meditations*, in fact, the principle is "I am deceived, therefore I am." He goes on to conclude that this "I" is a "thinking thing," an immaterial substance "housed" in a material body. As such, Descartes is a *dualist with respect to persons.

On the basis of this, most (including many theologians) have hailed Descartes as the originator of "subjectivity," finding certainty not in *God but in himself—thus making the *ego,* or subject, the new center of the universe. As the story goes, this turn to the subject gives rise to a new, almost godlike role for the subject and the gradual displacement of the Divine.

However, a closer reading of Descartes makes these claims problematic. While in the *Second Meditation* he seems to conclude that "I am, I exist" is certain, at the beginning of the *Third Meditation* this is again put back into doubt. For Descartes concludes "I exist" by inferring that anything that is deceived must exist in order to be deceived. But what if that inference is false? What if he is deceived even about that? Descartes goes on to show that he can overcome doubt only if he can demonstrate two things: first, that God exists, and second, that God is *good and not a deceiver. If both cannot be demonstrated, Descartes concludes, then nothing can be certain. He goes on to offer three arguments for the existence of God, including a version of the ontological argument. Thus, in the end, we find in Descartes what could be a radically theistic account of knowledge.

Descartes' influence on theology, often called "Cartesianism," has been significant. The Cartesian foundationalist model of rationality and the quest for certainty was followed for centuries. The Cartesian desire for certainty is almost pathological among certain theologians and *apologists. Although most current thinkers reject Cartesian dualism, it has contemporary adherents who believe it to be the best anthropology for Christian theology. Descartes is also one of the few Christian thinkers who maintain that God can do anything, even the *logically impossible.

See also Cause, Dualism/Monism, Enlightenment, Epistemology, Meta-physics/Ontology, Mind/Soul/Spirit, Modernity/Modernism, Omnipotence, Ontotheology, Self.

Bibliography. Tom Sorrell, *Descartes;* Richard Watson, *Cogito, Ergo Sum;* John Cottingham, ed., *The Cambridge Companion to Descartes;* Jean-Luc Marion, *Cartesian Questions.*

Dualism/Monism   "Dualism" is most broadly used to describe the conviction that there are two sorts of things in the world: material and nonmaterial entities. Dualism is opposed to monism, which holds that there is only one sort of thing in the world; *material monists* hold that reality is material, and *idealists* hold that reality is simply spirit or ideas. The most famous of the ancient monists was the pre-Socratic thinker Parmenides, who held that reality is one. The Real, according to Parmenides, is connected to *Truth, which is both one and never in conflict with itself; therefore, the Real must also be one. As a result, Parmenides drew a sharp distinction between the world as it appears and the world as it really is. He denied that change actually occurs; change is an illusion. This distinction led *Plato to contrast *reason (which can know the world as it really is) with experience (which only knows the world as it appears). By contrast, ancient materialists such as Democritus claimed that the world is as it appears and, as a result, believed that everything is matter. Modern materialism (*naturalism) is a form of materialist monism. Monists of the immaterial sort include George Berkeley, who believed that reality is ultimately spirit.

Most Christian traditions have been stoutly dualist (in this ontological sense). According to the Scriptures, *God is not a material being: God is spirit (John 4:24) and does not possess a body. So Christian thinkers have supposed that reality cannot be reduced to material things or events. But by way of balance, the affirmation of the "spiritual" dimension of reality has often led to a devaluing of the material world by certain Christian traditions or to a hierarchy of goods, with material pleasures at the bottom of the list. The challenge of Christian thinking in the present is to avoid the conflicts of spirit against matter or matter over spirit. In this respect, it is also important to recall the Christian doctrines of Creation (Genesis 1:31) and Incarnation (John 1:14), which affirm the *goodness of materiality.

In contemporary philosophical discussions, dualism normally refers to the distinction in humans between *mind and matter (and often the privileging of mind *over* matter). In theological terms, dualism refers to the distinction between body and soul. Debates rage as to whether one side of the distinction is reducible to the other and whether a reasonable description can be given to both sides. Theological dimensions of this debate have focused on questions of human identity and the soul's continued existence after death.

See also Atheism, Cause/Causality, Descartes, Essence/Essentialism, Human Nature, Idealism, Metaphysics/Ontology, Mind/Soul/Spirit, Naturalism, Plato and Platonism, Reductionism, Resurrection/Immortality, Substance.

Bibliography. W. K. C. Guthrie, *A History of Greek Philosophy*, vol. 2: *The Presocratic Tradition from Parmenides to Democritus*; Colin Gunton, *The One, Three and the Many*; Joseph Bracken, *The One in the Many*; Gordon Baker, *Descartes' Dualism*.

Enlightenment The eighteenth-century movement of "liberation" that elevated *reason above authority, thus seeking to liberate science from the control of religion. *Kant's charge in *What Is Enlightenment?* is clear: "Dare to use your own reason." Whatever cannot survive the scrutiny of reason—irrationality, prejudice, and superstition—must be discarded. Enlightenment thinkers such as Locke, Voltaire, Bayle, *Hume, Kant, and Wollstonecraft sought to rationally reconsider the nature of religion, morality, *philosophy, science, and society.

The revolutions and reformations of the sixteenth and seventeenth centuries created a bewildering variety of social, political, scientific, and religious options. Although the consequences were often dire, people had no clear method for making these choices. In an increasingly pluralist society, appeals to divine authority become increasingly problematic: which *God (the one of the Protestants, Roman Catholics, or Anabaptists) is the authority? And whose scriptural interpretation is true? As Hobbes writes, "If one prophet deceive another, what certainty is there of knowing the will of God, by other way than that of reason?"

Rejecting the notion that a human being ruled by divine right (the divine right of kings), Enlightenment thinkers sought a rational basis for human society. People were considered equal and endowed with natural rights to, for example, life and liberty. Liberal democracies were developed as systems of rights and laws that protected the individual from another, other nations, and capricious rulers. In the Enlightenment we thus find a correlation between what could be described as "*epistemological" and "political" revolutions: both sought to overthrow the control of authority and tradition over the individual.

Despite the Enlightenment's critique of authority, reason was not always used to discard traditional beliefs and values. Some Enlightenment thinkers were atheists, others were deists, and some were Christians. For example, Kant used reason rather than authority and Scripture to provide the justification for Christian beliefs and values. However, he believed that reason could not support rational belief in God. In removing the rational support for theism, Kant claimed to make room for *faith. The more characteristic view of the Enlightenment led to more revisionary understandings of Christian doctrines or to the rejection of Christian belief altogether.

Thomas Jefferson, for example, believed that *miracles were an abhorrence to reason and so desupernaturalized the Bible.

The autonomy of reason, the rejection of authority, and the denial of the miraculous would eventuate in a host of skeptical lives of Jesus and a loss of religious belief on the Continent and in the academy. In addition, post-Kantian assumptions gave birth to both classically liberal theologies such as Rudolf Bultmann's project of "demythologizing" the New Testament, and more recently, Gordon Kaufman's anthropological theology. William James at the turn of the twentieth century and reformed epistemologists at the end of the twentieth century would mount potent attacks on the presumptions of Enlightenment thinkers.

See also Common Sense Philosophy, Descartes, Epistemology, Hume, Kant, Modernity/Modernism, Natural Theology, Pascal, Reason/Rationality, Reason and Belief in God.

Bibliography. Roy Porter, *The Enlightenment*; Jonathan Israel, *Radical Enlightenment*; Peter Gay, *The Enlightenment*; James M. Byrne, *Religion and the Enlightenment*.

Epistemology Sometimes called "the theory of knowledge," epistemology concerns beliefs and their justification or warrant. Epistemology addresses such questions as, What is the origin and extent of human knowledge? What is the nature of human knowledge? Can we know anything at all? Epistemology became the central philosophical subject beginning with *Descartes and proceeding through the *Enlightenment. Insofar as both Christian confession and theology require knowledge of *God, epistemological questions are central to theological reflection.

The standard understanding of knowledge is *justified true belief*. A person p knows x if and only if p believes x, and p's belief in x is justified and p is true. One can believe something that is false,

but one cannot know, for example, that the earth is flat; one can only know true statements. And knowledge is more than mere opinion and so must be justified or warranted. There are many theories about how humans gain access to the various realms of knowledge and what justifies beliefs. Within theology, this question of "justified true belief" requires reflection on what justifies claims to knowledge about God.

Rationalism holds that the most fundamental items of knowledge are knowable through *reason; rationalists typically downgrade experiential beliefs. In the *modern era, they held to the doctrine of innate ideas—that there are fixed and immutable first principles that are etched onto the *mind, and these form the structure of our knowledge of the world.

Empiricism is an approach to knowledge that rejects innate (inborn) knowledge and holds that all knowledge derives from experience. Consider *Aristotle's claim that there is nothing in the mind that is not first in the senses. John Locke claimed that our minds are blank slates that can only be written on by experience. Although some empiricists are hostile to belief in God (most notably *Hume and the *positivists), some of empiricism's most noted defenders—Aristotle, *Aquinas, and Locke—are theists.

There are very few pure rationalists or pure empiricists. For the rationalist, it is difficult to move out of the mind and into the empirical world; pure rationalists are often *idealists who believe that all that exists is mind or spirit. For the empiricist, it is difficult to justify nonempirical items of knowledge such as *logic and mathematics. Pure empiricists may be led to skepticism about everything except present experience.

Foundationalism and coherentism are two pictures of the structure of justified belief. *Foundationalism* holds that some of our beliefs are self-justifying (logic and arithmetic) or immediately justified (perceptual beliefs) and so belong in the foundations of one's beliefs. The remainder of one's beliefs must be based on, by rules of inference, these immediately justified foundational beliefs. The resulting picture of justified beliefs resembles a pyramid. The most stringent forms of foundationalism (called classical or Cartesian foundationalism) have been rejected because the sparse set of beliefs permitted in the foundations are not adequate to justify any significant human beliefs and so would lead one to skepticism.

Coherentism holds that there are no basic beliefs, that all of one's beliefs are inferential. The coherentist picture of justified beliefs is a web consisting in a mass of interrelated beliefs. Some of the beliefs in the web are more central and others are more peripheral. Beliefs are justified insofar as they are part of a maximally coherent set of beliefs. Coherentism is often rejected because of the possibility that one's maximally coherent set of beliefs may have nothing to do with reality.

Postfoundationalist accounts of justified knowledge have begun to emerge, in both *philosophy and Christian theology. Alvin Plantinga has offered a powerful theistic account of warrant: A belief is warranted if it is produced by our properly functioning cognitive faculties working in accord with their design plan. He has used this account in a defense of warranted Christian belief. In theology, postliberalism (associated with Lindbeck and Hauerwas) has launched a critique of foundationalist theories of knowledge and offered a nonfoundationalist account for the warrant of Christian belief.

See also Common Sense Philosophy, Descartes, Enlightenment, Natural Theology, Nietzsche, Positivism, Realism/Anti-Realism, Reason/Rationality, Reason and Belief in God, Transcendence, Truth.

Bibliography. W. Jay Wood, *Epistemology*; Kelly James Clark, *Return to Reason*; Robert Audi, *Epistemology: A Contemporary Introduction*; George Lindbeck, *The Nature of Doctrine*; Alvin Plantinga, *Warrant*; idem, *Warrant and Proper Function*; idem, *Warranted Christian Belief.*

Essence/Essentialism   Belief in the distinction between essential and nonessential (contingent or accidental) characteristics of an object. Essentialism assumes that objects have essences and that an object's identity is its essence. The questions surrounding essentialism are normally associated with *metaphysics and the issue of *universals. Philosophers interested in metaphysics are especially interested in understanding reality "as it really (essentially) is."

*Aristotle distinguished between an object's essence and its existence. Its essence is "*what* a thing is." Its existence is "*that* a thing is." An object's essence is the collection of all the universals that it possesses, which if it did not possess them, it would cease to be. There are other sorts of properties that an object possesses but that do not make the object what it is. The property of "being owned by Mr. and Mrs. Smith" might be a property of Cato the cat but is nonessential, because Cato would still be a cat if she were owned by Mr. and Mrs. Jones (or not owned at all). However, Cato would not be a cat unless she was a furry animal, which suggests that the property of being a "furry animal" is essential to being a cat. The collection of all such properties that Cato possesses is its essence. Essentialism holds that natural things do have essences.

In contemporary *philosophy, modal notions (i.e., in terms of possibility and *necessity) of essentialism have come to the fore. In contrast to descriptive definitions of an object's essence, modal essentialism refers to those properties that it possesses necessarily. Contingent properties are those properties that an object possesses, but not necessarily. It could exist without having those properties. In medieval philosophy, *God's essence was a central metaphysical concern. Both *Anselm and *Aquinas affirmed divine *simplicity, that God's essence and God's existence are identical. Anselm further claimed that knowing God's essence makes it evident that God must exist.

Opponents of essentialism argue that "essences" are simply creations of language and culture. The "nature" of an object resides not in an objective property of the object itself but rather in a human description of the object. We assign the property of being a dog to Fido only because our community groups Fido together with other animals we have decided are similar. We organize these similarities under one conceptual umbrella that we arbitrarily call "dog." Contemporary anti-essentialists often see appeals to essences as disguised abuses of power. Some *feminist philosophers, for example, reject essentialism on the grounds that what is taken to be essentially human favors the male and disadvantages the female. For example, Aristotle believed that *reason is what makes us essentially human but that women, lacking in reason, are defective males. Males are by nature rational and domineering, while females (and slaves) are by nature emotional and subservient. For these reasons, some feminists reject essentialism altogether, while others, such as Mary Wollstonecraft, accept essentialism but argue persuasively that women are no less rational, that is, no less human, than men.

See also Anselm, Aquinas, Aristotle, Feminist Philosophy, Human Nature, Metaphysics/Ontology, Ockham, Simplicity, Substance, Universals.

Bibliography. Kelly James Clark and Anne Poortenga, *The Story of Ethics;* Brian D. Ellis, *The Philosophy of Nature;* Peter French et al., eds., *Studies in Essentialism;* Stephan Fuchs, *Against Essentialism;* Naomi Schor and Elizabeth Weed, *The Essential Difference;* Adrien Wing, ed., *Critical Race Feminism.*

Eternal/Everlasting   Without beginning or end. Classical theism holds that *God is eternal: God has and always will exist. Classical theism also claims that God is not bound by time and exists outside time. Time is a measure of change; a perfect being cannot change; therefore, God is outside time. A better term for this position is *timeless eternity*. The doctrine of timeless eternity is expressed most famously by Boethius (ca. 480–526), who defines eternity as the "perfect possession all at the same time of endless life." According to Boethius, everything exists for God in the eternal present. Strictly speaking, there is no past or future for God; for God every event occurs simultaneously now. Biblical support for this view is the "I am who I am" declaration of the divine name (*essence) to Moses, which is alleged to indicate God's unchanging existence in the eternal now.

Critics of this view allege that the doctrine of eternity is borrowed from *Platonic ideals of perfection and is read into Scripture. The chief obstacle to the doctrine of timeless eternity is the talk of change in the biblical narratives.

In biblical narratives God is presented as a character who changeably interacts with and responds to God's creatures within time. Nicholas Wolterstorff, who writes that we share time with God, contends that the biblical picture of God is everlasting rather than eternal. God exists without beginning and without end but freely chooses to enter into temporal relations with his creatures. Wolterstorff rejects the notion that God is *metaphysically or ontologically immutable (cannot change in any way whatsoever), yet he contends that the Bible teaches that God will never change in his loving purposes toward his creatures. While this understanding does justice to aspects of biblical revelation, it can also create difficulties for understanding God's knowledge of the future as seen in prophecies, for instance, regarding the birth of Christ.

See also Anthropomorphic Language; God, Nature of; Immutability and

Impassibility; Omniscience and Fore-knowledge; Plato and Platonism; Religious Language; Theistic Arguments.

Bibliography. Gregory E. Ganssle and David M. Woodruff, eds., *God and Time*; Nicholas Wolterstorff, "God Everlasting"; Alan G. Padgett, *God, Eternity and the Nature of Time*; Paul Helm, *Eternal God*.

Ethics   The theory of proper human conduct. There are two broad approaches to ethics. The first approach, *rule-based ethics,* is concerned with universal rules that tell us what to do in particular cases; value is located in actions. This approach would ask: "What should I do?" Moral admonitions might include negative prohibitions such as "Don't murder, cheat, or steal" and positive injunctions such as "Give to the poor and keep your promises." The second approach, *virtue ethics,* locates value in a person's character. This sort of approach, concerned primarily with virtues and vices, would ask, "What kind of person should I be (or become)?" Characteristic virtues are courage, *justice, moderation, and wisdom; characteristic vices include cowardice, injustice, immoderation, and foolishness. A virtuous person does not need the rules but will naturally do the right thing in each circumstance.

Rule (or duty) theories differ in how one determines what gives actions their value. *Consequentialism* is the view that good consequences (such as the maximization of pleasure over pain) justify the rules of conduct. This is sometimes called *teleological ethics* (from the Greek *telos*, "end" or "goal"). The most prominent consequentialists are utilitarians who affirm rules that maximize *happiness for the greatest number of people. On the other hand, *deontology* (from the Greek term for "duty") is the view that actions are right or wrong in themselves (intrinsically), regardless of their consequences. *Kant, the most famous deon-

tologist, contends that we should perform our duties without consideration of consequences. Even if one supposes that *God wills the rules, one might wish to know why. Did God will *x* because *x* is right *simpliciter* or because *x* will maximize human happiness?

Early virtue ethicists, like *Plato and *Aristotle, ground the virtues (strengths of character) in *human nature. The virtues expand (fulfill) while the vices diminish our nature. The flourishing human being is the one who gives proper expression to all of one's soul. Vices, say greed or gluttony, "take over" the soul and deny other parts of the soul (such as *reason, emotion, or other appetites) their proper satisfaction. Virtue ethicists often defend a *philosophy of moral education as essential to the process of moral development. But Plato and Aristotle disagree about how one discovers virtue. Plato contends that one withdraws from the world of experience and with the *mind's eye peers into the extramundane Good. Aristotle, on the other hand, thinks that virtue is discovered through rational reflection on characteristic human activities. This process sought the golden mean (say, courage) between the extremes of cowardice and foolhardiness. Within the Christian tradition, this virtue approach was most fully developed by *Aquinas, and revived in the work of Alasdair McIntyre and Stanley Hauerwas in the late twentieth century.

It should be noted that these two broad approaches are merely illustrative. Few thinkers are exclusively rule ethicists or virtue ethicists. Kant, for example, thought that consequences should not motivate our actions, but he believed that doing our duty will, in fact, result in good consequences. In addition, Kant was deeply concerned with the development of character. Aristotle, the most famous defender of virtue ethics, thought that, for example, murder and adultery were always wrong (and not right when done in moderation!).

Christian approaches to ethics include all of the above. Divine command theorists, who locate the good in the will of God, can be deontological ("God calls us to be obedient, not to be happy") or consequentialist ("Morality was made for man, not man for morality"). Divine command theorists may even be virtue ethicists: *Augustine's approach to ethics was influenced by Platonism and *Stoicism, and Aquinas's moral philosophy comes virtually straight from Aristotle.

See also Aquinas; Aristotle; Augustine; Essentialism; Ethics, Biblical; Happiness; Human Nature; Kant; Kierkegaard; Nihilism; Plato and Platonism; Relativism; Stoicism; Teleology.

Bibliography.   Kelly James Clark and Anne Poortenga, *The Story of Ethics*; William Frankena, *Ethics*; Alasdair MacIntyre, *A Short History of Ethics*; idem, *After Virtue*.

Ethics, Biblical

Ethics, Biblical   Although there is little in Scripture that would qualify as a systematic, theoretical treatment of *ethics, there are many pieces of a puzzle that, when put together, articulate a picture of "the good life" for human beings.

According to the Christian doctrine of Creation, everything depends on *God. The *divine command theory*, defended by Duns *Scotus and Calvin, is the view that morality too depends on God: the *good is what God wills and the bad is what God forbids. In the Old Testament, Yahweh imposed a series of moral, dietary, and ceremonial demands on the Hebrews. The Ten Commandments demand proper relations between people and Yahweh, as well as between people and other people. The prophetic writers assert that God is especially concerned for the plight of the weakest in society: children, orphans, widows, and the poor. Divine command theories are afflicted with the so-called *Euthyphro problem.

Jesus rejects the Pharisaical rule-keeping understanding of the Old Testament. He teaches that mere external behavior, without inner moral and spiritual transformation, is empty. In the Beatitudes (Matthew 5), Jesus proclaims that blessedness (fulfillment) is reserved for the poor in spirit, the meek, those who hunger for righteousness, the merciful, and the pure in heart. He later condemns those who believe that they are righteous simply because they have not committed murder or adultery. Anger, which we carry within, may betray our unrighteousness as much as our actions do. In addition to an emphasis on character over rules, Jesus' ethical message emphasizes a *communal* understanding of the good. We might say that Jesus' ethics is always already a *social* ethics. In particular, Jesus' disciples are to be a witness to the world by being the embodiment of the "peaceable kingdom." Thus Jesus' commandments regarding *love* point to a vision of peaceful social organization—one that encompasses even enemies (Matthew 5:44).

The apostle Paul develops Jesus' emphasis on inner moral transformation, coupled with an emphasis on the community in harmony. He commends love, joy, peace, patience, kindness, goodness, faithfulness, gentleness, and self-control as "fruit of the Spirit" (Galatians 5:22). In other words, the character transformation that is required to be "good" is not something that we can accomplish with our own resources. We require grace to be good. Christians demonstrate the truth of their confession *in their actions*. Thus Paul, echoing themes in 1 John, implores people to "serve one another in love," and concludes that "the entire law is summed up in a single command: 'Love your neighbor as yourself'" (Galatians 5:13–14). This love is demonstrated by the way that the church—as the "called-out" community *(ekklesia)*—embodies a spirit of unity and peace (Ephesians 2; Philippians 2). With this focus on character, it is little wonder that *Aquinas would develop Christian ethics as virtue ethics. But, unlike *Aristotle, Aquinas believes that we can obtain the grace necessary for the transformation of our lives from vice to virtue.

Christians are sometimes accused of "otherworldliness," of focusing so much on the life to come that they are of no good in this life. Yet the Bible is clear in its teaching that Christians are called to transform this world, in the here and now, rather than simply awaiting God to right everything in heaven.

Although some take rules approaches and others take virtue approaches to morality, most Christian ethicists have been eudaimonists, believing the good life to be the flourishing and happy life. God made us such that being good is conducive to human *happiness. The moral life, according to this view, satisfies our deepest human needs and desires. If, as *Augustine wrote, our deepest desire is for God, then the good life is not possible without God at the center of our being.

See also Aquinas, Aristotle, Augustine, Being and Goodness, Essence/Essentialism, Ethics, Euthyphro Problem, Happiness, Human Nature, Justice, Kant, Plato and Platonism, Teleology.

Bibliography. C. S. Lewis, *Mere Christianity*; John Hare, *Why Bother Being Good?*; idem, *The Moral Gap*; Daniel J. Harrington and James Keenan, *Jesus and Virtue Ethics*; Benedict M. Ashley, *Living the Truth in Love*; David John Atkinson, ed., *New Dictionary of Christian Ethics and Pastoral Theology*; Stanley Hauerwas, *The Peaceable Kingdom*; Robin Gill, ed., *The Cambridge Companion to Christian Ethics*.

Euthyphro Problem   An allegedly intractable problem first raised by Plato in the dialogue *Euthyphro*, for divine command theories of *ethics; it claims to show that morality cannot be based on the will of *God. Christians suppose that God is the source of morality; that is, that the *good is that which is willed by God, and the bad is that which is forbidden by God. The belief that goodness is the will of God may be taken in either of two ways: (a) something is good because God wills it, or (b) God wills something because it is good.

The problem with (a), something is good simply because God wills it, is that it seems to make morality arbitrary. God has laid down a particular set of moral commandments for our lives, but God could have laid down a very different set. God happened to command us to tell the truth, but what if God had willed that we lie instead? Would that have made lying good? Suppose, even worse, that God had commanded the torture of innocent babies for fun. If God's will is the source of all goodness, it looks as if such an act would make it good to torture innocent babies for fun. But surely it is not good and never could have been good to torture innocent babies for fun. Indeed, it seems that if God *had* willed that, *God* would have been wrong. But that suggests that there is a standard of morality to which even God is subject. The difficulty with (a) seems to lead the divine command theorist to accept (b), God wills something because it is good. If (b) is true, however, then God appears to be superfluous. If there is an independent standard of goodness that God recognizes and wills, then that standard is the source of morality, not God.

The Euthyphro problem raises an important issue for the relationship between God and morality: How can goodness both depend on God and not be arbitrary? Recent divine command theorists respond by locating divine commands not simply in the will of God but in God's character, which includes God's love that would constrain the types of commands God could will.

See also Aquinas; Augustine; Ethics, Biblical; Scotus.

Bibliography. John Hare, *God's Call*; Richard Mouw, *The God Who Commands*; Robert Merrihew Adams, *The Virtue of Faith*; idem, *Finite and Infinite Goods*; Philip Quinn, *Divine Commands and Moral Requirements*.

Evil, Problem of   The argument that *God cannot exist given the existence of evil. The problem of evil is raised against the backdrop of natural and moral evils. *Natural evils* arise solely from nature: earthquakes, pestilence, famine, drought, flooding, mudslides, and hurricanes. *Moral evils* are due to the free choices of human beings and include, for example, war, poverty, and racism. The basic argument from evil draws consequences from attributes of God and conjoins them with the simple fact of evil:

1. God is *omnipotent and wholly *good.
2. If God is omnipotent, God can eliminate evil.
3. If God is wholly good, God would want to eliminate evil.
4. There is evil.
5. Therefore, God does not exist.

This deductive argument is alleged to demonstrate the impossibility of God's existence given the fact of evil. The argument is classically formulated in *Hume's *Dialogues Concerning Natural Religion*.

By demonstrating the *logical consistency of God, *free will, and evil, Alvin Plantinga's free will defense shows that the deductive argument from evil is fallacious. Most atheists have conceded the success of Plantinga's refutation of the deductive argument from evil and have shifted their arguments. One form of the new problem of evil alleges that there is too much evil for God to exist. Another form says that there are certain kinds of evil (which involve apparently pointless suffering) that provide compelling reasons for believing that God does not exist. A final form contends that it is unlikely or improbable that God exists given the fact of evil.

The most satisfying response to the problem of evil would be a successful *theodicy*, which specifies God's reason for allowing evil.

See also Anthropomorphic Language; Augustine; Cause/Causality; Free Will; God, Nature of; Hell; Hume; Omnipotence; Omniscience and Foreknowledge; Reason and Belief in God; Theodicy.

Bibliography.   Michael Peterson, *God and Evil*; Kelly James Clark, *Return to Reason*; idem, *When Faith Is Not Enough*; Nicholas Wolterstorff, *Lament for a Son*; Marilyn and Robert Adams, *The Problem of Evil*; Alvin Plantinga, *God, Freedom, and Evil*; Daniel Howard-Snyder, *The Evidential Argument from Evil*.

Exclusivism   *See* Pluralism, Exclusivism, and Inclusivism.

Existentialism   An influential philosophical movement in the middle of the twentieth century, associated with Martin *Heidegger, Jean-Paul Sartre (1905–1980), and Albert Camus (1913–1960). The movement emphasizes the *choice* of the individual as determining her *essence. Sartre contends that existentialism simply draws out the consequences of a coherent atheistic position. Sartre sums up existentialism as "Existence precedes essence," which is in opposition to the classical doctrine that "essence precedes existence." By way of explanation, Sartre asks us to think about manufactured articles such as a paper cutter. A paper cutter is produced in a certain way and made for a definite purpose. No one makes it without knowing how to make it and what it is for. Its essence, the *what it is*, or its definition, precedes its existence. What it means to be a paper cutter is not up to the paper cutter. Sartre points out that traditionally human beings have been viewed in the same way. For Christians, *God was thought of as the artisan who creates human beings for a specific purpose and according to a conception already in God's *mind. As *Augustine classically formulated it, "You have made us for yourself and our hearts are restless until they rest in you." According to the tradition, human beings can no more determine their purpose than a paper cutter. The human task is to discover this preestablished human essence and then to order one's life according to it.

The claim "existence precedes essence" is a rejection of the idea that *human nature has an end or goal—or that there is any such thing as a "human nature." We are free to choose our own destinies and to create ourselves. In order to find fulfillment, we need not direct our lives toward any predetermined goal or way of life. We are free to direct our lives and find fulfillment as we see fit. As Sartre writes: "Man is nothing else but what he makes of himself. Such is the first principle of existentialism."

Atheistic existentialists are often associated with a very grim view of human existence without the consolations of the Divine. Although Camus was more hopeful than Sartre, he nonetheless viewed human life as ultimately absurd. This understanding of the absurdity of human life was embodied in the films of Ingmar Bergman, the leader of an existentialist school of film.

While Christians have rejected the atheistic existentialism of Sartre or Camus, the core emphasis on human responsibility or choice resonates with the Christian tradition. Existentialism has Christian predecessors in Augustine, *Pascal, and *Kierkegaard who emphasized the importance of radically free and passionate choice (it was also influential with early twentieth-century biblical scholars and theologians, such as Rudolf Bultmann). Authentic identity requires a *response* to that to which we are called. For Kierkegaard, we are only authentically human (and Christian) insofar as we resist conformity to "the crowd" and respond to the singular call of God. Thus for Kierkegaard, Abraham (in Genesis 22) would be the prime example of an authentic individual, a "knight of *faith."

See also Atheism, Essentialism, Heidegger, Human Nature, Kierkegaard, Nietzsche, Pascal, Self.

Bibliography. William Barrett, *Irrational Man*; Walter Kaufmann, ed., *Existentialism*; Robert Solomon, *From Rationalism to Existentialism*; Rudolf Bultmann and Hans Bartsch, *Kerygma and Myth*.

Faith   Belief, trust, commitment, way of life, a disposition of the soul whereby a person trusts in or is loyal to another. Christians are urged to have faith in *God through Christ. Faith in God involves an objective element (the existence of God, the fact that Jesus was God incarnate, etc.) and the subjective appropriation, moved by the grace of God, of those *truths. Some thinkers affirm, while others oppose faith to knowledge and even belief.

The history of discussion about faith has given rise to at least two significant and related controversies: the nature of faith as the core of the relation between God and persons, and the nature of faith as the means of reconciliation between God and sinful human beings. According to the first controversy, faith is viewed as a species of belief. But a belief in what? And what kind of belief? If Christians are urged to believe in God, what makes their faith different from or similar to the faith of other religions? The apostle Paul raised this issue by arguing that the faith of Abraham is analogous to the faith urged upon Christians. Paul's argument centered on faith as a trust in God, not on any performance of ritual religious works. But then questions emerged: Is there a specific content to the belief in God? The early church held that certain beliefs, like the special relation of Jesus to God and the sacrificial death of Jesus for our sins, were essential to faith. The medieval church would add specific views on the nature of Christ, the doctrine of the Trinity, and many other doctrines to the content of faith. Some contemporary thinkers have argued that faith is a trust in God, but not in any specific content about God or any specific revelation from God (promises or otherwise). So Paul Tillich and John Hick have claimed that faith is trusting in something ultimate, though each religion accordingly will give content to the ultimate; faith is not confined to Christianity or even belief in God. Others have argued that faith must always have some particular content attached to it.

The second controversy draws attention to the nature of faith as the means of reconciling God and sinful human beings. Leaving aside the debates about the nature of sin, the question is whether faith is an epistemic virtue of humans as they ponder what God has done on their behalf or whether faith is a gift of God as a means of their reconciliation. On one reading of the issue, "faith" is a synonym for trust in what God has already accomplished in Christ on a person's behalf, independent of that person's actions. Accordingly, faith cannot be a "work" with any merit attached to it, since reconciliation is entirely a work of God (Ephesians 2:8–10).

On the other reading of the issue, "faith" is a way to speak of faithfulness to God as a response to God's initiative in Christ. Faith is a kind of cooperation with God in this regard. According to the former, faith is not praiseworthy as such; according to the latter, faith merits divine favor and is indeed praiseworthy. This controversy is also tied to larger theological differences about the nature of grace and its mediation in and through the church. These controversies were particularly intense in the debates between *Augustine and the Pelagians and later in the Reformation. How one resolves this tension is ultimately determined by how one understands the effects of *sin*. According to the Augustinian line, because of the radical effects of sin, it is impossible for human beings to come to faith on their own. According to the Pelagian (or semi-Pelagian position of Roman Catholicism), the effects of sin are not so radical; therefore, there can be a "cooperation" or synergy between human effort and divine grace.

Many Christians identify faith with certainty (the absence of doubt). While certainty may be the goal of the Christian life, we, as the apostle Paul writes, see through a glass darkly, but then we shall see face-to-face. Certainty, like moral perfection, seems attainable only in the next life.

See also Faith and Reason; God, Belief in; Kierkegaard; Reason/Rationality; Reason and Belief in God.

Bibliography. Eric Springsted, *The Act of Faith*; Jonathan Edwards, *The True Believer*; William Lad Sessions, *The Concept of Faith*; Kelly James Clark, *When Faith Is Not Enough*.

Faith and Reason Christians have traditionally held that there are two sources of belief: *faith and *reason. Our rational faculties include reasoning (the ability to make inferences), intuition, and memory. They also include faculties that produce beliefs in the external world, the past, and inductive inferences. These God-given faculties are designed for the production of true beliefs. The deliverances of faith often involve beliefs that are not demonstrable by reason. Accepting these beliefs requires an act of the will on the part of the believer and involves an element of trust. What is the relationship between faith and reason, that is, between beliefs produced by the faculties of reason and those given in the deliverances of faith? Here we will not consider theistic belief but the relation of reason and faith as it pertains to Christian belief including, for example, beliefs about the nature and existence of *God, the Trinity, the incarnation, and the *resurrection. There are three dominant conceptions of the relationship between faith and reason: fideism, faith seeking understanding, and understanding seeking faith.

Fideism, the claim that Christian belief is contrary to reason, finds its most famous defender in Tertullian. Tertullian agreed with the apostle Paul that

Christianity is folly to the Greeks (the rational people), contending that faith is opposed to reason (1 Corinthians 1:18–25). The question, "What has Jerusalem to do with Athens?" is rhetorical. Tertullian famously retorts, "I believe because it is absurd." A more "chastened" fideism (Cornelius Van Til and Herman Dooyeweerd), called *presuppositionalism,* would still affirm a certain antithesis between faith and "reason," but only because "reason" itself is always laden with faith presuppositions. In other words, there is no "neutral" thing called reason, but only "Greek" reason or "Hindu" reason—at root, what goes under the name of "reason" depends on religious commitments. In this sense, one might still assert an opposition between Christian faith and the reason of the Greeks or *modernity. This position then slides toward the Augustinian pole.

*Augustine argued that all human inquiry begins with faith of some sort. Nonetheless, he believed that intellectual inquiry plays the positive and necessary roles of understanding, developing, and defending Christian beliefs. The role of reason with respect to faith is *faith seeking understanding (fides quaerens intellectum).* *Anselm's ontological argument is developed within this context. The argument begins with the prayer: "Help us, O Lord, to understand that thou art as we believe." *Aquinas is often taken as rejecting this Augustinian view. While Aquinas does believe that reason can attain some *truths about God, other divine truths are simply beyond the reach of human reason. The latter truths are accepted on the authority of God, but reason should be used to prepare people for faith and help people understand these revealed doctrines. Hence, with respect to the "articles of faith" (Trinity, resurrection, etc.), Aquinas is Augustinian on matters of faith and reason; but with respect to the "preambles of faith," Aquinas explicitly rejects Augustine's account of divine illumination and slides toward an *Enlightenment model.

The final view, *understanding precedes faith,* finds defenders in the Enlightenment. Because of the rejection or questioning of traditional authorities, reason was deemed necessary for the legitimate holding of significant beliefs. Moreover, reason is understood to be a *universal criterion common to all of humanity. John Locke, for example, held that items of faith are above reason, yet such beliefs cannot be contrary to reason. Although items of faith need not be deduced from reason, the revelation through which they are communicated must be justified by reason (to establish the reliability of the testimony, that it is indeed a message from God). Thus, Locke and his Enlightenment heirs require reason (understanding) before the legitimate assent to matters of faith.

See also Apologetics; Aquinas; Augustine; Cosmology; Enlightenment; Faith; Feuerbach; God, Belief in; Hume; Kant; Kierkegaard; Natural Theology; Reason/Rationality; Reason and Belief in God; Theistic Arguments.

Bibliography. C. Stephen Evans, *Faith Beyond Reason;* Paul Helm, *Faith and Understanding;* Alvin Plantinga, *Warranted Christian Belief;* William Wainwright, *Reason and the Heart;* Edward Grant, *God and Reason in the Middle Ages.*

Feminism/Feminist Philosophy

A primarily practical movement that seeks to eliminate the political, socioeconomic, and cultural oppression of women. Within contemporary *philosophy, it is a movement that has sought to highlight the role of gender in *ethics, *epistemology, science, and politics. Although feminism can be traced back to the eighteenth-century work of Mary Wollstonecraft, it did not flourish until the 1970s. Feminists demand equal rights for women, including access to all the modes of life required for human flourishing.

Historical injustices inflicted on women were justified by answers to the theoretical question, What does it mean to flourish as a human being? Historically important thinkers, including Christians such as *Aquinas and *Kant, believed that women are by nature inferior to men and incapable of human flourishing; women are deficient in *reason and more moved by emotions, passions, and desires. Emotions, passions, and desires are traits human beings share with animals, while reason is a property we share with *God. So according to this schema, men are more godlike, women more animal-like. In this patriarchal tradition, people should aspire to be all they can be: for men, to be like gods; for women, to be ruled by men. And society should be ordered in a manner consistent with these differences. Contemporary feminist philosophy seeks to unmask the pretensions of male privilege and power found in such models of human identity and the consequent understandings of human flourishing.

Liberal feminism accepts the traditional (*Enlightenment) views of the ideal person (as, say, rational and/or autonomous) and argues that women are just as capable of becoming fully human as men. At the end of the twentieth century, thinkers have begun to reject the traditional views of the ideal person because they enshrine male traits. These thinkers, sometimes called *difference feminists,* believe that men and women have different but equally valuable ideals to which to aspire. Still others believe that any so-called gender differences between men and women are cultural, not biological. This form of feminism is typically anti-essentialist.

Feminist philosophers tend to assume that sexual difference is philosophically significant. For example, Carol Gilligan, in *In a Different Voice,* has argued that because men are more rule-oriented, they have developed an ethic of *justice. Women, on the other hand, tend to relate empathetically to the other and so are more at home with an ethic of care. Other areas of political philosophy and

epistemology have been discussed from a feminist perspective as well.

Feminists also offer a variety of opinions on religious belief. Christian and nontheistic feminists alike agree that there are serious problems that demand discussion in the Christian tradition, most especially the use of Christian theology to justify the historical devaluation and subordination of women. Some feminists work from an explicitly Christian perspective and attempt to retrieve elements of the Christian tradition of equality that have been lost, which has involved a discussion of the nature of human persons as well as the nature of God. In biblical studies, feminist scholars such as Phyllis Trible (Old Testament) and Elisabeth Schüssler Fiorenza (New Testament) have paid close attention to the subjugation and marginalization of women within the biblical canon. In discussions of *religious language, feminist theologians have argued for the appropriateness of gender-neutral and feminine language for God. By continuing to call God "Father," some have argued, Christians continue to participate in an oppressive patriarchy that devalues women. In addition, feminist thinkers have urged a reconsideration of the traditional texts that have been taken to support the subordination of women in the church. Some feminist thinkers have more radical views of Christianity. Posttheistic feminists argue that the very notion of God is antithetical to genuine female freedom and equality. Other feminists argue that concepts of authority intrinsic to the Christian tradition ought to be abandoned to avoid the oppression of traditional patriarchy.

See also Epistemology, Essence/ Essentialism, Human Nature, Justice, Perspectivalism, Postmodernism.

Bibliography. Natalie Watson, *Feminist Theology*; Ruth Groenhout and Marya Bower, eds., *Philosophy, Feminism, and Faith*; Elizabeth Fox-Genovese, *Feminism without Illusions*; Serene Jones, *Feminist Theology*; Letty

M. Russell, ed., *Feminist Interpretation of the Bible*; Susan Parsons, ed., *The Cambridge Companion to Feminist Theology*; Francis Martin, *The Feminist Question*; Phyllis Trible, *Texts of Terror*.

Feuerbach, Ludwig (1804–1872)

German philosopher who developed a *philosophy of religion based on the assumption of *naturalism. Believing religion to be "illusionistic," Feuerbach reduced theology to anthropology—in the study of religion, we learn about human beings, not about some *transcendent reality. Feuerbach rejected *Hegel's view about the dependence of the individual on the Absolute. Humans, Feuerbach believed, created *God in their own image (as a projection of human ideals). Compared to this ideal, human beings are lowly and wicked. Feuerbach contended, therefore, that the invention of God alienated human beings from their true nature. If we could overcome religion, Feuerbach argued, we would overcome our alienation. Finally, Feuerbach grounded morality on physiology and anthropology instead of a spiritual, antinatural *essence of human beings. We are distinctively human not in virtue of our being image bearers of the Divine, but in virtue of our desire for community with other human beings. We are essentially social and physical, not spiritual, beings. Through his "unmasking" of Christianity, Feuerbach hoped to set human beings on the path of liberation and compassion. Feuerbach influenced the development of the atheologies of *Marx, *Freud, and *Nietzsche, the radical theology of Franz Overbeck, as well as more liberal forms of Christian theology. Karl Barth's theology can be understood as both indebted to and a response to Feuerbach's charge.

See also Atheism, Freud, Hegel, Marx, Naturalism, Nietzsche.

Bibliography. Van Harvey, *Feuerbach and the Interpretation of Religion*; Merold Westphal, *Suspicion and Faith*.

Foreknowledge *See* Omniscience and Foreknowledge.

Free Will The claim that some human choices are not coerced or determined either by outside forces or by one's genetic makeup. Free will is typically defined as *the ability to do otherwise*. For example, when faced with a choice to eat an apple, one is free only if one can choose the apple or can refrain from choosing the apple, or can choose the apple or an orange instead. If one is coerced (say, one's hands are tied and the apple is forced into one's mouth), then one's actions are not free—the one who is coercing the choice has removed the person's ability to do otherwise. There are three prominent conceptions of the human person that are concerned with the problem of free will: hard determinism, soft determinism, and libertarianism.

Hard determinism holds that all human actions are determined, either by our genetic inheritance, our social upbringing (or both heredity and environment), or by the decrees of *God. Hard determinism denies that there are any real choices and so denies free will. One cannot do otherwise than what one's heredity and environment have programmed one to do or that God ordains that you will do. A significant problem for determinism is that free will seems a prerequisite of moral responsibility. If a person is not free, then it is difficult to see how she could be blamed for her actions.

Soft determinism is still deterministic: it holds that all human actions are determined, but differs from hard determinism because it claims that some human actions are free. This view is sometimes called "compatibilism" because of its claim that determinism and free will are compatible. Since determinists deny that humans have the ability to do otherwise, soft determinists redefine free will. They do so by contrasting a free action with an unfree action. Free actions are those that a person wants to do and coerced actions are those that a person is forced to do.

*Augustine made a signal distinction between "freedom of choice" and genuine "free will." The sinner, according to Augustine, can choose many different options of sin; but because of the corruption of the will, he cannot choose the highest *good. As such, the sinner has freedom of choice but not genuine free will. In contrast, the redeemed person is empowered by grace to choose the good, and thus has genuine free will.

The *libertarian* rejects determinism, claiming that humans sometimes have the ability to rise above their heredity and environment and make free (i.e., uncaused) choices (hence, it is sometimes called "indeterminism"). Many libertarians believe that there is a nonphysical part of persons (soul, agent) that is not a slave to the *cause-and-effect conditioning of the body. It is this part of the person that stands above one's desires, heredity, and environment, and thereby freely makes its choice in the face of genuine alternatives.

Christian theologians, with their robust notions of human responsibility, usually fall within the compatibilist or libertarian camps. Many Augustinian Calvinists are compatibilists who believe in the strongest forms of sovereignty and providence: everything that happens, including human actions, are willed by God. Since they are soft determinists, they also claim that such actions are free. But how can human actions be free if they are the result of a causal chain, over which we have no control or choice, which terminates in God? Arminians deny that soft determinism adequately preserves the notions of free choice and moral responsibility and are, therefore, more inclined toward libertarianism.

See also Aquinas, Augustine, Cause/Causality, Human Nature, Justice, Mind/Soul/Spirit, Theodicy.

Bibliography. Ilham Dilman, *Free Will*; Augustine, *On the Free Choice of the Will*; Jonathan Edwards, *The Freedom of the Will*; Laura Ekstrom, *Free Will*; W. S. Anglin, *Free Will and the Christian Faith*.

Freud, Sigmund (1856–1939)   Austrian psychologist and founder of psychoanalysis. Freud, heavily indebted to an evolutionary worldview, conceived humans to be fundamentally constituted by "drives" or "instincts": a "pleasure instinct" directly related to libido and sexual pleasure, and a "death instinct," bent on a certain destructiveness. Because this drive toward destructiveness hampers the pursuit of pleasure, "civilization" develops in order to keep this instinct in check. However, civilization can function only if we also restrain the libido in some way and redirect that sexual energy toward constructive activities like work. As such, civilization requires both the "sublimation" of our instincts (redirecting them toward a different end) and the "repression" of our instincts (driving them down into our subconscious by mechanisms of guilt). This repression is what gives birth to the neuroses that attend the development of civilization.

Freud's account also includes a myth about primal origins: a father clan where sons desire their mothers. The father represses his son's desires to protect his interest in the mother. The son revolts, kills the father (embodied in the ancient play *Oedipus Rex*), and takes the mother for himself (hence Freud calls the desire for the mother the "Oedipus complex"). But the son then feels guilty for having murdered the father and deifies him. This is one account that Freud provides for the origin of religion (see *Totem and Taboo*). Another is the projection of human properties onto nature in the belief that the ultimate power is like a father (see *The Future of an Illusion*). We wish *God into existence—so begins the term "wish fulfillment"—and he hears our prayers: God can tame nature, help us accept our fate, and reward us for our sufferings. Thus religion represents a certain immaturity for those who do not want to face up to the frightening realities of nature.

See also Atheism, Feuerbach, Naturalism.

Bibliography. Armand Nicholi, *The Question of God*; William Alston, "Psychoanalytic Theory and Theistic Belief"; Merold Westphal, *Suspicion and Faith*; Herbert Marcuse, *Eros and Civilization*.

God, Belief in   There are many positions that a person may take with respect to belief in God or the gods. The most basic is *theism*, the belief that God exists. Theism comes in many varieties including *monotheism* (the belief that only one God exists), *polytheism* (the belief in many gods), and *pantheism* (the belief that everything is God). Monotheism is consistent with a number of religions, including Judaism, Christianity, and Islam.

Deism, a theistic position held by many *Enlightenment thinkers, is the belief that God created the universe like a watch, wound it up, and let it go on its own, but that God is not personally involved in the world now. Denying that God works *miracles such as the incarnation and resurrection, deists typically reduce Christianity to its moral teachings.

Those who are not theists may be *atheists*, who believe that God does not exist, or agnostics, who simply withhold belief in God (they neither affirm nor deny God's existence). *Agnosticism* holds that there is not sufficient evidence to prove or to disprove the existence of God; hence the rational position is to withhold belief either way. Christians often denigrate agnostics for their lack of commitment but are often agnostics themselves about, for example, extraterrestrial life due to the lack of evidence for or against it.

See also Cosmology; Enlightenment; Faith; Faith and Reason; God, Nature of.

Bibliography. James Turner, *Without God, Without Creed*; T. H. Huxley, *Agnosticism and Christianity*; John C. Polkinghorne, *The Faith of a Physicist*.

God, Nature of   Questions about the nature of God are concerned with matters of God's "*essence"—what God is like. This has traditionally included discussion of God's attributes or characteristics. In the past twenty years, Christian positions on the nature or concept of God divide into two major camps: classical theism and open theism. *Classical theism*, is the historically dominant position, holding that God has the attributes of *omnipotence, *omniscience, *immutability, aseity, perfect *goodness, and *eternity. Omnipotence is the ability to do anything (with some qualifications, as we shall see shortly). Omniscience means all-knowing, and immutability means unchanging. God's aseity means that God does not depend on anything and is usually attached to the doctrine of divine sovereignty, that everything depends on God. The attribute of eternity means that God is outside and, therefore, not bound by time. For classical theists the divine attributes are those that are necessary for a maximally perfect being. Open theists suggest that classical theism developed as the product of a synthesis between biblical revelation and Greek philosophical concepts. Thus the philosophical notion of a maximally perfect being was taken to be a way of expressing Scripture's affirmation of God's eminence. Or, the philosophical concept of omnipotence was taken up as a way of expressing the biblical claim that God is "Almighty."

There is a tight conceptual connection among all of the attributes of classical theism. For example, an immutable being must also be outside time (for time is the measure of change). Some thinkers contend that a perfectly good being must also be omniscient (to be good, one must know the good and how to maximize it); or perhaps it goes the other way around: an omniscient being is necessarily a perfectly good being. So the rejection of a single property might have ramifications for the entire set of properties contained in classical theism.

Some Christian thinkers have become suspicious that, in the synthesis of philosophical and biblical concepts found in classical theism, Greek concepts have superseded biblical revelation. They have seen fit to reject one or another of the divine attributes of classical theism. Arguments have been offered against divine eternity, immutability, omnipotence, foreknowledge, and even goodness. *Open* or *relational theists*, relying on the narrative portions of the Bible that portray God as a quasi-human actor in the drama of redemptive history, contend that the biblical view is that God enters into time, lacks exhaustive foreknowledge of the future, changes his plans and purposes, and is openly responsive to human failings, pleadings, and reminders. Some *process theists* go even further, denying both God's omnipotence and perfect goodness. If all of the attributes the classical theist ascribes to God are rejected, critics wonder just what is left that is distinctly divine in the nature of God.

See also Anselm, Anthropomophic Language, Aquinas, Augustine, Eternal/Everlasting, Hermeneutics, Immutability and Impassibility, Neoplatonism, Omnipotence, Omniscience and Foreknowledge, Ontotheology, Plato and Platonism, Process Thought, Religious Language, Simplicity, Stoicism, Transcendence.

Bibliography. Thomas Morris, *Our Idea of God;* Edward Wierenga, *The Nature of God;* Clark Pinnock et al., *The Openness of God;* John Sanders, *The God Who Risks.*

Good/Goodness   A term of moral approval. Philosophers have traditionally argued over whether goodness is objective or subjective. Does goodness reside in the nature of reality itself (objective), or does it designate the object of human desire or preference (subjective)?

Those who hold that goodness is independent of human feelings, desires, or preferences are called *moral realists.* Those who deny the extrahuman existence of goodness, locating it within the human psyche, are called *moral anti-realists.*

*Plato and *Aristotle, the first great Western moral thinkers, claimed that goodness is objective. Plato believed that there is an unchanging, *eternal standard (form) of goodness that actually exists in a spiritual realm. Aristotle believed that there is an objective *human nature that grounds objective morality. Christians historically identified goodness with *God, the ultimate good and the standard of goodness. Defining goodness by reference to God raises questions about the nature of divine goodness and its relationship to human goodness. Is the term *good* applied to both in univocal fashion? Is the goodness of persons the same as the goodness of God? Relating morality to God's will raised the *Euthyphro problem. *Utilitarians* suppose that goodness could be defined by appeal to the greatest benefit for the greatest number. That is, something is good if it makes the most people *happy and the fewest unhappy. They also think that what is right is what satisfies the most human preferences (without any means of distinguishing ignoble from noble preferences).

Many contemporary philosophers deny that goodness is objective or real. They think the world is best conceived by appeal to physical descriptions of matter and motion; value is simply not part of that conception of the world. Various theories have been offered to account for goodness in subjective or merely human terms. *Emotivists* claim that goodness is simply what people desire (and badness expresses human aversions); humans impose or project value onto the factual world according to their likes and dislikes. But if facts have no intrinsic value, what commends them? Likewise, what prohibits the condemnation of certain actions if there are no objective values attached to them?

Realists reject such theories because of a strong intuition that some actions or ends are good and bad in their own right, regardless of whether one is attracted to them or they maximize preference satisfaction.

See also Anthropomorphic Language; Aristotle; Augustine; Being and Goodness; Ethics; Ethics, Biblical; Euthyphro Problem; Evil, Problem of; Neoplatonism; Plato and Platonism; Realism / Anti-Realism; Religious Language.

Bibliography. Robert Adams, *Finite and Infinite Goods;* Kelly James Clark and Anne Poortenga, *The Story of Ethics.*

Happiness The state of human flourishing. The Greek word *eudaimonia* (often translated "happiness") means human flourishing or fulfillment. *Eudaimonism* is the view that ethical character and behavior produce (or are) human happiness. Human beings have an *essential nature that is fulfilled in *good character and actions. Eudaimonists do not consider happiness to be a psychological state (like giddiness or being "high"). Happiness is, rather, the state of a properly functioning soul. The pious assertion that *God calls us to obedience, not to happiness, would surprise Christian eudaimonists such as *Augustine and *Aquinas. They believed that humans naturally pursue happiness as part of our good, created nature.

Rejecting the idea that happiness is the gift of capricious gods or fortune, *Plato argued that happiness is psychic harmony; the just person is fulfilled in all levels of her personality—all the parts of her soul: reason, spirit, appetites. The vicious person necessarily represses or enslaves parts of his soul, allowing a particular desire to rule for its own satisfaction and not for the good of the whole person. Only in the just person are the parts of the soul ordered so that she can flourish.

*Aristotle argued that the goal or purpose (*telos*) of all human actions is happiness. Activities that fulfill our unique nature (or function) as humans result in human happiness. What makes humans unique, what distinguishes them from rocks, plants, and porcupines, is *reason. So happiness for humans is the excellent use of reason, which is a virtuous activity. Aristotle believed, unlike Plato, that we also require external comforts—food, shelter, clothing, health, family, and friends—for happiness. It should be noted that neither Plato nor Aristotle believed that happiness excludes pleasure. Both believed that the fulfilled person will find the proper satisfaction of her desires.

Augustine, following Plato, contended that human misery and wrongdoing is a matter of misplaced loves or desires (inordinate love of money, sex, food, etc.). Loving the right things in the right way, having a properly ordered heart, is human happiness. And the central love is of God, who fulfills our deepest desires. Aquinas, following Aristotle, argued that our nature is reason and that the most fulfilling human activity is contemplation. The only object capable of fulfilling our contemplative nature is God, so contemplation of God is happiness. But we see through a glass darkly, so the only truly happy person is the one who sees God face-to-face, that is, in the beatific vision in the next life.

More hedonistic views of happiness are on offer. Echoing themes in ancient Epicurus, hedonism says that happiness is the securing of pleasure and avoidance of pain. Jeremy Bentham's version of utilitarianism (the greatest happiness for the greatest number) employs the hedonic calculus where everyone's pains and pleasures are counted equally (the desire for a donut may have the same value as the desire to help a person in need). John Stuart Mill, believing Bentham's theory to be crass, argued for a hierarchy of pleasures with intellectual pleasures at the top and physical desires at the bottom. Some hedonisms, such as the Marquis de Sade's, reject traditional morality in favor of the pursuit of happiness (one's own pleasure) over others'.

The past four hundred years has seen a gradual divorcing of *ethics from happiness (ethics specifies what is right to do, whether or not it will make one happy). Any adequate Christian understanding of happiness should attempt to redress this decline. A biblical view of happiness is likely eudaimonistic: it holds that God made human beings such that the life of virtue fulfills one's nature and vice frustrates it. The biblical portrait of a God who will give us the desires of our hearts and who promises beatitude (happiness) to the merciful and the pure in heart is a God who graciously grants happiness to obedience.

See also Aquinas; Aristotle; Augustine; Being and Goodness; Essence/Essentialism; Ethics; Ethics, Biblical; Human Nature; Justice; Kierkegaard; Plato and Platonism.

Bibliography. Boethius, *The Consolation of Philosophy*; Kelly James Clark and Anne Poortenga, *The Story of Ethics*; Servais Pinckaers, *The Pursuit of Happiness—God's Way*; Jean Vanier, *Happiness*; Julia Annas, *The Morality of Happiness*; Ellen Frankel Paul, *Human Flourishing*.

Hegel, Georg Wilhelm Friedrich

(1770–1831)   German *idealist whose monumental and difficult ideas are contained in *Phenomenology of Spirit, Science of Logic,* and *Elements of the Philosophy of Right.* The central Hegelian theme is that history has a purpose or a meaning. Hegel contends that history is the rational outworking of *mind or spirit (the Absolute); indeed, the world is an extension of the self-actualization of *God. In Hegel's *Phenomenology of Spirit,* God is conceived primarily in terms of Spirit rather than Father or Son.

For Hegel, the rational process through which Spirit or Mind moves history and nature is *dialectical,* consisting in a movement of thesis, antithesis, and synthesis. For example, throughout history there are many ideologies that are dominant *(thesis).* Since these ideologies are typically partial and one-sided, they are opposed by other (partial and one-sided) ideas *(antithesis).* What often results is a new idea, which combines the virtues and eliminates the vices of the two opposing ideas *(synthesis).* The resulting synthesis is an improvement on the original and polarized ideas. The dialectic is teleological: it is a process of rational progress usually toward freedom. The new synthesis becomes a thesis that *must* eventually be opposed by a new idea (antithesis) that will issue forth a new synthesis. More concretely, Hegel suggests that the "synthesis" of Easter Sunday can only be achieved by passing through the horrors of Good Friday. This is important in two respects: first, it means that progress requires *evil as a necessary condition for completion. However, by making evil necessary, it would seem that Hegel's system mitigates its character *as evil.* Second, it reminds us why the "death of God" is central to Hegel's thought. For Hegel, the "death of God"—understood primarily in terms of the crucifixion—is the condition of possibility for the redemption of history.

Hegel's focus on history and knowing the Absolute (Mind) through history is quite different from the *Platonic tradition that views knowledge of the Absolute as a primarily intellective activity. Any historically based religion that believes that the Deity's purposes are revealed in space and time and that history is progressing toward an end *(telos),* such as Christianity, should have some sympathies for Hegel's vision.

Hegel's followers divided into two camps: those who believed that his system was compatible with Christianity (right-wing Hegelians) and those who did not (left-wing Hegelians). The vastly more influential left-wing Hegelians include D. F. Strauss, who wrote an early critical life of Jesus alleging that biblical narratives were myths that reflected the aspirations of the New Testament community. *Feuerbach claimed that theology is anthropology, where we learn about the idealized values of human beings in the study of religion. And *Marx claimed Hegel's dialectical view of history but eliminated the supernatural from the process. One of the most strident Christian critics of Hegel was *Kierkegaard.

Recently, Hegel's relationship to Christian orthodoxy has been reconsidered, particularly in light of his *Early Theological Writings* and *Lectures on the Philosophy of Religion*. Some have suggested that Hegel offers something of a Christian theology of Spirit. Others suggest that there is a deeply trinitarian thread to Hegel's *phenomenology. His *philosophy has also exerted significant influence on contemporary German theology, particularly in the work of Wolfhart Pannenberg and Jürgen Moltmann.

See also Cause/Causality; Dualism/Monism; Feuerbach; God, Nature of; Kierkegaard; Marx; Plato and Platonism; Transcendence.

Bibliography. Peter Singer, *Hegel;* William Desmond, *Hegel's God;* Karl Barth, *Protestant Theology in the Nineteenth Century;* Alan Olson, *Hegel and the Spirit;* Andrew Shanks, *Hegel's Political Theology;* Mark Wallace, *Fragments of the Spirit.*

Heidegger, Martin (1889–1976) German *philosopher of central importance to the *existentialist and *postmodern traditions and one of the most influential philosophers of the twentieth century. First trained within the Catholic philosophical tradition (writing a dissertation on *Scotus), Heidegger left the church and converted to Lutheranism (though he would later abandon

this as well). His earliest work (1919–1923) focused on the *phenomenology of religion, with special attention to *Augustine and medieval mysticism. His landmark work, *Being and Time,* was published in 1927, earning him the teaching post of his teacher, Edmund Husserl, at Freiburg.

Heidegger understood his *Being and Time* as a project in *metaphysics, attempting to understand the nature of "Being." To investigate the meaning of Being, Heidegger focused on "that being for whom its being is a question," viz., human beings. By this Heidegger meant that humans were the kind of beings who reflected on what it meant "to be." In order to avoid the static notions of the *self in *Descartes and *Kant, Heidegger did not describe the human person as a "subject." Instead, he named the human being *Dasein,* which literally means "being there." The human being—Dasein—is a finite, "located" being, conditioned by geography and history.

What, then, does it mean for Dasein "to be"? Through his analyses, Heidegger suggested that human beings are essentially *futural*—they are *called* to be something. As such, human beings are fundamentally directed toward the future (thus he concluded that Being *is* temporality). More specifically, Heidegger spoke about our "being-toward-death"—that the possibility of our nonexistence in death functions as a wake-up call for us. The authentic person is the one who answers this "call of conscience" and chooses to be that which she is called to be. It is this line that was seized on by existentialists such as Sartre and Camus. But the theologian Rudolf Bultmann also seized on this as unveiling the *truth about human existence. He then noted that a similar understanding of human existence could be found in the New Testament. Therefore, Bultmann appealed to Heidegger's "purely philosophical" analysis to prove the existential core of the New Testament. However, since Heidegger's early lectures have come to light, it has become clear that Heidegger's account mirrors that of the New Testament because it was derived *from* the New Testament. All of the basic pieces of Heidegger's *Being and Time* can be found in his 1922 lectures on Paul's letters to the Thessalonians!

Heidegger's later work moved even further away from Christian orthodoxy, toward a more pagan mysticism. But upon his death, he requested a mass of Christian burial. Heidegger also exerted considerable influence on Catholic theology in the last twentieth century, particularly in the work of Karl Rahner.

See also Deconstruction, Essence/Essentialism, Existentialism, Hermeneutics, Ontology, Perspectivalism, Phenomenology.

Bibliography. John Caputo, *Heidegger and Aquinas;* Laurence Hemming, *Heidegger's Atheism;* Theodore Kisiel, *The Genesis of Heidegger's Being and Time;* John Macquarrie, *Heidegger and Christianity;* Jean-Luc Marion, *God Without Being;* James K. A. Smith, *The Fall of Interpretation;* idem, *Speech and Theology;* Hugo Ott, *Martin Heidegger;* John Van Buren, *The Young Heidegger.*

Hell A place of *eternal punishment after death. The medieval church taught that those who stand outside the church are condemned to eternal, conscious, and usually physical torment in hell. Many medieval philosophers offered lengthy treatises describing and justifying *God's *goodness in the face of the suffering of the damned. To the question, how could those in heaven be happy knowing about those who suffered in hell? *Aquinas answered that seeing divine *justice meted out in hell will contribute to the *happiness of those in heaven. Or how could punishment be infinite when the sin and the sinner are finite? *Augustine contended that the punishment was infinite because the offense was against an infinite God. Dante gave a classic expression of the torments of hell in his *Inferno.* These convictions continued through the modern period in Roman Catholic, Protestant, and Orthodox traditions. This traditional doctrine has come under criticism by contemporary philosophers and theologians.

At stake in the controversy about the doctrine of hell is the question of divine justice. Traditionally, hell was viewed as the just recompense of actions of rebellion against God. The infinite holiness of God demanded an infinite punishment. Since infinite punishment could never genuinely be exhausted by a finite human being, punishment must last eternally. But belief in the disproportionality of the punishment (eternal torment) to the sin (finite in effect) led some to reject the eternality of hell. This view, known as *annihilationism,* holds that punishment is justly meted out in a temporally finite manner after death, after which the damned are annihilated.

Liberal Protestant traditions in the nineteenth century and some Roman Catholic traditions after the Second Vatican Council (1961–1964) defended *universalism,* the belief that all human persons will eventually be brought into a redeemed status before God; none is eternally lost or annihilated. Even some prominent conservative theologians have embraced universalism. Universalism is generally held for two reasons. First, the trajectory of the Bible suggests that in the end everything will be redeemed, every knee will bow and every tongue will confess that Jesus is Lord. Second, that in love God desires the salvation of all creatures and God's *omnipotence (infinite creativity) ensures that God can save all creatures without violating their *free will. But Jesus' affirmations of hell are problematic for universalism.

See also Aquinas; Augustine; Being and Goodness; Evil, Problem of; God, Nature of; Goodness; Justice; Pluralism; Resurrection/Immortality.

Bibliography. William Crockett, ed., *Four Views on Hell;* Edward Fudge and Robert Peterson, *Two Views of Hell;* Charles Steven Seymour, *A Theodicy of Hell;* Jerry Walls, *Hell.*

Hermeneutics The method and theory of interpretation (from the Greek *hermeneuo,* "to interpret," related to Hermes, the messenger of the gods). From the time of *Aristotle's *De interpretatione,* hermeneutics has been understood as an investigation of the conditions for interpreting texts and utterances—since both oral utterances and written texts require interpretation. The goal of interpretation was to understand the "meaning" of a text or utterance. Within the first centuries of the Christian church, this discipline became more focused on questions regarding the interpretation of Scripture, and thus emphasized the textual aspect. In particular, the focus was on methods that could be employed for interpreting the Bible (received as God's Word) in order to discern "what *God meant."

One of the first "manuals" of hermeneutics was *Augustine's *De doctrina christiana (On Christian Doctrine,* or better, *Teaching Christianity).* Written for preachers, this manual provided an introduction to the nature of language (as "signs"), and then discussed the different methods used to unearth the meaning of Scripture. For Augustine, the "author's intent" was only one of a number of possible meanings. Augustine emphasized what, in the Middle Ages, would be described as the "plenitude" of meaning in the Scriptures, uncovered not simply by "historical-grammatical exegesis," but also through reading the Bible allegorically (as Augustine did in his commentaries on Genesis). The precedent for this allegorical reading of Scripture was found in the apostle Paul's own interpretation of the Old Testament (for instance, his interpretation of the Abraham/Sarah/Hagar narrative in Galatians). In the end, for Augustine, the ultimate criterion of a "true" interpretation is that it build up the love of God and neighbor. While the Reformers railed against the abuses of the allegorical method, they did not advocate the narrow "historical-grammatical" method as we know it today. However, the Reformers were concerned about frameworks that placed the "true meaning" of a text in the hands of an authority such as the Roman magisterium. They emphasized instead the "perspicuity" or clarity of the Scriptures to the sincere reader illumined by the Holy Spirit.

With the advent of *modernity (particularly after the Renaissance), new attention was paid to questions of interpretation. Although new principles for scriptural interpretation were offered, principles for the interpretation of law and art were developed as well. The questions were analogous to those posed to Scripture: What does this painting or that law *mean,* and *how* can we know? At this point, hermeneutics still largely focused on texts. But with the groundbreaking work of Martin *Heidegger and Hans-Georg Gadamer (building on and responding to Friedrich *Schleiermacher and Wilhelm Dilthey), there was a new emphasis on the way in which all of life required interpretation—that simply "being-in-the-world" requires us to construe and understand the world around us, to *interpret* our surroundings. For Heidegger, for me to see a "cup," I must already see it *as* a cup, interpret this thing in front of me *as* the kind of thing that I can drink from. These interpretations or construals of my environment are conditioned by my heritage or "tradition"—the presuppositions (Heidegger called them "forehavings") that I bring to my perception of the world. Thus, especially after Heidegger, it is common to distinguish between "general hermeneutics" (a broad account of how we interpret our environment) and "special hermeneutics" (which focuses on how we interpret in particular spheres, such as art, law, and theology).

The development of *deconstruction posed a new challenge to both classical hermeneutics as well as Heideggerian notions. In particular, Jacques Derrida emphasized the way in which "signs" ("pieces" of language like words or bodily gestures) are susceptible to a multiplicity of interpretations—what Derrida would describe as a "play" of interpretation. "The" meaning of a text could not be stabilized, and the possibility of knowing the author's intention was problematized. Thus current debates in hermeneutics—between deconstruction and "speech-act theory"—have revolved around the question of authorial intent. While no confessional reading of Scripture that receives it as God's Word can simply jettison authorial intent, just how we discern the (multiple) meanings of Scripture remains debated. While the historical-grammatical method continues to dominate theological readings of Scripture, a new generation of scholars has come to appreciate both the premodern insights of Augustine as well as the legitimacy of some *postmodern accounts of interpretation.

See also Deconstruction, Heidegger, Religious Language, Schleiermacher, Semiotics.

Bibliography. James K. A. Smith, *The Fall of Interpretation*; Jean Grondin, *An Introduction to Philosophical Hermeneutics*; Roger Lundin, Clarence Walhout, and Anthony Thiselton, *The Promise of Hermeneutics*; Anthony Thiselton, *New Horizons in Hermeneutics*; Kevin Vanhoozer, *Is There a Meaning in This Text?*; John D. Caputo, *Radical Hermeneutics*; Hans Frei, *The Eclipse of Biblical Narrative*.

Human Nature The *essence of human persons. The answer to the question, What makes us human? has often been taken to mean a list of essential attributes all humans possess or a normative ideal to which humans should conform. The Christian tradition has long framed the concept of human nature using the language of creation in the image of *God (*imago Dei*). Christian treatments of the nature of human persons are often explanations of what separates humans from animals and angels. These can be discovered either by reflecting on similarities/differences between God and humans or between humans and animals. Concepts such as rationality, sociability, spirituality, and morality enter into the discussion.

With the advent of the *Enlightenment in the eighteenth century, it became increasingly common to suppose that God is not the ground of our humanity. Nonetheless, most believed that there is a universally common human nature underneath all the cultural and the individual differences of people. For without a common human nature, there would be no basis for a common *ethic to hold societies together, or so the reasoning went. The commonly accepted essence of humans in the Enlightenment was *rationality and *free will (in both respects women were considered defective).

Charles Darwin, in *Descent of Man,* paved the way for radically new views of human nature and fulfillment. According to Darwin, there is nothing special about human nature—we are the unexpected result of blind mutations, competition, and time, not the preordained plan of a loving God. We are apes without hair, not angels without wings. We must understand ourselves from below, not from above: "Man still bears in his bodily frame the indelible stamp of his lowly origin."

Since the time of *Nietzsche, the conviction of a common or universal human nature has been in some disrepute. Deeply influenced by Darwin's thought, Nietzsche speculates on human psychology, always keeping in mind the revolutionary thought that humans are not far removed from the animals. As he puts it in another work, "Formerly one sought the feeling of grandeur of man by pointing to his divine *origin:* this has now become a forbidden way, for at its portal stands the ape." He asks such questions as, Why do descendants of animals develop morality and a conscience?

Where do Christianity and morality come from? Although we seek to raise ourselves above nature through morality and religion, we are part of nature; we are hairless apes. Nietzsche peers deep inside our human/animal nature to see what will really satisfy our deepest desires.

In the twentieth century, the rejection of a shared and static human nature has come mostly because of the increasing appreciation for human differences (of ethnicity, race, gender, class, etc.) and the inability to rationally settle disputes about human nature without recourse to exercises of power. In addition, it is widely noted that traditional views of human nature have been used, with apparent divine and *metaphysical endorsement, to justify systemic and institutional injustice to women and slaves, the poor and the stranger. With the rejection of a common human nature, the belief has arisen that people are free to carve out their own characters without limit or constraint, to be exactly who or what they want to be without the conventional constraints of traditional religion or morality. It is difficult, however, to imagine that this project is possible without slipping back into some form of essentialism; that is, one must believe that humans are by nature radically free individuals who are sufficiently plastic to form themselves.

In recent times, reacting to "isolationist" models of human nature, philosophers have an increasing appreciation of the communal aspects of human nature. Functionalist (people defined by what they do) and essentialist (people defined by their individual characteristics) accounts inadequately capture the larger context of personhood as defined by their relations-in-community. A large voice in this revisioning has come from Christian thinkers, who have supposed that God's triunity is "relational" at heart. Thus the relational identity of the triune God is reflected in the creation of persons-in-relation. Human nature is a quality that belongs not simply to individuals

but to individuals-in-relationship. This would argue for thinking about ourselves not as isolated selves in possession of certain qualities or functions, but rather as complex in our characteristics and our relationships—including our relationship with God.

See also Being and Goodness; Dualism; Essence/Essentialism; Ethics; Ethics, Biblical; Existentialism; Feminist Philosophy; Free Will; Happiness; Justice; Mind/Soul/Spirit; Pascal; Self.

Bibliography. Roger Trigg, *Ideas of Human Nature;* Leslie Stevenson and David Haberman, *Ten Theories of Human Nature;* Alistair McFayden, *The Call to Personhood;* Ian Barbour, *Nature, Human Nature, and God;* Leroy Rouner, ed., *Is There a Human Nature?;* Hunter Brown, ed., *Images of the Human.*

Hume, David (1711–1776)   Scottish philosopher associated with the *Enlightenment. Working within the empirical tradition of John Locke (1632–1704) and George Berkeley (1685–1753), Hume reached decidedly more skeptical conclusions than his predecessors did. His most famous works are *Treatise on Human Nature* and the posthumously published *Dialogues Concerning Natural Religion.* Hume's project begins from the premise that one should "draw no conclusions but where he is authorized by experience." It is due to this emphasis on experience that Hume (like Bacon and Locke) is described as an empiricist. For Hume, all of our perceptions—what is present to the *mind—can ultimately be traced to two sources: impressions and ideas. Impressions are "lively and strong" perceptions conveyed to the mind by the presence of the external object. Ideas are "fainter and weaker" copies of impressions, and all of our ideas derive ultimately from impressions. This stands in contrast to rationalists such as *Descartes and *Leibniz who believed that the mind comes "preloaded" with innate ideas that are not derived from experience.

On this empirical basis, Hume erects a criterion for determining the validity or justification of our metaphysical ideas: Only those ideas that can be traced back to an original impression should be entertained. Ideas that cannot be traced back to original impressions are based purely on speculation and should be jettisoned. The effects of this strict criterion are felt in several areas; for example, things talked about in *metaphysics—things like *God and souls—cannot be empirically observed. And there are no sensory impressions of the external world (we only have appearances of what might be an external world). We have no sensory impressions of a *self that endures through time (we only have sensory impressions of some agent of sensation, but not of the same agent that persists through time). We also have no sensory impressions of the inductive principles that would justify beliefs about the future of the empirical world. We know nothing of causality; we only know when x occurs y occurs, but we cannot observe x causing y. So Hume takes empiricism and drives it to its logical (and skeptical) conclusion: If sensory information is our only access to the world, then we know very little about the world (including matter, God, causality, and the self). *Kant, who said that Hume woke him up from his dogmatic slumbers, endorsed Hume's critique of "metaphysics" as speculation without a tether.

Hume captured well the Enlightenment hostility to religious belief. He was a thoroughgoing naturalist, believing that nothing existed beyond what could be the object of sensory experience. Most especially he felt that the belief in a *transcendent God had no rational (i.e., empirical) basis. In his *Enquiry Concerning Human Understanding*, he famously argued that it would never be rational to accept any of the *miracles of the Christian tradition; the probability of a miracle claim being false is always greater than the probability that a universal law of nature had been violated. His posthumously published *Dialogues* contain both the classic expression of the problem of *evil and what many consider the final refutation of all theistic arguments.

See also Cause/Causality; Descartes; Enlightenment; Epistemology; Evil, Problem of; Kant; Miracles; Modernity/Modernism; Naturalism; Natural Theology; Positivism; Theistic Arguments.

Bibliography. Anthony Quinton, *Hume*; Ernest Mossner, *The Life of David Hume*; William Lad Sessions, *Reading Hume's Dialogues*; Keith Yandell, *Hume's "Inexplicable Mystery"*; David Fate Norton, ed., *The Cambridge Companion to Hume*.

Idealism   Philosophical theories that posit mental (ideas) or spiritual (nonmaterial) *phenomena as ultimate. It might better be called "idea-ism," as it posits the reality of only mental phenomena. Idealism stands in contrast to *materialism, which supposes that reality is material in nature. There are many different versions of idealism as well as many hybrid theories that combine elements of idealism and materialism. *Plato's contribution to ancient Greek thought is often thought to be a version of idealism since he believed that the most real exists in the world of Forms (Ideas); the sensory world is a shadowland. The full corpus of Plato's writing makes this designation difficult since he does, at other times, also affirm the full reality of the physical world.

Early Christians (e.g., *Augustine) argued for the philosophical primacy of the Creator over the created order. Because *God is not a material being, Christians supported the claim that the invisible world is more "real" than the physical world. There is some influence here of *Neoplatonism, which claims that merely material beings have less reality than the purely spiritual One.

This tended toward de-emphasizing the creation, the body, earthly sources of human *happiness, and human cultural activities.

Idealism became much more prominent in the early *modern period in the work of the Christian philosopher George Berkeley (1685–1753). Berkeley argued that our only evidence of the world is our perception of it. But perceptions are mental, not material; the only things we know to be real are ideas. They are the only entities to which we have immediate and certain access. They must be ultimately real. Berkeley maintained his idealist worldview in part to combat the increasingly materialistic and *atheistic worldviews of the *Enlightenment.

Throughout the modern period, it was commonly assumed that ideas are representations of material objects. This tradition reached its climax in the work of *Hegel, who propounded an idealist *philosophy of history. For Hegel, history moves with an inexorable internal purpose, the fuller realization of the Absolute Spirit, which pushes history forward and makes sense of the conflicts of ordinary history. The Absolute Spirit must transcend history if any final and ultimate meaning is to be given to the ordinary chaotic experiences in history. Hegel's philosophy entails that reality must ultimately reside in an ideal world. By the end of the eighteenth century, Hegel's British followers would drop all reference to a material world and hold that ultimate, ideal reality is abstract, unchanging, undifferentiated, and timeless.

As idealist philosophy became increasingly removed from the messy but insistent actual material world, it became increasingly ignored. Although it was the dominant philosophy in the West in the nineteenth century, it was finally rejected as irrelevant by philosophers moved by scientific and pragmatic concerns. No one refuted idealism, but no one found it appealing either. So philosophy simply moved on as though it had been rationally eliminated. There

are some signs in recent times that the death of idealism was prematurely pronounced by the *positivists. Contemporary anti-realists deny the fundamental postulate of materialism lying behind rejections of idealism. And contemporary Christian philosophers have fought to reinstate the conviction that reality (God) is ultimately spiritual. At stake theologically in these debates is how we understand the *goodness of the created order (Genesis 1:31) and how we can then conceive the relationship between Creator and creation.

See also Augustine, Hegel, Naturalism, Neoplatonism, Plato, Realism/Anti-Realism.

Bibliography. Jonathan Dancy, *Berkeley;* David Berman, *George Berkeley;* Robert J. Fogelin, *Routledge Philosophy Guidebook to Berkeley and The Principles of Human Knowledge;* Robert Merrihew Adams, *Leibniz.*

Immortality.   *See* Resurrection/Immortality.

Immutability and Impassibility
Immutability is the doctrine that *God does not change. Biblical support for the doctrine includes claims such as "I, the Lord your God, do not change" (Malachi 3:6), and Yahweh as the great "I am who I am" (Exodus 3:14). Divine impassibility rejects *patripassionism,* the belief that God the Father suffers. God's inability to suffer is entailed by immutability and aseity (God's radical self-dependence or independence). If God cannot change, God's emotions cannot change from a state of bliss to a state of unhappiness. And if God is radically independent of everything in the world, God cannot be emotionally affected by anything in the world. If God cannot change or be affected by things in the world, God cannot suffer. The multitude of passages smacking of passibility and mutability are interpreted as mere *anthropomorphism. Christians have recently come to

disagree on these questions, partly because of disagreements about just what it means to "suffer." If suffering entails some defect or lack, then a perfect being cannot suffer. But if suffering simply refers to an ability to "feel" (such as empathy), then this would not entail a defect but may be a virtue.

Divine impassibility does not preclude feelings on God's part. The doctrine of impassibility claims only that God does not suffer from any upsetting emotions, that is, those such as anger or sorrow that diminish *happiness. God is in a steady state of happiness from which grief has been banished, since grief would constitute a lack. This view of God was influenced by the Stoic ideal of happiness as uninterrupted, suffering-free bliss. God is completely lacking in *eros* (needy love or desiring love). Since God desires nothing, God cannot be disappointed. Hence, the love that God manifests is not eros or sympathy, but benevolence. God expresses God's love as benevolence—the unfaltering disposition to will good things for God's creatures. God's bliss is neither increased nor decreased by creaturely responses to God's well doing. God is *apatheia* (lacking disturbing passions). God's life is a steady stream of undisturbed joy that cannot be diminished by anything that happens in the world. Impassibility treats the biblical passages that state that God grieves or gets angry as mere anthropomorphisms.

To some modern theologians and philosophers, an immutable and impassible Deity seems to do injustice to both the biblical narrative and personal experience. We value a God who suffers with us, who is active in redemptive history, attentive to our needs, and heeds our prayers. Immutability and impassibility, it is alleged, were accepted only because of the unfortunate "hellenizing" influence on early Christian theology—the adoption of Greek philosophical categories that could not do justice to biblical theism. If one were to remove the Platonizing spectacles, a more natural reading of Scripture would clearly show a God that changes and suffers: "In all their distress he too was distressed" (Isaiah 63:9). The passages that suggest immutability are taken to imply merely that God never changes with respect to God's promises or love. The rejection of divine impassibility has implications for one's understanding of divine love. God's love for God's creatures entails that God has desires for God's creatures and their well-being. If God's desires are unsatisfied, that is, if human beings sin or suffer, then God's erotic or agapic love is expressed sympathetically—God's love is suffering love.

See also Anthropomorphic Language; Aquinas; Augustine; Eternal/Everlasting; God, Nature of; Happiness; Ontotheology; Plato and Platonism; Pseudo-Dionysius; Religious Language; Stoicism; Theodicy; Transcendence; Underdetermination.

Bibliography. Richard Creel, *Divine Impassibility*; Jürgen Moltmann, *The Crucified God*; Isaak August Dorner, *Divine Immutability*.

Inclusivism   *See* Pluralism, Exclusivism, and Inclusivism.

Justice   *Ethical concept concerning the ordering of a community's life together. Justice has two central meanings in moral *philosophy. *Retributive justice* is the proportional punishment for a wrong action. *Distributive justice,* on the other hand, is the equitable distribution of goods and resources according to a principle of fairness. Both notions of justice are seen in the biblical narrative, both have been subjects of controversy in *modern times, and both have significant theological implications.

Traditional notions of retributive justice are captured succinctly in the phrase, "an eye for an eye, a tooth for a tooth." The intent of the phrase in ancient Judaism was that the punishment must fit the crime. Crime and punishment should be proportional: the harm inflicted in punishment ought not be greater or less than the harm suffered by the victim of the crime. The practical question of retributive justice is determining what constitutes proportionality in punishment. In addition, retribution makes sense only if humans are responsible for their actions, that is, only if human beings freely choose their actions. If human choices are caused by our heredity and environment (or even *God), then human responsibility is diminished and retributive justice is unfair. Defenders of determinism tend to deny the morality of retributive justice; rather, they argue that retributive justice is to be meted out in accord with the power to deter future crimes. Deterrence becomes the criterion of justice.

A theological implication of retributive justice concerns the ethical dimensions of God's punishment of sinners. Questions of proportionality are raised for the traditional doctrine of *hell, and questions of responsibility are raised by the doctrines of total depravity and election. If persons cannot choose to be *good, because of being born into a condition over which they have no control, how can they be punished for their choices? Consider the following example: It would not be fair for the police to come to your house and arrest you for a crime your great-grandmother committed. How could it be fair for God to hold us responsible for the sin of Adam and the condition that Adam's indiscretion created? Finally, how can it be just for an innocent person to suffer (even voluntarily) for the crimes committed by another? Theological analyses of Christ's redemptive work must deal with hard questions like these.

The early church argued that the death of Christ satisfies the moral demands of God's justice while also expressing mercy toward sinners. This theory of the death of Christ, known as the penal substitionary view, has received stern criticism. Much of it echoes the charges of nineteenth-century religious liberalism that

satisfaction makes God out to be a surly judge who demands blood sacrifice while radically downplaying the importance of God's love. The controversy has revived earlier debates about legal and covenantal language in Scripture.

A second area of theological importance concerns the relationship between justice and forgiveness on the horizontal level of human relationships. The topic has found concrete embodiment in the Truth and Reconciliation Commission in South Africa. What would it mean to enact grace and forgiveness in the political order? Does forgiveness only come after retribution or restitution has been made? Does forgiveness take claims of justice seriously enough?

Since the time of Karl *Marx, a great deal of attention has been paid to the concept of distributive justice. The abundance of goods and resources created in modern industrial societies and the shocking differences in how those goods are created and distributed form the basis of the Marxist critique of capitalism. The great ideological debates in political philosophy of the twentieth century focused on the appropriate formula for the fair distribution of goods and resources. The Marxist tradition argued that need ought to determine allocation. The free-market tradition argued that markets left to themselves will determine appropriate allocation. Social democrats argued for a hybrid system whereby both market forces and governmental institutions control allocation. The most influential theorist of the twentieth century on these matters has been John Rawls (1921–2002). His book *A Theory of Justice* argues for an impartial notion of distributive justice by which one's social status would not be a determinant of allocation. In a genuinely just society, the least affluent members are treated the same as the most affluent. Given the patterns of distribution in Acts 2, there is a great deal of Christian reflection on these matters, ranging from Marxist liberation theologians to market-oriented Christian political thinkers.

See also Aquinas; Augustine; Ethics; Ethics, Biblical; Feminist Philosophy; Free Will; Goodness; Happiness; Hell; Kant; Marx; Plato and Platonism; Pluralism.

Bibliography. Richard John Neuhaus, *Doing Well and Doing Good;* Nicholas Wolterstorff, *Until Justice and Peace Embrace;* Miroslav Volf, *Exclusion and Embrace;* Gustavo Gutiérrez, *Theology of Liberation.*

Kant, Immanuel (1724–1804)   The central figure of the German *Enlightenment and arguably the most influential philosopher of *modern times. Kant was born, raised, and spent most of his life in the East Prussian city of Königsberg (now Kaliningrad). He was raised in a deeply religious home, studied theology in the university, but was generally impatient with traditional formulations of religious belief. He also had an abiding distrust in history as the vehicle of religious *truth. Being faithful to his own Pietist background, Kant attempted to safeguard religious belief from the inroads being made by rationalist dogmatism on the one hand and empiricist skepticism on the other (with mysticism as a third threat). His rendering of the relationship between *faith and *reason brings morality to the center of the discussion. In the preface to his *Critique of Pure Reason* (1781), he famously concluded: "I have found it necessary to deny reason in order to make room for faith." By this he meant that, while rationalist *metaphysics admitted no room for *God, morality demanded just such a belief. The "critique" of reason thus requires drawing the limits or boundaries of theoretical reason in order to preserve the room for this "moral faith." This project finds its completion in his later work *Religion within the Limits of Reason Alone* (1793).

Kant's central project concerned the grounding of the natural sciences in a critical framework that was influenced by both the empirical and rationalist traditions. He affirmed in *The Critique of Pure Reason* that human knowledge begins with sense impressions (following *Hume) but had to consist of more than mere sensations. His *epistemology ushered in "the Copernican revolution in *philosophy" where the *mind, not the external object, is the center of cognition; the mind is not a passive recipient but is the active organizer of human experience. There must be a habitual, intellectual ordering of empirical perceptions according to certain mental categories, such as the concepts of *substance and *causality. These categories do not exist "out there" in the world but rather "in here" as part of the mental apparatus. If for Locke and the empiricists the mind is a "blank slate" written upon by experience, then for Kant the mind is like a preformatted computer disk. Data are received onto the disk only within the structural parameters of the formatting. (To extend the analogy, for *Descartes and other rationalists the mind comes not just preformatted, but preloaded with data called "innate ideas.") These categories are filters through which the external world is apprehended and interpreted. They also provide the glue that holds sensory perceptions of the world together. Kant believed that there is something that grounds our sensory experience, something that exists independently of our sensations of it, but that we have no access to it. Kant called the inaccessible but real ground of human sensations the "thing-in-itself."

There are objects that cannot be filtered through our mental categories, most notably God and the *self (the "ego"). These are not the sort of things of which we could form any sense impression. Try as we might, God and the self (as the seat of consciousness) could never be seen or touched. Thus they cannot properly be objects of knowledge, but rather must be objects of faith. Our convictions about them rest not on any empirical evidence of their existence, but rather in their role as necessary postulates of moral reasoning. In matters of morality, for instance, Kant thought that it is rational to hope that being virtuous will result in human *happiness. Since virtue is not always rewarded with happiness in this life, we must believe that it will happen in the next life. In short, we must believe that there is a next life in which virtue and happiness coincide and that there is a God who ensures that this will happen. Our future existence and the existence of God are, for Kant, rational *postulates*. He rejected the classical proofs for God's existence, but in their stead argued on the basis of morality that we must nonetheless continue to believe in God if we are to be moral.

Hence we have Kant's reconfiguration or rational reconstruction of Christianity as offered in his *Religion within the Limits of Reason Alone*. Kant's Enlightenment project, concerned with universality and haunted by religious wars, required the rejection of the contingencies of tradition and hence "special" revelation (such as the Bible). Since tradition and special revelation were tethered to specific, particular, historical communities, any "religion" based upon them would be particular and contingent—and therefore disqualified from being a "universal" religion (the Enlightenment hope). Thus Kant offered a reconsideration of religion that revolved around the principles of *morality*, which were understood to be universal precisely because they were rational. He offered what he described as a "pure moral religion," devoid of the "cultic" particularities of confessional religion, such as Christianity. This project of a "moral religion" was the signal influence on the subsequent development of classical liberal theology.

See also Descartes; Enlightenment; Epistemology; Ethics; Ethics, Biblical; Faith; Faith and Reason; Feminist Philosophy; Happiness; Hume; Metaphysics/ Ontology; Modernity/Modernism; Natural Theology; Ontotheology; Pluralism; Postmodernism; Reason and Belief in God; Theistic Arguments.

Bibliography. Roger Scruton, *Kant;* Manfred Kuehn, *Kant;* Nicholas Wolterstorff, *Reason within the Bounds of Religion;* C. Stephen Evans, *Subjectivity and Religious Belief;* John Hare, *The Moral Gap;* Allan Wood, *Kant's Rational Theology;* Philip Quinn, ed., "Kant's Philosophy of Religion."

Kierkegaard, Søren (1813–1855) Danish philosopher who considered his task as a philosopher to discover what it means to be (or become) a Christian. Reacting against *Hegelian *philosophy and the externalist formalism of the Lutheran state church in Denmark, Kierkegaard provided an account of existence—and specifically Christian existence—that emphasized the role of inwardness or subjective appropriation. He reacted against both rationalism (which reduced *faith to what was reasonable) and dogmatism (which reduced faith to intellectual assent to objective propositions). Faith, for Kierkegaard, is a certain madness, a "leap" one makes beyond what is reasonable (echoing the apostle Paul's claim that the gospel is "foolishness" to the Greeks [1 Corinthians 1:18–25]). These themes are developed in key works (often written under pseudonyms) such as *Fear and Trembling, Philosophical Fragments,* and the *Concluding Unscientific Postscript.*

These claims are developed differently in different texts. In *Fear and Trembling,* Kierkegaard considers what it means to be an "authentic" individual, and more specifically, what it means to be authentically related to *God. The paradigm here is Abraham's response to God's command to sacrifice Isaac (Genesis 22). An authentic individual stands in a singular and direct relationship with the Absolute—like Abraham, who alone was the recipient of God's command to sacrifice Isaac. Making sense of this is an occasion for Kierkegaard to distinguish between different stages of existence. The first is the *aesthetic stage,* in which a person is committed to the satisfaction of his own desires. Here an individual is concerned only about himself and thus not in relation to anything other. In the *ethical stage*, the individual is drawn outside herself and sees her obligation to others as more important than her own pleasure. The ethical stage is the sphere of duty and law. So, for instance, one of the rules of *ethics is, "Thou shalt not kill" (and thou certainly shalt not kill thine own son!). If the highest stage humans could reach was merely to be ethical, how could Abraham be heralded as the hero of faith? According to ethics, Abraham was a murderer, or at least an attempted murderer. Perplexed by how to make sense of Abraham, Kierkegaard arrives at the third stage. The *religious stage* is where we move *beyond* the merely ethical into a singular relation with the Absolute. This relation "does not make sense" from the perspective of ethics or rationality—it is absurd.

In *Concluding Unscientific Postscript,* Kierkegaard offers the axiom, "Truth is subjectivity." By this he does not mean to deny that matters can be "objectively" true, only that such truth does not really matter until it is subjectively appropriated. For him, the paradigmatic example is how we see the truth of the incarnation. While it is objectively true that God was in Christ reconciling the world to himself, that truth only matters—only "becomes true"—when it is subjectively appropriated by the individual heart. And it is appropriated, not by merely rational assent to the truth of the proposition, but by the passionate commitment of the heart.

While playing a role in the development of existentialists such as Jean-Paul Sartre, Kierkegaard exerted significant influence on both Martin *Heidegger and Karl Barth, and thus was one of the central influences on twentieth-century Protestant theology. The emphasis on choice, on subjectively appropriating, and hence of becoming a certain kind of person influenced both Barth and Paul Tillich. Barth was impressed by Kierkegaard's belief in "the infinite qualitative difference" between people and God, and so God as "wholly other," beyond humanly available categories, became central to his theology. This led to his famous rejection of *natural theology and his corresponding endorsement of God's revelation in the Word as the source of theology. Kierkegaard's critique of objective reason and emphasis on subjective appropriation is seen as a precursor to the *postmodern critiques of rationality and have influenced figures such as Jacques Derrida and John Caputo.

See also Enlightenment, Ethics, Existentialism, Faith, Faith and Reason, Happiness, Hegel, Human Nature, Kant, Modernity/Modernism, Postmodernism, Pseudo-Dionysius, Reason and Belief in God, Transcendence, Truth.

Bibliography. C. Stephen Evans, *Kierkegaard's "Fragments" and "Postscript"*; idem, *Passionate Reason*; idem, *Faith Beyond Reason*; Merold Westphal, *Becoming a Self.*

Leibniz, Gottfried (1646–1716)

German philosopher and mathematician associated with the rationalist tradition of the seventeenth century, which includes *Descartes and Benedictus Spinoza. Leibniz was a prodigious and complex thinker, at home in the world of mathematics, *philosophy, theology, politics, science, and history. He corresponded with all the major figures of his time and made numerous influential intellectual contributions, including breakthroughs in mechanics, the codiscovery (with Newton) of the calculus, and authoring *Theodicy*, the most important book-length treatise on the problem of *evil in the early eighteenth century.

Leibniz's most enduring philosophical contributions come in the areas of *metaphysics and philosophy of religion. With respect to the first, Leibniz is well known for the claim that the universe consists ultimately of simple substances called *monads.* Leibniz's motivation for this conception was to preserve the "life" of the world, in contrast to the mechanistic views of the universe, which were becoming common. For Leibniz, the basic "stuff" of the universe, though material, is also "charged" with an immaterial *transcendence (what he describes as "substantial forms"). Part of Leibniz's concern here is to provide an account of the universe as *created*; as such, his motivations are largely theological.

Another important feature of Leibniz's metaphysics is also theologically motivated: his claim that each *substance is causally isolated. Again, this stems from his desire to construct an account of creation that is "worthy" of the Creator, as well as an attempt to account for Providence. According to him, this requires honoring the "integrity" of creation. *God has created the world in such a way that it has a qualified autonomy. It has autonomy because a good Creator created a sufficient universe that can "run on its own," but this autonomy is qualified since it is the direct result of being created. For Leibniz, each substance is "preloaded" by the Creator, and thus contains *within itself* all the resources necessary for everything it will ever become. Leibniz described these resources as an internal "law" that brings about the entire series of states the substance will ever be in throughout its existence. Thus when one billiard ball hits another, the first does not *cause the second to move. Rather, at the creation, God brings it about that there is a *preestablished harmony* between all substances. So when the balls come in contact, the second one moves in such a way that it *appears* to be moved by the first, when in fact its movement springs from its own "law of the series." Needless to say, many of Leibniz's critics argued that the view was viciously deterministic, a charge he firmly, if not always convincingly, denied by redefining freedom in a compatibilist manner.

Leibniz argued that God is the creator of all monads. But since God is perfect, Leibniz held that God must create the best possible set of monads, that is, *the best of all possible worlds*. This left Leibniz with some explaining to do, since one is inclined to think that the best possible world would not be as bad as the actual world is, as Voltaire famously and pointedly shows in his later work *Candide*. Leibniz takes on this worry in *Theodicy*, his only published book-length work, by arguing that the overall harmony and ultimate perfection of the universe makes this the best possible world, appearances to the contrary notwithstanding. Here we find echoes of accounts offered by *Augustine.

In addition, Leibniz coined the *principle of sufficient reason*, which he and the later tradition widely employed in *cosmological-style arguments for the existence of God. According to the principle, every true claim must have some sufficient reason that explains why it, rather than its denial, is true. Leibniz used the principle to show that the contingent universe as a whole must require some sufficient reason for its existence, and the sufficient reason is God. Many revised variants of the principle have been offered in recent years in an attempt to defend cosmological-type arguments for the existence of God.

See also Augustine; Cause/Causality; Evil, Problem of; God, Nature of; Metaphysics/Ontology; Necessity; Theistic Arguments.

Bibliography. Robert Merrihew Adams, *Leibniz*; Donald Rutherford, *Leibniz and the Rational Order of Nature*.

Logic   The science of argument. Logic is centrally concerned with the form or structure of arguments as opposed to the substance or content of the arguments themselves. Logic proper is not concerned with whether the premises in an argument are true, but rather, supposing the premises to be true, does the conclusion follow from the premises. Arguments are divided into two types: inductive and deductive. In *inductive logic* the conclusion follows from the premises with some degree of probability (and, hence, some degree of uncertainty). In *deductive logic* the conclusion follows from the premises with *necessity (hence is certain given the *truth of the premises).

The form of an argument is the way in which the conclusion is inferred from the initial premises. Logically valid deductive argument forms are those where if the premises are true, then the conclusion must be true. Further, an argument is considered sound if the argument form is valid and the premises are true. *Aristotle, the first great logician, suggested that all good arguments have similar argument forms. For example,

1. All men are mortal
2. Socrates is a man
3. Therefore, Socrates is mortal.

This particular argument is of the form, All A are B, C is A, therefore C is B. If the premises (1 + 2) are true, then the conclusion (3) necessarily follows. New forms of deductive logic—using terms like "For every x," "There is an x," "Possibly," and "Necessarily"—were developed in the nineteenth and twentieth centuries that dramatically extended the scope and application of deductive logic.

With the advent of the scientific revolution, logicians began to pay greater attention to inductive patterns of inference. These forms argue from particular instances to a generalization. For example, if one sees ten instances of black ravens, one might conclude that all ravens are black. The problem with inductive inferences is the possibility that there are exceptions to the generally perceived instances. In this regard, induction may be said to deal with probability and not necessity. Inductive arguments vary from the highly probable on down.

While deductive certainty is desirable, more often than not human decisions must be made with less than a complete set of data. As Bishop Butler wisely noted, "Probability is the guide to life." That is, most human decisions

must be made inductively with the attendant uncertainty that attaches to inductive arguments. In theological reasoning, deductive arguments are seldom in play. More often one's arguments are based either on religious intuitions, biblical texts, or theological norms depending on probability and induction. Although theological reasoning might aspire to the certainty ensured by deductive reasoning, the inductive methods of interpretation and exegesis preclude it.

There are many ways an argument could go wrong, that is, be fallacious. A *fallacious argument* possesses an invalid inference somewhere in its chain of reasoning. There are many different types of inferences and also many different types of fallacies of inferences. *Formal fallacies* are those that purport to follow an acceptable logical form but that deviate from it in critical aspects. The deviations are often unnoticed to those not looking for them or by those not trained to see them. *Informal fallacies* are faulty according to a wider sociolinguistic context of acceptable arguments that do not strictly have to do with logical laws.

The oldest and still most influential list of informal fallacies came in the work of Aristotle, which most contemporary textbooks in logic still follow. A small sampling of informal fallacies include: *Ad hominem:* the use of an attack on the person holding certain views as a substitute for a criticism of the views themselves. By discrediting the person, one allegedly discredits the views of that person. *Begging the question:* an argument whose premises include the conclusion that the premises are supposed to prove. *Straw man argument:* the weakening of another's argument in order to make it easy to criticize. *Equivocation:* when a key term in an argument changes meaning from the beginning to the end of the argument, thereby blunting the validity of the argument as a whole.

The matter of fallacies has become especially significant in an era where matters of religious belief are highly contested. Arguments of many different kinds are offered for the validity or invalidity of religious belief or for or against the moral and social convictions of Christians. Understanding the fallacies involved in much of the argumentation will greatly aid the clarity of the issues—though it probably will not end the conflicts.

See also Aristotle, Necessity, Reason/Rationality.

Bibliography.   M. R. Haight, *The Snake and the Fox;* John D. Mullen, *Hard Thinking;* Morris Engel, *With Good Reason;* John Woods, *Argument.*

Logos   An ancient Greek term roughly translated as "word," it can also have the senses of "an account of" or "the study of." In its philosophical usage in ancient Greece, logos is a cosmic principle by which all of reality is ordered. Although the cosmos is diverse and apparently disunified, the logos provides an underlying unity and rationality to all of these aspects. In *Aristotle, logos came to mean the central argument or explanation of a theory; it was identified with *logic in contrast to a *metaphysical principle. The Stoic tradition identified logos with a rational principle of harmony in the universe. It is not only the supreme organization and unity of the universe, but the ground of rationality as well. Logos also has the connotation of the laws of the universe. Logos, manifested in the orderly progression of the seasons, is the law behind nature, that which gives nature an intelligible structure. It was akin to the early *modern notion of "natural law."

The Christian tradition took over many of these nuances of meaning and attached them to Jesus Christ as the logos. In John's Gospel in particular, Jesus is the principle of order behind creation and the final purpose of creation. John expressed his conviction that Jesus is a human person but much more: Jesus, the Logos, is a figure of cosmic significance as well. Several early Christian theologians went further and suggested that the logos is the principle of universal divine wisdom.

The importance of logos for modern theological discussion lies in its conceptual power to capture the intuition that wisdom can be found outside Christian circles, while also recognizing wisdom's unique expression in the gospel of Jesus Christ. Modern theology continues to wrestle with how best to express the particular scandal of the cross while affirming that *reason and purpose are not unique to the Christian tradition. However, the adoption of the term *logos* by early Christianity was also the basis for the charge made by Harnack and others that Christian thought had been "hellenized" by adopting Greek categories.

See also Aristotle; Augustine; Cause/Causality; God, Nature of; Neoplatonism; Plato and Platonism.

Bibliography.   David Fideler, *Jesus Christ, Sun of God;* David Winston, *Logos and Mystical Theology in Philo of Alexandria;* Walter J. Ong, *The Presence of the Word;* Sharon Ringe, *Wisdom's Friends;* Adolf von Harnack, *What Is Christianity?*

Marx, Karl (1818–1883)   Prussian-born thinker who developed the intellectual underpinnings of Communism. Marx was an ethnic Jew but his family practiced Christianity. He abandoned any religious beliefs and made *atheism the foundation of his *philosophy. Marx's starting point was the nineteenth-century working conditions of laborers. Due in part to the industrial revolution, workers were exploited with menial labor, low wages, and long hours. Children often worked fifteen to eighteen hours a day and were given just enough food to sustain their existence so they could continue working. Workers were treated as a commodity, according to the law of supply and demand: easily replaced workers (i.e., economically unvaluable people) could be paid little. As they were paid less and had access to fewer resources (which were going to the factory), they had to work harder and longer in order to survive. In short, they became "wage slaves." With his almost prophetic passion for *justice, these conditions of injustice motivated Marx's philosophical analyses, which include several key themes.

First, Marx offered a *materialist conception of *human nature*. In fact, he argued that there is no such thing as a stable human nature per se; rather, human nature is created by the material conditions in which humans find themselves. For example, in industrialist, capitalist societies, human beings are conditioned to be economic animals, formed largely for production and consumption in the service of capital. But because of the malleability of human "nature," a change in the material conditions or environment can engender a change in humanity itself.

This insight is coupled with a second regarding the *structural injustice* of society. According to Marx, all of society has been a history of class struggles, where there is a ruling or dominating class with power that exploits a powerless class (freeman/slave, lord/peasant, etc.). In *modern society, the two classes were the bourgeoisie (the owners of the means of production) and the proletariat (those who sell their labors to the bourgeoisie). Because the bourgeoisie have *capital* (resources beyond what is necessary to survive), they have the power to purchase the labor of others. In exchange for their labor, the workers receive a *wage*. However, this entails what Marx describes as the *alienation of labor:* by selling the fruit of their labor for a wage, the workers no longer enjoy the fruit of their hands—nor the profit that such products yield. Because the increase of wealth becomes the possession of the bourgeoisie, workers are reduced to pieces of equipment, which can be exploited because they are expendable. And the structures of society make it impossible for the proletariat to move out of their condition of oppression. Marx went on to criticize religion as a tool for maintaining the status quo of oppression, by urging the proletariat to accept their conditions of oppression in *this* life in exchange for the hope of something better in "heaven."

For Marx, this situation of oppression is rooted in the very structures of society. It is not that individual employers are mean, but that the economic structure disempowers the oppressed class. The only way to undo this injustice is to revolutionize the structures of society. Reform would not be enough; the advent of justice would require revolution.

Marx's passion for justice and insight into the structural nature of injustice has had a massive impact on theology since the 1950s. Gustavo Gutiérrez's liberation theology closely follows Marx and demonstrates how his concerns parallel those of both the prophets and Jesus of Nazareth. Jürgen Moltmann's eschatology of hope finds an ally in Marx's vision of a future classless society. Many theologians, including Pope John Paul II and John Milbank, have criticized Christian theology for adopting Marx's framework, which is rooted in a worldview antithetical to Christian *faith. Nevertheless, Marx's impact continues to reverberate in contemporary theology.

See also Atheism; Ethics, Biblical; Feuerbach; Happiness; Hegel; Justice.

Bibliography. Peter Singer, *Marx*; Gustavo Gutiérrez, *Theology of Liberation*; John Milbank, *Theology and Social Theory*; Jürgen Moltmann, *Theology of Hope*; Merold Westphal, *Suspicion and Faith*.

Materialism *See* Naturalism/ Materialism.

Metaphysics/Ontology The branch of *philosophy concerned with the nature and structure of reality; sometimes called "ontology," or the "science of Being." The term can be traced to *Aristotle's *Metaphysics*, which investigated

Being qua being, or what kinds of things exist. In philosophical terms, the nature of being is not about particular things, but rather about the ultimate *kinds* of things. Is reality ultimately material or immaterial? What is *substance—is there a substrata in which sensory appearances inhere? What is the relationship between material and immaterial reality (say, *mind and body, or *God and world)? Do *universal terms or numbers exist? Do moral values exist? What is the relationship between things that exist contingently and those that exist necessarily? In the medieval era, with the development of Christian and Islamic philosophy, these questions were asked in an explicitly theistic context. While Aristotle's metaphysics included a "prime Mover" as the first *cause of reality, medieval philosophers further developed Aristotle's "theistic" metaphysics. Philosophical reflection on these questions informed early Christian theological reflections about the nature of God and the relation of God to the world. Creedal formulations regarding the Trinity and the nature of Christ's divinity (one *substance*, three *persons*) were influenced by Aristotelian metaphysics. Although early modern thinkers defended substantive metaphysical commitments, later David *Hume and Immanuel *Kant would contend that the metaphysical realm is beyond the reach of human cognitive capabilities.

Since the beginning of the twentieth century, metaphysics has developed in two directions: the continental and *analytic traditions. The continental tradition, following the lead of Martin *Heidegger, still tends to investigate matters in terms of the Aristotelian question, "What is Being?" More radically, *postmodern thought, following Kant, has called into question the very project of metaphysics as *ontotheological.

In the analytic tradition, metaphysics has followed two paths. The rise of natural science and the legacy of *logical *positivism have led some thinkers to be deeply suspicious of traditional meta-

physics. They take *Ockham's razor as their principal tool of ontological inquiry and seek the theory that posits the fewest kinds of things that exist (that are necessary to explain everything). W. V. O. Quine claimed that most phenomena could be adequately explained with reference solely to physical entities, and therefore *naturalism is ontologically preferable to every other theory. Others, influenced by Saul Kripke, David Lewis, and Alvin Plantinga, have defended traditional and revisionary metaphysics based on new developments in modal logic (the logic of possibility and *necessity).

Basic metaphysical issues often indicate fundamental differences in worldviews. Christianity, for example, believes that all of reality traces back to one ultimate source, God, who created us to freely worship him. So Christian philosophers typically believe that reality is both material and immaterial, that the material world is *good, that humans are significantly free and, until recently, that humans are composed of mind (soul) and body. Naturalistic metaphysics, on the other hand, seeks to explain the nature of persons, the mind/body relationship, and human freedom in terms of matter and natural law.

See also Analytic/Continental Philosophy; Aquinas; Cause/Causality; Cosmology; Dualism/Monism; Enlightenment; Essence/Essentialism; Free Will; Heidegger; Hume; Idealism; Kant; Naturalism; Necessity; Positivism; Process Thought; Universals.

Bibliography. William Hasker, *Metaphysics*; Peter Van Inwagen and Dean Zimmerman, *Metaphysics*; Michael Loux, *Metaphysics*; L. Gregory Jones and Stephen Fowl, eds., *Rethinking Metaphysics*.

Mind/Soul/Spirit   An   enduring immaterial *substance; the center of a person's consciousness. The English term *soul* translates the Greek word *psyche* and the Latin term *anima;* the English *spirit* translates the Greek *pneuma* and Latin *spiritus*. The terms are sometimes used interchangeably, but in other contexts are carefully distinguished. "Soul" (and "spirit") in both Greek *philosophy and Christian thought typically refers to an immaterial aspect or part of the human person. The soul is generally linked to the center or "seat" of consciousness and thought. Both *Plato and *Aristotle thought the soul was the principle of life in a cosmic sense—every living thing has a soul. Plato believed that there is a world-soul from which all individual souls came and on which he grounded the claim that the soul must be *eternal. He also believed that individual souls could "migrate" from body to body. Aristotle, on the other hand, supposed that souls were inextricably bound to their bodies, though divided into two parts, an animal aspect and a rational aspect (*Aquinas would follow Aristotle). Aristotle's view anticipated some versions of *materialism. In early *modernity, "mind" (Greek *nous*) replaced the language of "soul." While he did not accept Plato's theory of reincarnation, *Descartes would later rearticulate Plato's *dualism. For both Plato and Descartes, the mind is the immaterial core or *essence of the human person—the ground of personal identity that survives the death of the body.

Because of affirmations regarding life after death, the Christian theological tradition also affirmed that mind or soul is an immaterial reality. Yet the Hebraic narratives rarely discuss the relationship between body and soul, pressing rather the manner in which each person stands in relationship to Yahweh. Though the New Testament appears to distinguish more sharply between body and soul, its affirmation of the *resurrection of the body emphasizes the integral union of the two. A small minority of Christians have supposed, as did Plato, that a person is divisible into three distinct parts—body, soul, and spirit (trichotomy)—owing to the oblique reference in 1 Thessalonians 5:23. They believed the soul was a mediating presence between the material world of the body and the immaterial world of the spirit. The vast majority of Christians, however, have been traditional dualists, affirming two distinct but related parts to the person: body and soul. Contemporary debates in Christian philosophy and theology about the resurrection have considered whether the biblical position could be consistent with some versions of materialism.

With the advent and growth of *naturalism—the belief that all of reality is only matter—the notion of an immaterial mind has been challenged. Instead, many philosophers hold that all we have are physical brains, animated by firing neurons. Thus positions on mind tend to reduce to classical *dualism* (material body, immaterial mind), *reductionistic materialism* (only matter), or *nonreductionist materialisms,* which still describe the "emergence" of a mental reality, but ultimately emerging from (or constituted by) material bodies.

Mind/body issues raise the question of the Christian's relationship to the material world and the *goodness of creation. Ancient forms of Gnosticism supposed that the physical world, including the body, was evil. Gnosticism was often a rival to early Christianity, shunning revelation in creation as well as in Scripture in favor of esoteric speculations. The upshot was a denigration of the body and an exhaltation of human *reason. A Christian theory of the mind ought to protect both the intrinsic goodness of the body and the proper appreciation of the mind.

See also Aquinas, Aristotle, Descartes, Dualism/Monism, Essence/Essentialism, Human Nature, Hume, Metaphysics/Ontology, Modernity/Modernism, Naturalism/Materialism, Plato and Platonism, Resurrection/Immortality, Self.

Bibliography.   Paul McDonald, *History and the Concept of Mind;* John Cooper, *Body, Soul, and Life Everlasting;* Kevin Corcoran, ed., *Soul, Body, and Survival;*

Warren S. Brown, *Whatever Happened to the Soul?* Peter Geach, *God and the Soul;* Richard Swinburne, *The Evolution of the Soul;* William Hasker, *The Emergent Self;* Stephen Stich and Ted Warfield, eds., *The Blackwell Guide to Philosophy of Mind;* Charles Taliaferro, *Consciousness and the Mind of God;* Richard Warner and Tadeusz Szubka, eds., *The Mind-Body Problem.*

Miracles Supernatural events of divine causation within the natural order; sometimes defined as violations of the laws of nature. Orthodox Christian faith rests on the miracle par excellence, the *resurrection of Christ. Simply stated, the revivification of corpses is not a "natural" occurrence. In fact, it runs counter to what we would expect given the general workings of the natural world and our prior experience of the natural order. As such, miracles have been a long-standing target of critics of Christianity from the first century to the present.

One of the most articulate criticisms of miracles was offered by David *Hume, in his *Enquiry Concerning Human Understanding.* Hume adopted the common definition of a miracle as a "violation of the laws of nature" and attempted to demonstrate that, given this very definition, experience itself afforded proof that miracles were impossible. Why? Because the "laws of nature" are based on "a firm and unalterable experience" or "uniform experience." In other words, for Hume, the very uniformity of our experience is what establishes the so-called laws of nature, so laws of nature are maximally justified. But we know that people sometimes lie or make mistakes, so no testimony could ever be maximally justified by the uniformity of experience. Thus when we compare the maximal justification of a natural law with the less than maximal justification of the testimony that a miracle occurred, there could never be sufficient testimony to dislodge our confidence in the laws of nature. It is

far more likely that the person reporting the miracle lied or was deceived than that a law of nature be violated. "No testimony," he concludes, "is sufficient to establish a miracle."

Hume's argument, then, rests upon demonstrating the impossibility of adequate testimony to believe a miracle. Even if a miracle had occurred, it would never be reasonable to accept it. However, his empirical views do not permit a demonstration of the ontological impossibility of such an event. As naturalism becomes more widely accepted, the belief in the universe as a closed system has been taken to preclude miracles. However, the metaphysical assumption that nothing can interfere with the operations of the universe makes it hard to see how such assumptions avoid begging the question. Even some theologians have been unable to resist the assumption of naturalism. Most famously, such a naturalistic starting point motivated Rudolf Bultmann's project of "demythologizing" the New Testament of its miraculous elements, leaving only its "*existential *truths" in place.

See also Apologetics, Atheism, Hume, Naturalism.

Bibliography. C. S. Lewis, *Miracles;* Norman Geisler, *Miracles and the Modern Mind;* Richard Swinburne, *Miracles;* idem, *The Concept of Miracle;* John Earman, *Hume's Abject Failure.*

Modernity/Modernism The advent of an epoch now described as "modernity" is generally traced to *Descartes; it then crystallized during the *Enlightenment of the eighteenth century. This constituted a break with the Middle Ages or medieval period, largely over the role of "authority," in both knowledge and society.

Descartes is seen as the father of modernity because of two important shifts in his thought: first, the equation of knowledge with certainty (achieved solely on the basis of *reason rather than revelation); second, his mathematization of the world (seeing the world as a geometrical object of investigation rather than a living organism). The first theme—the focus on certainty—would later engender the hegemony of reason in determining what is rational and true. This fed into the second theme, which gave rise to science—and ultimately scient*ism*—which tended to construe the world as an object for investigation and mastery.

After Descartes, modernity is identified with the Enlightenment, first on the Continent, and then in England and Scotland. The Enlightenment particularly focused on freedom, in two ways. First, intellectual freedom from the constraints of church and tradition resulted in the development of *autonomous reason;* that is, a notion of reason as a universal, neutral arbiter of *truth that was not conditioned by any prior commitments. Second, this fed an emphasis on political freedom or the *autonomy of the individual.* This side of modernity gave rise to classic liberal politics, which begins from principles of individual rights and freedoms. The modern notion of a universal, autonomous reason has been the primary target of the *postmodern critique, and the individualistic emphasis on human rights has been the object of critique by communitarians.

Theologically, the *epistemological aspects of modernity have been a point of contention, particularly in the area of *apologetics. Classical apologetics assumes something like a modern notion of universal, autonomous reason. Presuppositional apologists argue that this is untenable, and thus also tend to be critics of modernity and have sympathy with postmodernism. Postliberal theologians call into question the individualistic politics of modernity, particularly insofar as it has come to infect the church.

See also Apologetics; Descartes; Enlightenment; Epistemology; Faith and Reason; God, Belief in; Hume; Kant; Ontotheology; Perspectivalism; Postmodernism; Reason and Belief in God; Relativism; Scholasticism.

Bibliography. Philip Clayton, *The Problem of God in Modern Thought;* James L. Marsh, John D. Caputo, and Merold Westphal, *Modernity and Its Discontents;* William C. Placher, *The Domestication of Transcendence;* Alasdair McIntyre, *After Virtue;* John Milbank, *Theology and Social Theory;* Genevieve Lloyd, *Man of Reason.*

Monism *See* Dualism/Monism.

Naturalism/Materialism A form of *atheism that maintains that the universe is a closed system that operates entirely according to natural laws. *Metaphysical naturalism* is the view that the world is a series of natural processes governed by *cause and effect, which is, therefore, closed off to *miracles or perhaps to *free will. If everything that exists is in space and time, everything that can be known is knowable through scientific methods. Although the progress of science and the decline of religious explanations of natural phenomena are taken as evidence in support of naturalism, it is more a worldview assumption than a well-derived conclusion. Nevertheless, it is one of the most prominent contemporary worldview assumptions and dominates both contemporary *philosophy and science.

Metaphysical naturalism, with its denial of the supernatural, is assumed by a variety of biblical scholars, influenced by such diverse figures as philosopher David *Hume, theologian D. F. Strauss, and New Testament scholar Rudolf Bultmann, who contended that in our *modern, scientific age it is no longer possible to believe in miracles. Since a great deal of Holy Writ involves miracle stories, such portions of Scripture must be "demythologized," that is, purged of the purely mythical elements (i.e., those involving miracles and of dubious historicity). The resulting "gospel" involves a desupernaturalized Jesus who typically holds the philosophical or social views of the biblical scholar or theologian (such as *existentialism or *Marxism).

Methodological naturalism is the more modest claim that science should proceed by restricting itself to the search for natural explanations of empirical phenomena. For example, the methodological naturalist seeks natural explanations of both the weather and the origin of species. This practice is open to theists and nontheists alike.

Materialism, a species of naturalism, is the monistic view that the only things that exist are matter and energy in various forms. Materialists are attempting an account of human persons in terms of matter without reference to an immaterial soul.

See also Atheism, Cause/Causality, Cosmology, Dualism/Monism, Enlightenment, Ethics, Feuerbach, Free Will, Hume, Marx, Metaphysics/Ontology, Mind/Soul/Spirit, Philosophy, Positivism, Renaissance Humanism.

Bibliography. J. P. Moreland and William Lane Craig, *Philosophical Foundations for a Christian Worldview;* J. P. Moreland and William Lane Craig, eds., *Naturalism;* Michael Rea, *World Without Design;* James K. Beilby, ed., *Naturalism Defeated.*

Natural Theology The attempt to prove the existence of *God on the basis of *reason and experience without reference to information gained from divine revelation. Supporters of natural theology range from *Aristotle through *Aquinas to present times. The locus classicus of natural theology is Romans 1:20: "For since the creation of the world God's invisible qualities—his eternal power and divine nature—have been clearly seen, being understood from what has been made, so that men are without excuse."

Classical natural theology is the attempt to prove the existence of God on the basis of premises that all rational creatures are obliged to accept. If one could make an easy inference to the existence of God on the basis of universally acceptable (and, reputedly, obvious) premises, then one could show that unbelief is irrational and the unbeliever is accountable for her lack of assent to God's existence.

Unfortunately, the project of classical natural theology failed. Arguments for the existence of God employ key premises, the *truth or falsity of which are difficult to determine. Although theistic arguments are often rooted in experience, they always rely on controversial *metaphysical principles about which rational people rationally disagree. Virtually every argument in *philosophy is afflicted with this sort of problem. There are few universally acceptable premises, at least in matters of fundamental human concern. In areas of deep human concern—*ethics, for example, politics, and *human nature—reasonable people simply judge fundamental truths differently from other reasonable people. The attempt to justify *any* philosophical argument to everyone's rational satisfaction is a snare and a delusion. Nonetheless, many contemporary apologists are classical natural theologians.

Since the 1950s there has been a shift among Christian philosophers away from classical natural theology toward more reasonable standards for *theistic arguments. Recognizing the likelihood of rational disagreement, they reject the claim that theistic arguments must be restricted to premises that *all* rational creatures are obliged to accept. Instead they claim that one can argue from premises that are rationally acceptable even if others might disagree. So the question for the premises is not, Are all rational creatures obliged to accept them? but, Could one reasonably accept them (in the face of rational disagreement)? If it is reasonable (but not universally coercive) to accept the premises of a theistic argument, then it is reasonable to accept what follows from those premises (namely, God). Thus, freed from the intellectual imperialism of classical natural theology, theistic arguments have found new life in recent times.

Many Calvinist thinkers have been critical of the project of natural theology. They believe that knowledge of God is a gift, not the work of reason. And they note that the Bible assumes God's existence ("In the beginning . . .") and nowhere attempts to prove it.

See also Apologetics, Reason and Belief in God, Theistic Arguments.

Bibliography. Kelly James Clark, *Return to Reason;* David Hume, *Dialogues Concerning Natural Religion;* Jaroslav Pelikan, *Christianity and Classical Culture;* Basil Mitchell, *The Justification of Religious Belief.*

Necessity A characteristic of propositions and beings that applies when there is no possibility of not being free or not existing. A proposition is said to be necessarily *true when that proposition could not possibly be false. Various propositions that have been considered necessarily true are "1+1=2," "All bachelors are unmarried men," and "God exists." A necessary state of affairs is one that holds in all possible conditions. For example, in every possible condition, squares are always four sided. A necessary being is one that exists and whose nonexistence is not possible (in contrast to a contingent being, whose nonexistence is possible). *God is the most obvious example of a necessary being, but other candidates include numbers and *ethical truths. A *possible being* is one that might have existed (if it does not already) and might cease existing (if it already exists).

The science of necessity and possibility is called *modal *logic.* Modal logic employs the apparatus of "possible worlds," imaginative constructions of the infinite ways things might be or might have been, to designate those conditions that are possible but that might

not be actual. For example, it is logically possible that cows jump over the moon. This would mean that it is possible to conceive of a situation (a possible world) where the earth, moon, and cows exist, but where things are so different from the actual world that, in that possible world, cows can jump over the moon. "Cows jumping over the moon" is actually false, of course, but it is possibly true. This example is far-fetched for illustrative purposes, but modal logic gives us a way of philosophically understanding possible things such as "I could have been two inches taller" or "I might have been born in a different time and place." Finally, propositions are necessarily true if they are true in "every possible world," that is, under every possible condition, the proposition is still true.

Modal logic has proven theologically useful in at least three ways. First, it illuminates the Christian belief that God's existence is necessary, unlike every object and person in creation. Whereas it is conceivable that any human person might not exist (i.e., their existence is merely possible or contingent), God is the sort of being who cannot be conceived not to exist. The nature of this divine necessity is explored in the ontological and the *cosmological arguments for God's existence. Second, modal logic has helped understand the nature of *free will. There are events, choices of the will, which do not appear to follow natural laws. They are not necessary, even in light of all the preceding conditions. Finally, Alvin Plantinga's free-will defense employs modal logic to refute the deductive argument from evil (the claim that if evil exists, it is impossible for God to exist).

See also Anselm; Essence/Essentialism; Evil, Problem of; Free Will; God, Nature of; Leibniz; Logic; Metaphysics/ Ontology; Mind/Soul/Spirit; Theodicy.

Bibliography. Kelly James Clark, *Return to Reason;* Kenneth Konyndyk, *Introductory Modal Logic;* Alvin

Plantinga, *God, Freedom, and Evil;* idem, *The Nature of Necessity;* idem, *Essays in the Metaphysics of Modality.*

Neoplatonism Philosophical school in the tradition of *Plato, emphasizing mystical ascent to a vision of the divine; Neoplatonism significantly shaped early Christian thought. A major influence on ancient and medieval theology was the Egyptian philosopher Plotinus (204–270 C.E.), considered the founder of Neoplatonism. In Plotinus's grand *metaphysical scheme (found in the *Enneads*), inspired by the works of Plato, all of the progressively less significant things emanate from the nonmaterial central unity (the One or the *Good) like ripples in a pond; the further removed a thing is from the Good, the less goodness the thing has. However, everything that is *participates* in the One. A person's life project is to contemplate the Good (whose emanations may be found in everything) and to find the proper place of one's divine Soul within this orderly cosmos. *Philosophy is redemptive as it liberates the Soul from its preoccupation with lesser goods to contemplation of the Good and so brings the Soul into unity with the One. In "theurgical" Neoplatonists such as Porphyry (ca. 232–305 C.E.) and Iamblichus (ca. 250–325 C.E.), liturgical rites were a means of attaining this ascent of the soul. Many Christians, including *Augustine and later *Aquinas, have found Plotinus to be a helpful framework for articulating a Christian account of the soul's vocation. Augustine's Neoplatonism (in his writings they are called "the Platonists") had a tremendous influence on the development of Christian orthodoxy from the early medieval period to the seventeenth century and exerts renewed influence today in *postmodern thought and radical orthodoxy.

The distinctive doctrine of Neoplatonism is that of the *transcendent One or Good, a single being upon whose Intelligence (divine *Mind) the rest of reality depends. Out of goodness, the One projects its goodness and power into all lower and weaker beings. The transcendence of this supreme being is stressed with an emphasis on *God's ineffability (that God's ultimate nature is unknowable by humans). Human intelligence is incapable of attaining knowledge of what this being is. God is superior to any concept that humans could understand. Therefore, we are limited to negative theology—saying what God is not. God is not this or that (not finite, not limited in power, not limited in knowledge, without sin).

According to Plotinus, all of reality is generated by the One in levels according to each thing's participation in perfection. The highest level is the One, with Mind just below (the One, Mind, and Soul are the three divine elements of reality). All natural beings are souls. These many things all seek to return to the One. Human beings, just below Mind, are both divine and material. They have a godlike soul, a "real *self" in which intelligence resides, temporarily trapped in an earthly body. The human project is to free oneself from the confusing world of the senses and desire and return in spirit to the divine intelligible world to which we really belong, a world infinitely superior to the physical world. This requires tremendous effort on our part to discipline both our intellect and our heart. When this is accomplished, as with Plato, the life of the righteous person will mirror the order of ultimate reality.

One can see in Neoplatonism much that early Christian thinkers might welcome. Augustine, for example, cited Neoplatonism's role in moving him away from the Manichean doctrine that all of reality (including the ultimates, Good and *Evil) is material. In addition, Plotinus's claim that human thought cannot grasp the divine reality informs doctrines of divine transcendence. Finally, the Neoplatonic view of the interactions among the One, Mind, and Soul were used to understand the

Trinity as Father, Son (*Logos), and Spirit. But Neoplatonism also had adverse affects on Christian thought. Taking Jesus as Mind (Nous) led to a conception of the Christian life as primarily intellectual and the belief that the contemplative life was the superior life. Not unrelated, the hierarchical view of reality led to a downgrading of the physical world and the body.

See also Aquinas; Augustine; Being and Goodness; Ethics, Biblical; God, Nature of; Mind/Soul/Spirit; Ontotheology; Plato and Platonism; Pseudo-Dionysius; Religious Language; Transcendence.

Bibliography. John Gregory, *The Neoplatonists;* Kevin Corrigan, *Reading Plotinus;* Dominic J. O'Meara, *Neoplatonism and Christian Thought;* Gregory Shaw, *Theurgy and the Soul.*

Nietzsche, Friedrich (1844–1900)

A radical German critic of Christianity described (along with *Marx and *Freud) as one of the "masters of suspicion." Nietzsche's project calls into question the traditional core values of Western thought from *Plato to *Kant. This can even be seen in the style of his work, often written in complex, mystifying aphorisms (as in *Beyond Good and Evil*) or literary mythology (as in *Thus Spake Zarathustra*). In both content and style, his project is a precursor and source for *postmodern criticisms of the Western tradition. We can delineate three key (and related) themes of his critique: what we might call his *ethics of the will to power, his rejection of *reason in favor of *perspectivalism, and his account of religion (especially Christianity).

One of the fundamental tenets of Nietzsche's thought is his valorization of *power.* For Nietzsche, notions of morality that appeal to something like moral law or divine commands are misguided and weak. "*Good" and "*evil" are not based on some divine law; rather, Nietzsche contends, what is "good" is what is *powerful,* or more specifically, what is *active.*

Correlatively, we should describe as "bad" not that which violates moral law, but rather those intentions and actions that are *reactive* or weak. Now, for Nietzsche, to be powerful and active requires a person to affirm existence and life, with all of its trials and tribulations. Rather than seeing violence or trauma as "evil," the powerful individual absorbs such assaults on existence and is strong enough to affirm them as "good." Thus Nietzsche's paragon of the powerful individual—the Overman (*Übermensch*) —is able to say to *all* of existence, "Let's do that again." This is what Nietzsche describes as the affirmation of the myth of the "*eternal return of the same." The weak, reactive individual cannot make such an affirmation. He cannot handle the trauma of existence and wishes things were different. When something befalls the weak person, she says, "I wish this wouldn't happen," and then describes such things as "bad" or "evil." The very notion of there being "evil," then, is traced to weakness. As such, Nietzsche distinguishes between what he describes as "slave morality"—which is the morality of the weak and reactive—and "noble morality"—which is the ethical system of the powerful and active.

Based on the above notions, Nietzsche calls into question the long-standing notion of a neutral, autonomous "Reason" as the guarantor of *truth. In *Twilight of the Idols* and "On Truth and Falsity in an Extra-Moral Sense," Nietzsche traces the ascent of *logic to Socrates's influence on Western *philosophy. In fact, he argues that philosophical infatuation with the invisible world of *essences and reasons is a symptom of weakness: trying to escape the difficulties of this world by positing another world where the weak rule. So what counts as "rational," according to Nietzsche, is in fact very particular and conditioned by weakness. Therefore, there is no such thing as a universal reason, but rather only a plurality of *perspectives.*

Finally, the critique of slave morality and the otherworldliness of philosophy coalesce in Nietzsche's critique of Christianity. For Nietzsche, Christianity is characterized by the same "weak" rejection of earthly existence in favor of an otherworldly hope. This is famously depicted in the passage from *The Gay Science* where a madman enters the square, screaming "*God is dead." The "death of God" entails, for Nietzsche, the "transvaluation of values."

While his thought constitutes a radical critique of Christianity, he has had a long influence on Christian theology, beginning with the work of Franz Overbeck, the "radical theology" of Thomas J. J. Altizer, and more recently, Mark C. Taylor's "deconstructive a/theology." A more orthodox appropriation of his critique can be found in Jürgen Moltmann.

See also Atheism; Ethics; Ethics, Biblical; Existentialism; Human Nature; Modernity/Modernism; Nihilism; Perspectivalism; Plato and Platonism; Postmodernism; Reason; Relativism; Truth.

Bibliography. Michael Tanner, *Nietzsche*; Gilles Deleuze, *Nietzsche and Philosophy*; Mark C. Taylor, *Erring*; Merold Westphal, *Suspicion and Faith*.

Nihilism   From the Latin word *nihil* (nothing), a theory that claims there is no meaning and value to life. We can distinguish between *ontological nihilism*, which makes *metaphysical claims about the "nothingness" of reality, and *existential nihilism*, which makes claims about the lack of *meaning* in human existence (though the two are often related). It is often grounded in the denial of any objective moral values and the denial of the consolations of the *eternal. Nihilism is most often associated with *Nietzsche, who proclaimed that *God is dead and embraced the consequences of living in a world abandoned by God. The picture of such a world can be found in the novels of Dostoevsky, some of whose characters affirm that "without God, everything is permitted." Abandonment by God is metaphorical for a loss of a *transcendent moral, intellectual, and teleological grounding of reality. In God's place: nothing. There are no transcendent values, there is no mind-independent structure of reality, and there is no goal of human history.

The French existentialist tradition of Jean-Paul Sartre (1905–1980) and Albert Camus (1913–1960) emphasizes nihilism as capturing the meaninglessness or absurdity of life. Both Camus and Sartre were overwhelmed by the devastation of Europe in World War I and then again in World War II. Although World War I was supposed to be the war to end all wars, it was followed by even greater decimation of the European continent. Given the profundity of this *evil and the inevitability of death, the wars manifested the utter hopelessness of life. Camus captured this sense in his book-length essay, *The Myth of Sisyphus*. Recalling the ancient Greek myth, Camus suggested human existence was like Sisyphus, who was punished by the gods and eternally condemned to push a heavy ball up a slope, only to have the gods kick it back down. Life is neither just nor rational. Sartre's novel *Nausea* suggests that there is no purpose to the accident of human existence; human beings are superfluous. The existentialist's reflections resonated with the feeling in Europe in the aftermath of the wars that life does not "make sense."

Each of these thinkers suggested a positive aspect of nihilism. Following Nietzsche, Sartre relished the possibilities of absolute human freedom in a world without God. Nietzsche thought this provided the opportunity for full human creativity without the constraints of conventional morality. Sartre argued that humans were responsible for their actions and used this as a ground for morality; this responsibility held the moral key to creating a better society. Camus presented the existentialist hero who, without the light of the transcendent, courageously navigated the present chaos of existence. By taking responsibility for his actions, fighting against the suffering that would rob us of meaning and life itself, the existentialist hero creates whatever meaning he can. But, of course, there is no meaning and so our hero is back with Sisyphus, rolling his ball back up the hill.

In addition to being an influential source for *postmodernism, nihilism has also influenced popular culture, as embodied in the long-running sitcom *Seinfeld:* a "show about nothing." Christian theology and the church will speak to culture only insofar as they address the most fundamental assumptions of a nihilist framework. "Radical Orthodoxy"—a theological movement linked with John Milbank, Catherine Pickstock, Graham Ward, and others—has recently confronted nihilism "head-on" with a theological response.

See also Atheism; Evil, Problem of; Existentialism; Naturalism/Materialism; Nietzsche; Postmodernism.

Bibliography. Conor Cunningham, *A Genealogy of Nihilism;* Michael Allen Gillespie, *Nihilism Before Nietzsche;* Glen Martin, *From Nietzsche to Wittgenstein;* John Milbank, *Theology and Social Theory.*

Ockham, William of (1280–1349) British philosopher, born in Ockham (near London), who is renowned for his "razor" and nominalism. Although trained at Oxford, his main teaching career was at Paris until his theology incited opposition. Defending the life of poverty as the Christian ideal (against the lavish lifestyle of Pope John) led to imprisonment and excommunication, and accusing the pope of heresy did not help his cause. His thought, along with that of Duns *Scotus, exerted significant influence on early modern philosophers such as *Descartes, as well as the thought of Reformers such as Martin Luther.

Ockham is most famous for *nominalism*: the claim that universal terms are simply mental names or tags that do not point to existent *universals (like *Platonic forms); universals are not *substances outside the human *mind. He also endorsed what has come to be known as *Ockham's razor,* a kind of *metaphysical minimalism articulated in the axiom: "Don't multiply entities beyond *necessity." He opposed the needless population of the metaphysical world with universals and abstractions. However, he also offered criteria for when to posit the existence of entities. *Reason (which gains information from self-evident *truths, experience, and Scripture) could affirm the existence of entities.

In his theology, Ockham was a *voluntarist* who maintained *God's absolute freedom: God was under no necessity or external obligation to create the world or to redeem humanity. The creation of the world and the plan of salvation were effected solely for the pleasure of God. Even the crucifixion and *resurrection were not necessary, as God could have freely decided that forgiveness without satisfaction was adequate for salvation. This view of divine freedom would influence Calvin and Reformed theology.

Ockham believed that the authority of the church derived from the authority of the Bible. And, although the Bible is infallible, its interpreters (the pope and councils) are not. The Bible is the only infallible authority in matters of *faith and practice. This view contains the seeds of Luther's revolt against the Catholic Church.

See also Aquinas; Aristotle; Augustine; Free Will; God, Nature of; Metaphysics/Ontology; Plato and Platonism; Realism/Anti-Realism; Universals.

Bibliography. Marilyn McCord Adams, *William Ockham;* Heiko Oberman, *The Harvest of Medieval Theology.*

Omnipotence The doctrine that *God is all-powerful (from two Latin terms: *omni* meaning "all," and *potentia* meaning "power" or "ability"). This attribute arises from biblical claims regarding God as "Almighty." However, this claim raises questions. Can God, for example, do the *logically impossible such as make a square circle? Many people have heard (and snickered at) the so-called paradox of omnipotence: Can God create a stone so big that God cannot lift it? Various answers are no (a stone that God cannot lift is impossible and God can only do the logically possible) and yes (God *can* make a stone that God cannot lift and, being omnipotent, can lift it!). This paradox does raise a serious problem for omnipotence: Can God do just anything? Challenges to omnipotence have led some schools of theological thought to reject the notion, as in *process theology.

Theologians have suggested that "God is almighty" does not mean that God can do anything; rather, it means that God has dominion over God's creation. God's omnipotence, therefore, is linked to God's providence and sovereignty. The Bible itself states or implies that there are things that God cannot do, such as sin or change the past. Therefore, Christian thinkers have typically argued that God cannot do anything that is contrary to God's own nature. So some limits on what God can do are relative to God's nature. But it is also widely believed that God cannot do the logically impossible (*Descartes is an exception). This is essential to *free will *theodicies, which hold that God cannot *cause free (i.e., uncaused) actions.

See also Descartes; Evil, Problem of; Free Will; God, Nature of; Process Thought; Theodicy.

Bibliography. Edward Wierenga, *The Nature of God*; Alvin Plantinga, *God, Freedom, and Evil*; Charles Harts-horne, *Omnipotence and Other Theological Mistakes*.

Omnipresence The attribute of being present everywhere, motivated by biblical claims such as Psalm 139:7–9.

*God's omnipresence is not defined physically or spatially. Since God is not a spatial or material being, God cannot be physically present at every point in space. Rather, God exercises God's powers and *goodness in all places at every moment. God is spacelessly present everywhere.

By contrast, *pantheism* maintains an identification between God and everything else, so it may be said that everything is God and God is everything. *Panentheism* is the view that God is the soul of the universe. God's soul enlivens the whole universe as the human soul enlivens the body. The overwhelming majority of the Christian traditions reject both of these views.

There are two important issues surrounding the discussion of omnipresence. The first concerns the difference between God's presence in general and God's presence in redemption. Omnipresence does not mean that God is everywhere in identically the same manner. Christians believe that God is uniquely present at the cross of Christ. God is also present in an unusual manner in the sacraments of the church. The second significant issue surrounding omnipresence concerns God's relationship to time as well as space. If God is present everywhere, is God also present at all times? Some have argued that being spacelessly present everywhere implies being timelessly present at every moment (past, present, and future). Others have argued that though God may be present everywhere in space (in the present), God cannot be everywhere present in time (say, in the past or the future); divine action requires a before and after.

See also Eternal/Everlasting; God, Nature of; Ontotheology.

Bibliography. Luco van den Brom, *Divine Presence in the World*; Richard Swinburne, *The Coherence of Theism*.

Omniscience and Foreknowledge The doctrine that *God knows everything (from the Latin words *omni* meaning "all" and *scientia* meaning "knowledge"). Christians have affirmed this attribute on the basis of biblical claims regarding God's knowledge of our innermost thoughts (Psalm 139), knowledge of the future (in prophecy), and governance of the world. However, omniscience is not without challenges, both in itself and in conjunction with other properties. If, for example, God is outside time, can God know what time it is now? Since time is ever-changing, doesn't this sort of knowledge require that God be ever-changing (hence, creating a problem for *immutability)?

The most pressing problem for omniscience is the *problem of foreknowledge and human freedom*: God's infallible knowledge of everything that will happen in the future. God's complete and clear prevision of the future seems inconsistent with libertarian understandings of *free will. Free will involves the ability to do otherwise—to be able to accept or refuse, say, that tempting piece of chocolate. But if God infallibly knows that you are going to accept that piece of chocolate, then you must do so. For, if you were not to choose that piece of chocolate, God would have had a false belief. But this is impossible. So you must, of *necessity, do whatever God has already foreseen that you will do. And if one cannot do otherwise, one is not free. Let us consider three responses to this problem.

The most influential solution to the problem of foreknowledge and human freedom was offered by Boethius (ca. 480–525 C.E.), the medieval philosopher who, while awaiting execution, wrote *The Consolation of Philosophy*. If God is *eternal (outside time), strictly speaking God cannot have foreknowledge (because "before" is a temporal predicate). For God, everything is in the eternal present, everything is now. So God sees everything—past, present, and future—at once or simultaneously, while it happens. But just as our seeing a human choice as it happens does not remove that person's ability to do other-

wise, so God's seeing it as it happens does not remove that person's ability to do otherwise. God knows all things—past, present, and future (as present)—but God's mode of knowing does not preclude the ability to do otherwise.

An *Aristotelian response, favored by some open theists, places God within time. According to this view, the future as it pertains to the choice of free agents (future contingents) is a blank slate: there are no true (or false) statements about what free creatures will freely do in the future. If Aristotelianism is correct, then God knows everything that can be known (past and present) and is thus omniscient. In addition, God's knowledge grows as free creatures continue to make free choices. According to other theists, there are *truth values concerning what free creatures will freely do in the future, but God voluntarily restricts God's access to this knowledge.

A third solution, called *middle knowledge*, claims that God does not have prevision or any direct knowledge of the future. Rather, God knows the future indirectly by way of knowing what free creatures would freely do in every possible circumstance. If God knows what one would freely do in every possible circumstance and God knows what circumstance will occur, God will thereby also know what one will freely do in that circumstance. God's middle knowledge preserves foreknowledge and a robust notion of free will.

See also Eternal/Everlasting; Evil, Problem of; Free Will; God, Nature of; Immutability and Impassibility; Onto-theology; Theodicy.

Bibliography. James Beilby, *Divine Foreknowledge*; John Sanders, *The God Who Risks*; William Lane Craig, *The Only Wise God*; Thomas Flint, *Divine Foreknowledge*; Jonathan Kvanvig, *The Possibility of an All-Knowing God*.

Ontology   *See* Metaphysics/Ontology.

Ontotheology

A *metaphysical system or theory that posits *God as a solution to a problem. Though the term is often employed loosely and without precision to refer to any kind of *realist understanding of God, "onto-theo-logy" entered the philosophical lexicon through an important essay by *Heidegger entitled "The Onto-Theo-Logical Constitution of Metaphysics." The central question for Heidegger was, "*How does God enter *modern philosophical thought?*" In other words, when we look at the system of a particular philosopher such as *Descartes or *Hegel, what role does God play in the system? Focusing especially on Hegel, Heidegger contends that in modern metaphysical systems, "God" is merely "admitted" in the system in order to solve a problem or gap within the system. As such, God is *reduced* to a piece of a metaphysical puzzle and constitutes something of an afterthought, brought in only to fill the gaps. God, then, simply becomes the *causa sui* of a metaphysical system, not the living God of biblical revelation. Thus Heidegger himself protests the inappropriateness and reductionism of such a metaphysical God, asking, "Is this a God before whom we can dance and pray?" Thus, contrary to popular belief, Heidegger's critique is aimed at the metaphysical reduction of God in *modernity and harbors within it a respect for the *transcendence of God vis-à-vis finite thought.

As such, Heidegger has both an important precursor and an heir. First, Heidegger himself was deeply influenced by *Pascal's critique of philosophical conceptions of God. In his *Pensées*, Pascal contrasts the reductionistic "God of the philosophers" to the robust, revelational "God of Abraham, Isaac, and Jesus Christ." The "God of the philosophers," we could say, is an "onto-theo-logical" reduction of the biblical God. In contemporary thought, Heidegger's critique of ontotheology has been appropriated most forcefully by Jean-Luc Marion. In his *God Without Being*, Marion distinguishes between conceptual "idols" of God that reduce God to just one Being among beings, and conceptual "icons" of God that begin not from metaphysical systems but from the revelation of God in Christ, re-revealed in the Eucharist. In both cases, Heidegger's critique of ontotheology is linked to a theological project that takes revelation seriously enough to challenge the god of metaphysical gaps.

See also God, Nature of; Heidegger; Pascal; Postmodernism.

Bibliography. John Caputo, *Heidegger and Aquinas*; Martin Heidegger, *Identity and Difference*; Philip Clayton, *The Problem of God in Modern Thought*; Jean-Luc Marion, *God Without Being*; Merold Westphal, *Overcoming Onto-Theology*.

Ordinary Language Philosophy

A philosophical movement that focused attention on the way in which language functions in ordinary discourse as opposed to its technical use in abstract philosophical contexts. The movement flourished in Britain after 1945, and its central figures were J. L. Austin, Gilbert Ryle, and John Wisdom. Its continuing significance has been in the development of speech-act theory so central to contemporary *hermeneutical debates in *philosophy and theology.

Ordinary language philosophy was inspired by the later work of *Wittgenstein, who insisted that traditional philosophical puzzles can often be solved by paying closer attention to the way in which words are used in ordinary conversation. His admonishment to philosophers, "Don't think, look," discouraged philosophical abstraction in favor of leaving language as it is in ordinary human discourse. Words have meaning in the contexts of whole language systems and ought not be torn asunder from their frameworks. Granting words a special meaning outside their ordinary contexts often creates artificial conundrums rather than solving them. For example, wrenching terms like "*truth" or "*mind" out of ordinary conversation and attaching special meaning to them, as philosophers do, leads to the hypostatization of terms that are understood perfectly well in their ordinary context. Words are meant to do a certain duty in a certain linguistic context *(meaning is use)* and lack meaning when they are discussed in abstraction as one does when one discusses theories of truth or mind.

Attending to language resulted in a renewed interest in the way words are used to perform a variety of functions in ordinary contexts. Austin's *How to Do Things with Words* is indicative of this method. Language is not primarily a conceptual tool as much as it is a means of action. This insight led to the development of speech-act theory. The words "open the door" are aimed primarily not at describing a state of affairs, but rather are an attempt by the speaker to get a listener to do something, that is, to act. Speech-act theory cautions us that referential statements (sentences that refer to objects in the world), those favored by many philosophers, are only one small part of language.

Ordinary language philosophy, particularly speech-act theory, has come to the fore in Christian reflection on the nature of revelation and questions of *hermeneutics. Paying attention to the way words are ordinarily used helps to illuminate the meaning of words in Scripture. We are reminded that the Bible is not a technical theological treatise but a collection of narratives written in a variety of mostly ordinary styles and situations. Its authors speak in historically conditioned ordinary language rather than in the abstract language of *metaphysics and theology. An appreciation for the language in which the Scriptures were originally written will also push us away from reductionistic theological claims that seek to find only narrow meanings for terms.

See also Hermeneutics, Positivism, Religious Language, Wittgenstein.

Bibliography. Charles E. Caton, *Philosophy and Ordinary Language;* Oswald Hanfling, *Philosophy and Ordinary Language;* Tim Ward, *Word and Supplement;* Nicholas Wolterstorff, *Divine Discourse.*

Pascal, Blaise (1623–1662)   French mathematician who, after a dramatic conversion, devoted his prodigious intellect to the defense of Christianity. Because of his early death, the project was not finished, but his notes and ideas were posthumously collected under the title *Pensées* (thoughts). Part of his project was to shock indifferent and apathetic people into caring for ultimate questions concerning *God, immortality, and the meaning of life.

Pascal was a trenchant critic of philosophical *reductionism as contrary to the particularity of belief in the God of Jesus Christ. Thus he often opposed the *god of the philosophers* to the God of Abraham, Isaac, and Jesus Christ. Part of this stemmed from his *epistemology— deeply influenced by *Augustine— which emphasized the importance of the *affective* to our beliefs. Thus one of Pascal's most famous claims is that "the heart has reasons that *reason does not know."

Pascal is most famous for what has come to be known as *Pascal's wager.* The wager offers a cost-benefit analysis of the rationality of belief in God. Given the possibilities that God exists and that the unbeliever will be punished with eternal damnation and the believer rewarded with *eternal bliss, Pascal argues that it is rational to wager that God exists. Using a rational decision procedure, he asks us to consider placing a bet on God's existence. If one bets on God's existence, then either God exists and one enjoys an eternity of bliss, or God does not exist and one loses very little. On the other hand, if one bets against God and wins, one gains very little; but if one loses that bet, then one will suffer in *hell forever. Pascal demonstrates that even if the evidence is incapable of settling whether God exists, prudence demands that one should nonetheless believe in God's existence. As Pascal says at the end of his defense of the wager, "Wager, then, that God exists."

There are three standard criticisms of Pascal's wager. First, Pascalian wagering only works if one has an exhaustive listing of the possibilities. Pascal only considers whether one ought to believe in the Christian God. Consider how difficult it would be to use his method to decide which of all the religions one ought to accept. Second, believing simply to avoid the torments of hell and to gain the pleasures of heaven is a crassly self-interested basis for belief and cannot provide a suitable foundation for genuine *faith in God. Third, even if one were persuaded that it is in one's best interest to believe in God, it does not follow that it is possible for one to acquire that belief. Beliefs, by and large, are not within our direct, voluntary control. For example, close your eyes and think of your belief in God; now, if you believe in God choose not to believe, and later, choose to believe again. This and countless similar examples, suggest that we do not just choose what to believe.

Pascal's replies to the objections typically go unnoticed. The wager is just one of his many tools for shocking people into caring about their eternal destinies. After arguing that our desires affect our abilities to discern the *truth, he tries to get our desires appropriately oriented toward the truth. The wager can stimulate the desire to seek the truth about God and, after one's desires are changed, the ability to judge the evidences for Christianity properly.

See also Apologetics; Augustine; Descartes; Enlightenment; Faith and Reason; God, Belief in; Hell; Ontotheology; Reason; Reason and Belief in God.

Bibliography. Thomas Morris, Making Sense of It All; Marvin R. O'Connell, Blaise Pascal.

Perspectivalism The claim that human cognition is relative to a perspective or framework. Hard perspectivalism, often linked with anti-realism, claims that reality is relative to the perspective in which it is cognized. This entails that something might be real for one person but unreal for another person (depending on the cognitive frameworks and sociohistorical location of the different believers). For hard perspectivalism, there is no objective "thing" of which one has a perspective; rather, we might say, perspective "goes all the way down." Soft perspectivalism claims more modestly that one's perception of the world is conditioned by the particular perspective or horizon of the perceiver. Thus it asserts that there is an extraperspectival reality—a world of which one has a perspective—but that access to this world is always mediated by a particular perspective. In contrast to perspectivalism, then, would be a kind of naïve *realism, which claims both to know an objective reality and to perceive this reality without any conditioning by perspective horizon.

*Nietzsche is a representative of radical perspectivalism. His declaration that *God is dead was intended to signal the end of Christianity's influence in the West, and also to claim that all absolutes were exhausted. Nothing remained but the individual in search of his or her own meaning. All human understanding is interpretation: "reality" is filtered through a perspective. According to Nietzsche, there are no objective or neutral—"God's eye"—perspectives; hence there is no objective world. All cognition is finite, perspectival, and provisional. There is no world "out there" to which our view of the world corresponds. Reality is a matter of convention and consensus; it always bears the marks of the contexts in which it was developed. In this he was a clear forerunner of *postmodernism.

Many hard perspectivalists are motivated by the sincere and noble desire not to pronounce judgment on other groups of people (as though they had a superior perspective, i.e., were gods). However, it is difficult to stomach the consequences. For if hard perspectivalism is right, the killing of Jews or female genital mutilation is *good for those within a certain perspective.

Soft perspectivalism has become prominent as well since the mid-twentieth century. Sociohistorical enquiry has elicited a greater appreciation of the profound influences of historical context on human understanding. The death of *Enlightenment foundationalism in the twentieth century, coupled with the claims of *phenomenology, has meant the rejection of the conviction that there was a single, objective foundation upon which all knowledge could be (scientifically) constructed. Rather, the project of understanding is intertwined with sociohistorically conditioned perspectives that deeply influence what one sees and believes. This has brought an appreciation of the way in which assumptions and beliefs interact. Soft perspectivalism is one of the great and nearly universally accepted insights of postmodernism and is also consonant with orthodox Christian *faith. The apostle Paul teaches that after the Fall, human "perspective" is darkened, such that unredeemed humanity cannot properly perceive the structure of created reality. This influenced Abraham Kuyper's (Dutch Reformed theologian and statesman, 1837–1920) view of scientific knowledge as governed by prior commitments. We might say that presuppositional *apologetics assumes something of a perspectivalism.

Soft perspectivalism raises many thorny issues. How can a person have any assurance that her perspective is better than anyone else's? How does a person adjudicate *truth claims from different perspectives? In science, the perspectives of Newtonian mechanics and quantum physics appear at odds with each other. In religious matters, the claims of Christianity seem to be in conflict with other religions. In both cases, how could such differences be adjudicated, if the different claims are made from within different perspectives? Some soft perspectivalists assume that standards of rationality are constituted by traditions but that traditions can "talk" to one another. It is also possible that traditions or perspectives may change because of either internal difficulties or external evidence (as when confronted with better explanations from other traditions).

In our time of deep religious *pluralism, conversation across diverse perspectives has become central to contemporary theology. This is important both across diverse religions (e.g., Christianity and Islam) and within diverse religious traditions as well (e.g., within Roman Catholicism). Tolerance of disagreement across or within religious traditions ought to be taken seriously without supposing that tolerance of diverse perspectives is paramount to *relativism.

See also Common Sense Philosophy, Deconstruction, Enlightenment, Epistemology, Hegel, Hermeneutics, Metaphysics/Ontology, Nietzsche, Postmodernism, Realism/Anti-Realism.

Bibliography. Richard Middleton and Brian Walsh, *Truth Is Stranger Than It Used to Be*; Peter Berger and Thomas Luckmann, *Social Construction of Reality*; Ian Hacking, *The Social Construction of What?* John Searle, *The Construction of Social Reality*; Kenneth Gergen, *Social Construction in Context*; Richard Rorty, *Philosophy and the Mirror of Nature*; idem, *Objectivity, Relativism and Truth*.

Phenomenology A philosophical school stemming from Edmund Husserl (1859–1938), and later *Heidegger, focused on the careful description of experience of consciousness. In its broadest sense, then, phenomenology designates methods of description. Initially trained in the *philosophy of arithmetic and then concerned with *logic, Husserl focused on describing the *appearances* (Greek *phenomena*) of objects for consciousness. Thus, beginning with his *Logical Investigations* (1901), through the *Ideas* (1913), and up to his later *Cartesian Meditations* (1928), and *Crisis of European Philosophy* (1933), Husserl developed what he described as the "phenomenological method," which has several key elements.

The entrée to phenomenology is what Husserl described as the "phenomenological *reduction.*" The reduction involves "bracketing" or "putting out of play" my interest in the cup as it exists, and rather being concerned with how the cup *appears* to me. This move reduces our sphere of concern to the *experience* of things. When we turn to experience, we discover three important characteristics. First, consciousness is characterized by *intentionality* (from the Latin *intentio*, "to aim"); that is, consciousness is always consciousness of something, some phenomenon. In other words, every experience of consciousness has an intended object—it aims at something. A second aspect of conscious experience is *constitution:* while I am confronted by an influx of "data" (what Husserl calls "intuition") from the cup in front of me, that "raw data" have to be "put together" in order for me to experience the object *as* a cup. Thus consciousness constitutes or "puts together" the data of my experience. There is thus an active role that consciousness plays in constructing the world of our experience. Finally, this process of constitution happens within *horizons* of perception; in other words, how I constitute a phenomenon is relative to the horizons of my experience, including my past. Thus I can constitute the object in front of me as a cup because I have a history of encounter with such objects. But sometimes I am encountered by intuitive data for which I have no previous experience. In such cross-cultural cases, conscious-ness struggles to constitute the phenomenon because of the conditions of my particular horizons.

Central to phenomenology, then, was the post-Kantian sense that our world of experience is in some sense "constructed" by us, and such constructions are conditioned by our horizons, which are themselves conditioned by tradition, history, culture, and so forth. These core insights were picked up and developed in later twentieth-century thought, particularly in the "*hermeneutic phenomenology" of Heidegger, Hans-Georg Gadamer, and Paul Ricoeur, but also in the more radical thought of Jacques Derrida.

While influential for a variety of schools of "phenomenology of religion" (Mircea Eliade, Rudolf Otto, and Gerardus van der Leuuw), phenomenology has also been appropriated by different strains of theology, as seen in the work of Edward Farley and Jean-Luc Marion. Hovering in the background of Husserl's concerns has always been a sense of "*transcendence." This element has been developed in late-twentieth-century French phenomenology, particularly in the work of Jean-Luc Marion and Emmanuel Levinas.

See also Deconstruction, Existentialism, Heidegger, Realism/Anti-Realism.

Bibliography. Edward Farley, *Ecclesial Reflection;* Edmund Husserl, *Cartesian Meditations;* Herbert Spiegelberg, *The Phenomenological Movement;* Sumner Twiss, *Experience of the Sacred;* Robert Sokolowski, *Introduction to Phenomenology;* J. Kockelmans, *The Phenomenology of Edmund Husserl;* Emmanuel Levinas, *Of God Who Comes to Mind;* Jean-Luc Marion, *God Without Being;* James K. A. Smith, *Speech and Theology.*

Philosophy The love of wisdom (from the Greek words *phileo*, which means "to love," and *sophia*, meaning "wisdom"), which *Plato suggested begins in "wonder." *Aristotle opened his *Metaphysics* by claiming that "all humans by nature desire to know." To some, philosophy is the grandest of all intellectual pursuits, attempting to delineate the first principles of all knowledge about the world. To others, it is much more practical: it offers a way of negotiating through life. In both senses, philosophy concerns questions and issues that most ordinary people think about at one time or another, such as the meaning of life, the practice of virtue, the nature of *evil, ultimate reality, the existence of *God. One could say that philosophy seeks answers to the foundational questions that are then assumed in other areas of inquiry. For instance, the theologian asks, How can we know God? But that question presupposes something about knowledge and about God. The philosopher asks the more fundamental questions, How can we know at all? and Who or what is God? The historian asks whether Jesus rose from the dead. But the historian's method assumes beliefs both about existence (of Jesus, Jerusalem, the crucifixion, etc.) and knowledge (how do we determine the *truth about the distant past?). Philosophy is that realm of investigation that asks these most basic questions and is, therefore, an important way of understanding God's creation and our place in it. When the apostle Paul warns against "deceptive philosophy" (Colossians 2:8), he has in mind a particular philosophical doctrine, not philosophy as such (he himself employs philosophical reasoning in service of the gospel in Acts 17).

In the ancient world, philosophy was the umbrella under which all other intellectual endeavors were pursued. For Plato, Aristotle, and the *Stoics, philosophy was also a way of life. Wisdom is not only understanding the world but understanding how to live well in that world. As a result, philosophical "schools" resembled religious orders. With the emergence of Christendom in the West, philosophy was a tool for thinking clearly about *faith and seeing the implications for living. Thus *Augustine makes no clear distinction between philosophy and theology.

The era of *modern philosophy began with *Descartes and departed from the older integration of knowledge and action. The modern tradition (in its rationalist, empiricist, and *idealist stages) thought of philosophy as a second-order discipline that helps clarify the first order claims of the natural and human sciences. The twentieth century has seen the rise of the professional philosopher and increased specialization. In addition, Western philosophy has divided, roughly, into two schools: *analytic and continental.

When the oracle of Delphi proclaimed Socrates the wisest of all, Socrates at first rejected it but then affirmed it: "I don't know anything, but at least I know that I don't know anything." Socrates' philosophical humility is somewhat exaggerated, as he certainly had strong beliefs about many things. But his point is clear: on questions of fundamental human concern, the answers are extremely difficult to discern. Philosophy is often criticized because it provides few definite answers (for every philosophical theory there is an equal and opposite philosophical theory). But the problem may not be with philosophy. The problem likely lies in the enormity of "the big questions" and our puny cognitive equipment. If there is a lesson to be learned from the history of philosophy, it is that intellectual humility is a virtue worthy of cultivation.

See also Analytic/Continental Philosophy, Augustine, Descartes, Faith and Reason, Metaphysics/Ontology, Underdetermination.

Bibliography. Robert C. Solomon, *A Passion for Wisdom*; Kelly James Clark, *Philosophers Who Believe*; David Karnos and Robert Shoemaker, *Falling in Love with Wisdom*; James F. Sennett, *The Analytic Theist*; Pierre Hadot and Arnold Davidson, *Philosophy as a Way of Life*.

Plato (470–399 B.C.E.) **and Platonism**
Student of the Athenian philosopher
Socrates and arguably the founder of
Western *philosophy. His writings
include dialogues with Socrates as the
central figure, the most famous being the
Republic. These dialogues, along with
Plato's own more systematic thought,
have exerted a lasting, indelible impact
on Western philosophy. Alfred North
Whitehead famously suggested that all
of Western philosophy is but a footnote
to Plato. The Platonic tradition was first
mediated through *Neoplatonism and
then was taken up by the Christian tradition. The most significant appropriation of Platonism in Christian theology
was in the work of *Augustine, who in
his *Confessions* (book VII) indicated that
the books of the Platonists (the Neoplatonists) led him toward his conversion to
Christian *faith. This influence persisted
throughout the Middle Ages (as seen in
*Aquinas), during the Reformation (in
Calvin), and into contemporary thought
(in the work of Radical Orthodoxy).

Plato's philosophy places a special
emphasis on *transcendence, or what he
sometimes describes as the "intelligible
world." According to Plato's *ontology,
there is a certain "scale" to reality, with a
marked distinction between the physical, material world of our experience
and the intelligible, immaterial world of
thought. What is "really real" for Plato is
not the sensible objects that we taste,
hear, or see, but rather the "Forms" or
*essences of such particular things. Par-
ticular, sensible things participate in
these intelligible forms but are only
copies of the Forms. For instance, while
we can see many different chairs in the
room perceived by our eyes (visual
organs), there is only one Form of a chair,
which cannot be seen with our eyes but
is grasped by the *mind (what Plato calls
"intellection"). For Plato, what is "really
real," then, is the invisible world of the
Forms (which are *eternal and unchanging), not the visible world of things
(which, as temporal, are subject to generation and decay). The material world

is "less real" than the Forms. One can
see, then, how Christian theologians
would be drawn to such a philosophical
framework that emphasizes that humans
are called to set their minds on the
"things above."

When we consider Plato's account of
human persons and immortality, as discussed in the *Phaedo*, however, we see
the beginnings of a tension between Platonic and Christian thought. For Plato,
the essence of the human person is a disembodied, immaterial soul. That human
souls are embodied constitutes a kind of
punishment. Indeed, Plato describes the
body as a prison for the soul, from which
the soul seeks release and liberation. The
way to achieve such liberation from the
imprisonment of the body is to pursue
philosophy, which requires an ascetic
rejection of material, worldly pleasures
in order to reflect on the Forms. The
human being who lives a life of philosophy will, upon death, escape the prison
of the body. The human being who is
absorbed with material pleasure will
be reincarnated. While the critique of
absorption with material pleasure echoes
New Testament themes, at root this
conception of the person runs counter
to the biblical witness. According to
Scripture, we are created as embodied
beings; therefore, bodies are not prisons.
Further, the hope of the Christian is
*resurrection of the body, whereas the
hope of the Platonist is escape from
the body. These differences regarding
the *goodness of material creation signal
a point of deep tension between the
Christian and Platonic traditions—tensions that can be found within Christianity itself, as demonstrated in the
corpus of Augustine.

Platonism (or some version of Neoplatonism) dominated Christian thought
from the church fathers up to early
*modernity. However, in the nine-
teenth century, particularly in German
theology following Harnack, Christian
theology became suspicious of the
"hellenization" of Christianity—that is,
the importing of doctrines that were

Greek (especially Platonic), not Christian. Twentieth-century Christian theology was dominated with a concern to de-Platonize Christianity. As the dominant cultural stance has tended toward materialism and immanence, however, Christianity has again turned to Platonism as a resource for countering materialism. This can be seen in the work of Radical Orthodoxy, which explicitly draws on Plato's notion of "participation" as a way of affirming both the immanence and the transcendence of the created world.

See also Aquinas; Aristotle; Augustine; Being and Goodness; Dualism/Monism; Epistemology; Essence/Essentialism; Ethics; Ethics, Biblical; Euthyphro Problem; God, Nature of; Good/Goodness; Happiness; Human Nature; Idealism; Metaphysics/Ontology; Mind/Soul/Spirit; Neoplatonism; Resurrection/Immortality; Teleology; Transcendence; Universals.

Bibliography. Julia Annas, *Plato;* C. C. W. Taylor, ed., *Greek Philosophers;* Michel Despland, *The Education of Desire;* John Rist, *Platonism and Its Christian Heritage.*

Pluralism, Exclusivism, and Inclusivism

Positions on the status of non-Christian religions. The problems of religious diversity are pressing. Sincere truth seekers about the nature of ultimate reality reach widely divergent conclusions, and one's religious beliefs seem to be closely connected with how, where, and when someone was raised. The idea that our salvation or transformation depends on believing just the right things about *God (or Ultimate Reality) and doing just the right things to gain access to God (or heaven or nirvana) raises important and pressing questions: Is our salvation dependent on sociohistorical accident? Is it fair to make salvation dependent on historically particular beliefs? Is it theologically and morally acceptable to

maintain that one religion is uniquely true and that the others are crucially incomplete or even false? There are three major Christian theories concerning the relationship of Christianity to divergent religious beliefs. The first two, exclusivism and inclusivism, maintain that the central claims of Christianity are true and that Christianity is the only salvifically efficacious religion. The third view, pluralism, rejects the exclusive truth of Christian beliefs and maintains that salvation is possible through most major religious systems.

Exclusivism, the traditional view, holds that only people who have explicit (usually antemortem) *faith in Jesus will be saved. Other religions that depart from the central claims of Christianity are false. Salvation, requiring confession of and belief in the incarnation, death, and *resurrection of Jesus, is not to be found in other religious traditions. Thus, according to exclusivists, salvation requires both the ontological accomplishment of Christ's death and resurrection as well as the individual's *epistemological trust in Christ's work (Romans 10:9–10).

Inclusivism holds that people without explicit faith in Jesus may be saved, but no one is saved apart from the redemptive work of Jesus. That is, although Jesus' atonement is necessary for everyone's salvation, God has made it available through non-Christian religions; people in other traditions have (nonconscious) access to salvific faith in Christ. Just as people in the Old Testament (chronologically B.C.E.) are saved apart from explicit faith in Christ, so such salvation is possible for practitioners of other religions (informationally B.C.E.). Christian inclusivists often appeal to the alleged unfairness of making explicit faith in Jesus a requirement for salvation when most people lack access or inclination to that information.

Religious pluralism is the view that all religions are equally efficacious in achieving the salvation or transformation of their adherents. John Hick, pluralism's most powerful defender, affirms a plurality of valid and equally efficacious transformational responses to the ultimate divine Reality. Hick roots religious pluralism in *Kantianism when he distinguishes between "the Real *an sich*" (in him/her/itself) and the Real as humanly experienced and thought. The various religious traditions are formed out of the awareness of the Real as experienced. We may have access to the phenomenal world of religious experience, but we have no access to the divine noumenal world. We cannot encounter Reality in itself. Pluralists reject the belief that God has revealed himself in any unique or definitive sense in Jesus Christ. Christian faith is merely one of many equally legitimate responses to the same divine reality.

See also Anthropomorphic Language, Hell, Justice, Kant, Perspectivalism, Realism/Anti-Realism, Relativism, Theodicy, Underdetermination.

Bibliography. John Hick, Dennis Okholm, and Timothy Phillips, eds., *Four Views on Salvation in a Pluralistic World;* David Basinger, *Religious Diversity;* John Hick, *God Has Many Names;* Philip Quinn and Kevin Meeker, eds., *The Philosophical Challenge of Religious Diversity;* Amos Yong, *Beyond the Impasse.*

Positivism   The belief that natural science, the codification of sense experience, is the sum total of all human knowledge. Positivism was christened by the nineteenth-century French philosopher Auguste Comte (1798–1857), who claimed that science has historically proceeded through three successive stages: the theological, the metaphysical, and the positive (see his *Course in Positive Philosophy*). Science has progressed from the darkness of attributing the occurrence of natural events to the will of *God or to abstract metaphysical principles to now attributing them to the light of positive knowledge, wherein science is firmly grounded in sense experience.

In the early 1920s, logical positivists such as Moritz Schlick (the founder) and Rudolf Carnap (the most brilliant) gathered together to develop their ideas in Vienna and came to be called the Vienna Circle. *Logical positivism* (also called logical empiricism) accepted Comte's empiricism and also incorporated the recent breakthroughs in formal *logic. Following David *Hume, Bertrand Russell, and the early *Wittgenstein, logical positivism holds that the content of knowledge is provided by sense experience and is structured by formal logic. Logical positivists disdained *metaphysics (traditional *philosophy), believing it to be not false but meaningless.

Logical positivists held the *verification theory of meaning*: all meaningful assertions (sentences or statements) must be empirically verifiable (i.e., their *truth or falsity must be "checkable" by the senses). All nonempirical assertions—those in metaphysics, theology, and *ethics—are cognitively meaningless. Such statements may have emotive power but are cognitively empty (they could not possibly be proper items of knowledge). Some positivists offered an account of ethical statements consistent with the criterion of verifiability. According to the *emotive theory of ethics*, ethical statements are expressions of emotion, so "That action is bad" means "Boo!" and "That action is *good" means "Hooray!" One can imagine that few outside the circle found the "Boo-Hooray" theory of ethics appealing.

The logical positivists were their own best critics. They recognized, for example, the impossibility of meaningfully stating the verification theory of meaning (because the verification theory of meaning is not empirically verifiable). They also recognized that many entities in science, like atoms and the center of the sun, are unobservable and hence meaningless according to the criterion of verifiability.

Positivism, for all its flaws, recognized that the single, universally accepted branch of knowledge is the natural sciences. In nearly every other domain of human belief, including religion and theology, there is widespread disagreement about both content and method. Nonetheless, the failure of logical positivism to establish the foundations of science (content and method), especially as argued by Thomas Kuhn in *The Structure of Scientific Revolutions,* played a significant role in the rise of *postmodernism.

There is no philosophy, once discredited, that has not found influence among theologians, and logical positivism is no exception. Although most sober-minded Christians found positivism to be an enemy of the faith, some of the so-called "death of God" theologians made it the foundation of their faith and reduced theological statements to their emotive and motivational content.

See also Analytic/Continental Philosophy, Atheism, Epistemology, Ethics, Hume, Logic, Metaphysics/Ontology, Naturalism, Postmodernism, Underdetermination, Wittgenstein.

————

Bibliography. Allan Janik, *Wittgenstein's Vienna*; A. J. Ayer, *Language, Truth, and Logic*; Frederick Ferré, *Language, Logic and God.*

Postmodernism A term loosely used to describe the critique of *modernity across disciplines ranging from architecture to physics. Unfortunately, the term is often used simply to label any contemporary bogeyman of theology or Christian practice. But more particularly, "postmodernism" is often used to describe the specifically theoretical or academic accounts, whereas "postmodernity" is used to refer to a broader cultural milieu. If Jacques Derrida is a proponent of postmodern*ism*, MTV and the rise of the Internet would be symptoms of postmodern*ity*. In any case, the term is very slippery and is used to denote a vast array of positions and *phenomena. This slipperiness has led even Richard Rorty to suggest that the word is "causing more trouble than it is worth."

So the term should be used with both caution and qualification.

Postmodernism is, to some degree, reactive and perhaps even parasitic insofar as it is oriented by a critique of modernity and the fundamental convictions of modernism, particularly the epistemological convictions of modern philosophers such as *Kant and *Descartes. This *epistemological critique then entails criticism of and revision in the area of *ethics. For instance, the postmodern rejection of a notion of universal *reason entails the rejection of anything like Kant's categorical imperative. Instead, postmodern ethics tends to focus on the particular and concrete. As such, postmodern ethics has sometimes been described as a kind of casuistry.

One of the epistemological tenets of modernity has been described as "foundationalism," which held out the promise that scholars and scientists—freed from religious and political biases—could know the world as it "really" is. According to Descartes, for instance, knowledge properly acquired is constructed from the ground up, on the basis of "certain" foundations. The most basic beliefs are supposed to satisfy the criteria of being self-evident and irrefutable. In Kant and others, this account of knowledge gave birth to the notion of a universal, neutral, autonomous reason as guarantor of truth. This foundationalist account of objective knowledge is one of the primary targets of postmodern critique.

According to philosophers such as *Heidegger, Gadamer, and Derrida, all knowledge is always already prejudiced. This is because our very perception of the world is conditioned by our "horizons," and these horizons are relative to our particular sociocultural histories; there can be no universal, neutral, "objective" knowledge, but only "stories" about the world told from within particular commitments. Michel Foucault intensified this critique by arguing that knowledge is conditioned by *power*—that our "prejudices" stem from interests of power and domination.

Jean-François Lyotard has defined post-modernism most famously as "incre-dulity toward metanarratives." By meta-narratives, he does not mean simply "large-scale" stories, but rather accounts of the world that seek to ground them-selves by appeal to a universal, auton-omous reason (as in Kant, *Hegel, *Marx, or *positivism). For Lyotard, all accounts of the world—even scientific ones—ultimately appeal to a founding "narrative," analogous to a religious story or "myth." As such, all knowledge is rooted in the particularity of *faith sto-ries. One of the effects of this insight about knowledge is what is called (by both Lyotard and Jürgen Habermas) a "legitimation crisis": if we cannot appeal to universal rationality to justify or legit-imate our account, then how can there be "agreement"?

Postmodernists are less sanguine about achieving such consensus than modernists. But it should be noted that most Christian philosophers and post-foundationalist theologians also affirm the reality of this state of affairs. In a sense, then, "narrative theology" could be seen as a kind of postmodern theol-ogy. However, postmodernism has also produced more "radical" theologies in the vein of "death of God" theologies, particularly in the work of Mark C. Tay-lor and Donald Cupitt.

Some Christian theologians have suggested that insofar as postmod-ernism rejects "metanarratives," it must entail the rejection of the Christian story. While some versions of a radical (and less responsible) postmodernism might reject the very notion of a global story, Lyotard's critique does not. Therefore, the Christian story would only fall prey to Lyotard's criticism of metanarratives if one assumes that the biblical narra-tive is a story grounded by neutral rea-son. While classical *apologists might assume something of this sort, presup-postionalists and nonfoundationalists do not; therefore, Christian theology might in fact *share* postmodernity's incredulity toward metanarratives.

While postmodernism is often con-strued in negative and almost amoral terms (and admittedly, some of its more *Nietzschean strains suggest this), at its core is a very positive concern about *justice. It is important to recognize that in "responsible" postmodernists, such as Derrida, Levinas, Lyotard, Rorty, and Foucault, we find a trenchant critique of the way in which social and institutional structures marginalize and dominate the powerless and oppressed. While in Fou-cault this is informed by a broadly Marx-ist concern regarding domination, and Rorty's concern for justice is informed by democratic liberalism (with a dash of Marxism), in Levinas this is directly informed by the biblical concern for "the widow, the orphan, and the stranger." Levinas has thus introduced deeply Hebraic conceptions of ethics into contemporary postmodern dis-course, exerting a signal influence on Derrida. According to Levinas, and in contrast to the "rights talk" of moder-nity, I am not first and foremost an indi-vidual with "rights," but rather I find myself always already obligated to the face of the Other. The "Other," for Lev-inas, is the other human being who at the same time "incarnates" the Otherness or "alterity" of God. In the postmodern concern for alterity, in contrast to the hegemonic "sameness" of modernity, Christian theologians have found an important biblical basis for cultural cri-tique and engagement.

See also Deconstruction, Descartes, Enlightenment, Epistemology, Kant, Modernity/Modernism, Nietzsche, Per-spectivalism.

Bibliography. John Caputo and Michael J. Scanlon, eds., *God, the Gift, and Postmodernism*; Stanley J. Grenz and John R. Franke, *Beyond Founda-tionalism*; David Harvey, *The Condition of Postmodernity*; Gavin Hyman, *The Predicament of Postmodern Theology*; Jean-François Lyotard, *The Postmodern Condition*; John Milbank, *Theology and Social Theory*; Merold Westphal, ed.,

Postmodern Philosophy and Christian Thought.

Pragmatism A distinctly American philosophical tradition that values beliefs according to their practical consequences; *philosophy is not considered primarily a cognitive enterprise but is more concerned with the acquisition of beliefs that help us cope with life. Harvard philosopher William James (1842–1910), the founder of pragmatism, contends that human inquiry reflects not just the world but also our temperament, needs, concerns, fears, hopes, and passions. Our inclinations are essential to our worldview because of the *underdetermination of theory by data: for any set of data, there are competing hypotheses that adequately account for the data but that are mutually incompatible. Because the divergent hypotheses equally account for the evidence, no appeal to the evidence could determine which hypothesis is true. How does one reasonably decide which to accept? According to James, we must consult our passional nature—passions, intellect, *reason, and even "dumb conviction." The test of *truth is the proven usefulness of a belief in the practice of our lives. The pragmatist mantle has been most recently carried by Richard Rorty, who continues James's emphasis on "usefulness" when judging social arrangements.

Although many later pragmatists would be *atheists, James used the pragmatic approach to defend immortality, human freedom, and belief in *God. His encyclopedic *Varieties of Religious Experience* (1902) is one of the best treatments of the topic. In "The Will to Believe," James defends religious belief against the *Enlightenment demand for evidence. In certain cases one is forced to make a decision in the absence of adequate evidence. To believe in God or not is one of those forced choices, and the stakes are so high that, even in the absence of evidence, each person has a right to believe in God based on an assessment of the benefits and costs of belief or unbelief. As one brings one's passional nature to the question of God's existence, one helps create the kind of reality, involving a personal relationship with God, that the person seeks and desires. Thus belief in God proves its usefulness, that is, truth.

Some theological traditions—particularly stemming from Wesley—have found an ally in pragmatism because of their emphasis on the relationship between truth and practice. For Wesley, the "truth" of Christian doctrines is determined by their effects in *love*; in other words, the only ortho*doxy* is that which produces ortho*praxis.*

See also Analytic/Continental Philosophy, Enlightenment, Modernity/Modernism, Philosophy, Positivism, Postmodernism, Realism/Anti-Realism, Truth, Underdetermination.

Bibliography. Louis Menand, *The Metaphysical Club;* Charles Taylor, *Varieties of Religious Belief Today;* William Wainwright, *Reason and the Heart;* Hunter Brown, *William James on Radical Empiricism and Religion;* Cornel West, *The Cornel West Reader;* Richard Rorty, *Consequences of Pragmatism.*

Process Thought A school of thought emphasizing the priority of events (processes) over *substances. In this scheme, becoming is more fundamental than being. By contrast, classical Western thought has conceived of ontology as consisting of things or substances at their most basic level. Process thought's ontology is restricted to events —processes that occur through time.

Process thought as a formal philosophical tradition receives inspiration from the work of the ancient philosopher Heraclitus and from Plato's *Theaetetus*, both of whom saw change as fundamental to reality. Alfred North Whitehead (1861–1947) was the originator of the movement. Other names associated with this tradition include Henri Bergson and Charles Hartshorne. A theological tradition, process theology, is closely aligned with the work of Whitehead, and its chief proponents are Shubert Ogden, John Cobb, and David Ray Griffin.

In process thought, the fundamental fact of *cosmology is the unfolding of events, not substances. Reality is like a large wave (or set of waves) that rolls through time, defined more by its motion than by the volume of water it contains. The theory of relativity is in the background as a major influence. Central is the notion that mass is not fixed and unalterable, but is a function of, and interchangeable with, energy. As a way of capturing this insight, Whitehead supposed that reality consists of "actual occasions." These are not enduring entities in themselves, but rather are processes of becoming held together progressively by being apprehended. The act of apprehension is itself an occasion held together in a network of processes. Whitehead rejected a *dualism of *mind and matter, fearful that the ontological distance between the two would always create an *epistemological crisis: How could one thing (mind) actually know something completely different in kind (matter)? Process thought effectively reduces mind and matter to a process that has an intrinsic unity-in-diversity. Though Whitehead's original desire was to remove the abstractness of the more traditional *metaphysical philosophies, his work ended up far more abstract than the philosophers whose work he sought to leave behind.

Process theology accepts the general framework of process *philosophy but sees *God as the deepest and most profound process in the world. Process theologians reject the classical, static notions of God as *immutable, *omniscient, *omnipotent, and *transcendent. Rather, their desupernaturalized God is the primordial occasion to which all other occasions relate. God changes as the world changes. God does not determine history but rather acts like a magnet that "pulls" or persuades other events toward him. God never violates the freedom of others nor does God ordain *evil. Rather, God is striving to overcome evil even as God seeks to persuade others to do likewise.

There are resemblances between process theology and open theism. Both schools of thought view God as existing within time rather than outside time. Both think of God as neither knowing nor determining the future. And both think the problem of evil is insuperable given classical understandings of divine sovereignty and foreknowledge. However, important differences are present. Open theism maintains God's *transcendence as well as God's immanence, and is also not typically committed to a process ontology as opposed to a substance ontology. Finally, open theism views God as entirely and maximally *good.

See also Cause/Causality; Evil, Problem of; God, Nature of; Eternal/Everlasting; Immutability and Impassibility; Metaphysics/Ontology; Naturalism; Omnipotence; Omnipresence; Omniscience and Foreknowledge; Ontotheology; Substance; Teleology; Theodicy; Transcendence.

Bibliography. John Cobb and David Griffin, *Process Theology;* John Cobb and Clark Pinnock, *Searching for an Adequate God;* Lewis Ford, *Transforming Process Theism.*

Pseudo-Dionysius   Author of several treatises (such as *The Divine Names* and *Mystical Theology*) in which he developed Christian doctrine from the perspectives of *Neoplatonism and mysticism. His claim to be Dionysius the Areopagite (Acts 17:34) was taken at face value, so until the nineteenth century his works were considered to have apostolic authority. Because of the Neoplatonic influence, his works have come to be dated around 500. This unknown author is now referred to as Pseudo-Dionysius.

Pseudo-Dionysius is associated with "negative theology," which affirms God's radical *transcendence from human conception and experience (God's otherness and ineffability) and denies the power of human cognition to grasp God's nature. Humans cannot know what God is, they can only know what God is not: God is *eternal (i.e., not temporal), God is *omnipotent (not impotent), God is *immutable (not changing), God is *omniscient (not limited in knowledge), and so forth. Humans have concepts of and can grasp temporality, impotence, change, and limited knowledge, but have no concept of eternality, immutability, omnipotence, and so forth. In describing God, the Wholly Other, all we can say is that God is not like us (in this or that respect).

Pseudo-Dionysius does not deny that affirmative theology is possible. He believes that some affirmations of (i.e., comparisons to) God, using humanly available images, symbols, and analogies, are appropriate. But as we ascend to God, we find that God is beyond all human concepts; at that point, we must abandon all speech and thought, even negations.

The influence of Pseudo-Dionysius has been remarkable. His negative theology was embraced by, for example, *Aquinas and Bonaventure, and his mystical writings were affirmed by Meister Eckhart, Teresa of Avila, and John of the Cross. In the late twentieth century his thought experienced a *postmodern revival, spearheaded by the work of Jean-Luc Marion.

See also Anthropomorphic Language, Neoplatonism, Plato and Platonism, Religious Language, Transcendence.

Bibliography. Paul Rorem, *Pseudo-Dionysius*; Jean-Luc Marion, *Idol and Distance*; idem, *God Without Being*.

Rationality   *See* Reason/Rationality.

Realism/Anti-Realism   Realism is a *metaphysical theory about the existence outside the *mind of, variously, *universals, *goodness, beauty, unobservables in science (like atoms), numbers, or even the world itself. Anti-realism, then, is the metaphysical theory that denies the extramental existence of some class of things, or even the world itself. For example, a moral realist holds that goodness exists independently of human attitudes, desires, emotions, or beliefs. The moral anti-realist would deny the independent existence of goodness and might claim that goodness is simply an expression of human preferences or emotions. Realism/anti-realism is typically subject-specific. For example, someone might be a realist about unobservables in science but an anti-realist about goodness. There are a few prominent global anti-realists, that is, people who deny the existence of a world independent of human beliefs. Followers of *Kant contend that we cannot conceive of the world independent of human concepts or linguistic structures, so we cannot conceive of the world independent of human beliefs. But Kant's claims are *epistemological and thus not properly "anti-realist."

Outside *philosophy, the terms *realism* and *anti-realism* are often used less precisely to describe not metaphysical claims about extramental existence, but rather epistemological claims about *access* to the extramental existence of various realities. In such cases, "realism" is confused with an overly optimistic, classical foundationalist epistemological theory often described as *naïve realism*. According to this view, realism aspires to attain a God's-eye view (a view that transcends the particularity and finitude of the human believer) to see reality as it is in itself (independent of human beliefs). But it must be noted that realism's claims about extramental existence do not entail any particular epistemological theory, so not all realists are naïve realists. Indeed, it should be noted that very few contemporary philosophers defend the epistemological thesis that anti-realist nonphilosophers reject; rather, most would concede that, though extramental realities exist, our access to them is difficult and conditioned by the particularities of culture, horizons of perception, and so forth.

Theology has a stake in the realism/anti-realism debate. Given that orthodox Christian theology asserts the *transcendence of *God vis-à-vis creation, it is often associated with realism in respect to its metaphysical claims. But again, this does not necessarily entail a naïve account of our *access* to the extramental structures of the divine reality. Postliberal theology, for instance, would retain an ontological claim about the existence of a transcendent God, but would assert that any epistemological access to God would be mediated by communal constructions. There are also more radical (i.e., metaphysical) anti-realist theologies on offer (often influenced by *Wittgenstein) that remove the existence of God from theology, reducing theology to religious practices.

See also Analytic/Continental Philosophy, Aristotle, Epistemology, Essence/Essentialism, Ethics, Kant, Metaphysics/Ontology, Modernity/Modernism, Nietzsche, Perspectivalism, Pluralism, Postmodernism, Reason/Rationality, Religious Language, Transcendence, Truth, Wittgenstein.

Bibliography. George Lindbeck, *The Nature of Doctrine*; Michael Loux, *Metaphysics*; D. Z. Phillips and Timothy Tessin, eds., *Religion without Transcendence?* D. Z. Phillips, ed., *The Concept of Prayer*; Andrew Moore, *Realism and Christian Faith*; George Lindbeck et al., *The Nature of Confession*; William Alston, ed., *Realism and Antirealism*.

Reason/Rationality

Reason is the human capacity to reach the *truth or "get in touch with" reality, sometimes described as a "faculty" of the human *mind. Being rational is a quality of the person who has done her best to acquire true beliefs. The goal of being rational is to acquire true beliefs. We are truth seekers and reason is a means to that end.

Rationality is a matter of *how* one believes, not *what* one believes. Rationality is not identical with truth since a person may hold a belief for "good reasons" and yet believe what is false. Suppose Sam believes the testimony of an otherwise reliable person about an event. Unknown to Sam, that person is lying, though Sam has no good reason to believe that person is lying. Sam believes what he is told and appears to have followed rational procedures and yet believes falsely. So a person may rationally hold a false belief.

Rationality is also *person-* and *situation-specific*. That is, what is rational for one person at a particular sociohistorical time and place might not be rational for another person at a different time and place. It was rational for most people two thousand years ago to believe that the earth was flat but is no longer rational for most people to believe now. This is not *relativism, for a relativist would hold that it was true that the earth was flat to those who believe it, and also true that it is round for those who believe that.

In order to grasp reality, we must use and trust our cognitive faculties or capacities such as memory, perception, induction, and deduction—they are the sum total of our rational powers. But we also know that we get things wrong. We ought to trust the beliefs produced by our cognitive faculties in the appropriate circumstances unless we have good reason to reject them. When belief formation follows normally reliable processes, true beliefs normally result. If we are sincere truth seekers on these matters, we should be willing to do two things that may help us attain true beliefs and eliminate false beliefs. First, we ought to seek, as best we can, supporting evidence for immediately produced beliefs of fundamental human concern; evidence is truth-conducive and can lend credence to a basic belief. Second, we ought to be open to contrary evidence to root out false beliefs.

Some Christian traditions have been deeply suspicious of reason. Luther asserted that reason is the devil's whore. Blaise *Pascal passionately believed that *faith involved the heart, not just reason.

In both cases, however, there were good reasons to be suspicious of the notions of rationality they rejected, that of *Scholasticism and of the *Enlightenment. Scholasticism was overly optimistic about the powers of reason, and the Enlightenment was overly restrictive in what it countenanced as rational. Some Christians denigrate reason in deference to the authority of the Bible. But Christians must make reasoned judgments as to which Scripture is God speaking, what a passage means in its literary context, how it should be interpreted, and the role it should play in a larger theological context. In short, Christians cannot dispense with reason as a tool for grasping theological truth.

See also Common Sense Philosophy; Descartes; Enlightenment; Epistemology; God, Belief in; Natural Theology; Perspectivalism; Reason and Belief in God; Relativism; Scholasticism; Truth; Underdetermination.

Bibliography. W. Jay Wood, *Epistemology;* Kelly James Clark, *Return to Reason;* Alvin Plantinga, *Warranted Christian Belief;* Alfred Mele, ed., *The Oxford Handbook of Rationality.*

Reason and Belief in God

What is the relationship of belief in God (an *omnipotent, perfectly *good creator of the universe) to *reason? One extreme contends that rational belief demands proof of a rather stringent sort (evidentialism), and the other extreme claims that belief in God should be maintained contrary to or in defiance of reason (fideism).

The most recent debate on reason and belief in God centers around *evidentialism,* which maintains that one must have evidence or arguments for one's beliefs (in God) to be rational. The evidentialist objection to belief in God holds that it is irrational to believe in God without sufficient evidence or argument, and there is not sufficient evidence or argument for the existence of God. Hence, although

God might actually exist, in the absence of evidence, it is irrational to believe in God. The evidentialist attempts to discredit belief in God, not disprove God's existence.

Some theists endorse *theistic evidentialism,* which affirms evidentialism but claims that there is sufficient evidence for the existence of God. *Sensible evidentialism* is the view that belief in God is rational because someone in the theistic community has evidence for God's existence. It concedes that there is a need for evidence for belief to be rational, but resists the awkward implication that each person is under some sort of obligation to become a quasi-philosopher— carefully studying all of the alleged proofs and disproofs of God's existence.

Fideism holds that belief in God ought to be accepted and maintained in the absence of or even contrary to reason. If reason were to oppose belief in God, then so much the worse for reason. It is difficult to find many recent defenses of fideism, it being a term as unpopular in Western *philosophy as "communist" or "fundamentalist." However, the term *fideism* is sometimes loosely used to describe those who reject evidentialism (as in *Kierkegaard or *Pascal), or who argue that what constitutes "evidence" is, in fact, already determined by *faith (as in Cornelius Van Til [1895–1987] or Herman Dooyeweerd [1889–1977], both working within the Reformed tradition).

The most prominent recent defense of reason and belief in God is called *Reformed *epistemology,* which holds that belief in God does not require the support of evidence or argument in order for it to be rational. This view has been defended by Alvin Plantinga and Nicholas Wolsterstorff. Although Reformed epistemology is often associated with Calvin, its tenets are also found in thinkers such as *Augustine and *Aquinas. The evidentialist objector claims that rational belief requires sufficient evidence but that there is insufficient evidence for God's existence; hence belief in God is irrational. The problem with the evidentialist's universal demand for evidence is that it simply cannot be met in a large number of cases with the cognitive equipment that we have. No one has ever been able to prove the existence of other persons, or that we were not created five minutes ago with our memories intact, or the reality of the past, or that in the future the sun will rise. This list could go on and on. There is a limit to the things that human beings can prove. We cannot help but trust our cognitive faculties. If we were required to prove everything, there would be an infinite regress of provings. There must be some *truths that we can just accept and reason from. We have been outfitted with cognitive faculties that produce beliefs that we can reason *from*. The kinds of beliefs that we reason *to* is a small subset of the kinds of beliefs that we do and must accept without the aid of a proof. In most cases, we must rely on our God-given intellectual equipment to produce beliefs, without evidence or argument, in the appropriate circumstances. Is it reasonable to believe that God has created us with a cognitive faculty, the *sensus divinitatis*, which produces belief in God without evidence or argument?

There are at least two reasons to believe that it is proper or rational for a person to believe in God without the need for an argument. First, because most of our cognitive faculties produce beliefs immediately, without evidence or argument, there are good inductive grounds for thinking that the *sensus divinitatis* produces belief in God immediately. Second, belief in God is more like belief in a person than belief in a scientific hypothesis. Human relations demand trust, commitment, and faith. If belief in God is more like belief in other persons than belief in atoms, then the trust that is appropriate to persons will be appropriate to God.

See also Apologetics; Common Sense Philosophy; Enlightenment; Epistemology; Faith and Reason; Freud; God, Belief in; Hume; Kant; Kierkegaard; Modernity/Modernism; Natural Theology; Pascal; Reason/Rationality; Theistic Arguments.

Bibliography. Nicholas Wolterstorff, *Reason within the Bounds of Religion;* Kelly James Clark, *Return to Reason;* Stephen Davis, *God, Reason and Theistic Proofs;* Pope John Paul II, *Fides et Ratio;* Alvin Plantinga, ed., *Faith and Rationality;* Alvin Plantinga, *Warrant and Proper Function.*

Reductionism   A philosophical strategy by which one set of facts or events is thought unnecessary because of the existence of another, more fundamental, set of facts or events. The term is often used in a pejorative sense; that is, a position will be described as "reductionistic" because it tries to make things more simple than they really are by *reducing* what should be a complex phenomenon to only one of its components. But not all reductions are bad—for example, reducing chemistry to physics. A contentious reduction is the claim that the existence of immaterial mental entities (*minds) is an unnecessary postulate. Eliminative materialists believe that all mental events could be explained in terms of events about material states (brain waves, neural processes, etc). Talk about minds (according to this way of thinking) is reducible to talk about material objects; hence, we do not need to believe in minds.

Reductionist strategies are often criticized for ignoring essential aspects of the phenomena to be reduced. Early in the twentieth century, for example, some philosophers fashionably defended emotivism, the claim that moral values could be reduced to human desire. They argued that the sentence "X is good" could be reduced to "Most people like X." Morality was thought to be explainable by (or explained away by) evolutionary science, because *justice or goodness is simply an expression of human wishes. The obvious problem with this strategy is that there are aspects of "*good" that are simply not reducible to human desires. Indeed, often the good is contrary to human desire. Christian theology has also been guilty of various reductionist strategies—sometimes reducing the *miraculous to the natural (Bultmann), or reducing revelation to inspiration (*Schleiermacher), or reducing revelation to divine dictation. Given the complexity of creation, Christian theology should expect our theoretical accounts of the world to honor this creational complexity rather than oversimplifying it.

See also Ethics; Ethics, Biblical; Justice; Naturalism; Mind/Soul/Spirit; Simplicity; Underdetermination.

Bibliography. Terrance Brown and Leslie Smith, eds., *Reductionism and the Development of Knowledge;* David Charles and Kathleen Lennon, eds., *Reduction, Explanation, and Realism;* Philip Clayton, *Explanation from Physics to Theology;* John W. Cook, *Wittgenstein, Empiricism, and Language.*

Relativism

The claim that there are no absolutes, that *truth and value are determined by historical contexts and cultures. Cognitive (or ontological) relativism holds that there are no universal truths about reality. Reality is not fixed. It is nothing more than whatever one perceives and interprets it to be. Ethical relativism claims that there are no universal standards of *good and *evil. There are no universal moral principles. Good is nothing more than what a person or community determines is advantageous to its well-being and thus is "conventional." Cultural relativism is the descriptive claim that cultures do in fact, believe differently and behave differently on the basis of different standards.

Cognitive and ethical relativism have ancient roots. Protagoras is said to have uttered the famous claim that "Man is the measure of all things." Ancient hedonism supposed that pleasure was the only moral guide. But as what one person found pleasurable differed from what another found, so morality must differ from person to person. In the contemporary setting, Richard Rorty has defended the claim that reality is simply the name we give to the idea about what we currently believe is going on. Some contemporary defenders of religious *pluralism (John Hick) have claimed that all of the world's great religions are equally valid responses to a divine reality. If this is so, the argument proceeds, then all religious truth claims ought to be treated equally and deference shown to every religion. This is our only protection against a dominant and domineering religion.

The critique of relativism is as old as relativism itself, arguing that relativism falls prey to the horns of a dilemma. Either relativism is true or it is not. If relativism is true, it is self-defeating, since there is one belief that is not relative, viz., the belief in relativism. If relativism is not true, then there is no need to take it seriously. On either ground, relativism is defective. And in either case it would seem to be unreasonable to be a relativist. But relativism is typically rejected because it is wildly counterintuitive. For example, either *God exists or God does not exist. Our beliefs about God's existence do not affect the nature of reality.

Arising out of the *modern discussion of relativism has come a greater attention to cultural relativism. Historical, cultural, and psychological factors appear to influence us in profound ways. Consensus on matters of religion and morality seems futile. This recognition has left us with two conflicting intuitions. On the one hand, we are more cognizant (and appreciative) of the tolerance required to sustain a civil society. On the other hand, we also realize that truth and goodness are necessary to a civil society. Although truth and tolerance make strange bedfellows, the Christian *faith requires a commitment to both. Tolerance is rooted in the Christian virtue of love of neighbor, and truth is rooted in the Christian virtue of love of God. Neither cancels the other out.

Bibliography. Francis Beckwith and Greg Koukl, *Relativism*; Stanley Fish, *The Trouble with Principle*; P. T. Geach, *Truth and Hope*; Kenneth Gergen, *Social Construction in Context*; Ian Markham, *Truth and the Reality of God*; Richard Rorty, *Objectivity, Relativism and Truth*.

Religious Language   The issue of how humans may speak of *God. The problem of God-talk involves the difficulty of using words that gain their meaning from ordinary human experience and applying them to a Being who lies outside ordinary human experience. How is it possible that we could know whether our human words about God "reach" their destination? How could finite concepts be predicated of an infinite being? In other words, how is talk of God possible?

Three diverse traditions emerged in the medieval period. The mystical tradition asserted that all human language is *equivocal* with respect to God. No human term is appropriate as a description of God. At best humans can only assert what God is not. This tradition informs the "negative theology" common to Eastern Christian theologians and has been revived in *postmodern discussions.

A more common tradition, associated with *Aquinas, asserted that our language about God is *analogical*. There are important similarities as well as important differences between God and humans, and, therefore, words used of God reflect this similarity and difference. The *goodness of God is similar to but different from the goodness of humans. A modification of the analogical position is found in Karl Barth's notion of the *analogia fidei*. Barth rejects

Aquinas's *analogia entis* (analogy of being), which posits a kind of "natural" ability of human language to speak of God. For Barth, language's inherent poverty cannot do justice to the Wholly Otherness of God. Nevertheless, God in his revelatory grace—operating by *faith—utilizes human language. The Scriptures, for instance, while characterized by the paucity of human speech, can be the site for the *event* of revelation where God can be spoken of almost *in spite of* language. (Barth sometimes gives the impression that this revelation is unconditioned, but it is difficult to understand how an unconditioned revelation could communicate to conditioned, finite, linguistic beings.)

The third tradition, represented by Duns *Scotus, is that our language about God is *univocal*: terms that apply to God (such as love, mercy, and power) mean the same as they do when applied to humans (though God may possess the properties in greater degree). If our terms are not univocal when used of God, how could it be possible to know wherein lies the difference? The end result of denying univocal language of God, so argued Scotus, is skepticism.

Religious language was rejected in the twentieth century by *logical *positivists and post-*Kantian theologians. The positivists' verification theory of meaning imperialistically declared religious language cognitively meaningless. Post-Kantian theologians, such as Gordon Kaufman, declared God cognitively inaccessible to human beings. Kaufman claimed that God transcends ordinary human experience. The concepts of human language can apply only to those experiences that are part of ordinary experience, and therefore our terms cannnot apply to God.

In more recent times, there has been a retrieval of the medieval and early *modern discussions of analogy as a way to speak of God. There has also been a greatly expanded discussion of the multiple uses to which language can be put. Using the tools of *ordinary language *philosophy inspired by the later work of *Wittgenstein, many philosophers of religion today are trying to clarify the conceptual conundrums and opportunities to speak meaningfully of a God who is both unlike us (*transcendent) and like us (immanent). So also the manner in which God "speaks" through rich literary venues of narrative, parable, and poetry has begun to play a prominent role in understanding how God uses language to shape us even as we use language to embrace God.

See also Aesthetics, Anthropomorphic Language, Aquinas, Hermeneutics, Kant, Naturalism, Ordinary Language Philosophy, Positivism, Pseudo-Dionysius, Scotus, Transcendence.

Bibliography. Dan R. Stiver, *The Philosophy of Religious Language;* Janet Martin Soskice, *Metaphor and Religious Language;* James K. A. Smith, *Speech and Theology;* William Alston, *Divine Nature and Human Language;* Richard Swinburne, *Revelation;* Nicholas Wolterstorff, *Divine Discourse.*

Renaissance Humanism   A fifteenth- and sixteenth-century movement that held that the Greek and Latin classics contained everything needed to lead a flourishing life. The Renaissance in Europe saw the rebirth ("renaissance") of Latin and Greek languages and classical literature. Renaissance humanism involved a revival of humanistic studies, which included disciplines outside theology and natural science (grammar, rhetoric, history, literary studies, and moral *philosophy). It opposed the pretensions of *scholastic *logic and theology and sought to humanize scholarship and learning. Denying the scholastics' claims to dogmatic certainty, Renaissance thinkers were more tolerant of differing theological views. With its assertion of personal independence and individual expression, the Renaissance was the beginning of the end of the medieval reliance on

religious authority, and would provide fertile ground for the Reformation.

Petrarch (1304–1374), one of the early figures of the Renaissance, was influenced by Cicero's philosophy and *Augustine's theology. Cicero's insistence that philosophy serve the public *good led to the focus on the importance of philosophy and theology to the civic (that is, human), realm. Rejecting abstract *scholastic theology, Petrarch embraced Augustine's view that the proper study for a human being is oneself, which later leads to the development of the central humanist doctrine of the dignity of humanity. This version of humanism found theological justification in the belief that humans are the special creation of *God and hold a special place in God's creation.

With newly developed linguistic tools, Renaissance scholars reexamined the Bible, especially the New Testament. With their newly acquired knowledge of Greek language and grammar, they criticized the extant Latin texts and sought the original meaning of the older Greek texts. These efforts inspired the Reformation's *ressourcement* attitude of "returning to the sources"—jumping over medieval tradition to return to the New Testament and early church fathers as a resource for contemporary *faith and life.

See also Aristotle, Augustine, Plato and Platonism, Scholasticism.

Bibliography. Paul Johnson, *The Renaissance;* Donald J. Wilcox, *In Search of God and Self;* Jill Kraye, ed., *The Cambridge Companion to Renaissance Humanism.*

Resurrection/Immortality   Resurrection is the belief that life continues after death in an embodied state. Immortality is the belief that the human soul has always existed and will always continue to exist in spite of the destruction of the body at death. *Plato believed that death frees the soul from the body and then enters into an immortal state, liberated from change and decay. The disembodied soul returns to an eternal realm from which it came. Neither Plato nor most ancient Greek thinkers had a notion of resurrection. Rather, the *essence of the human person was taken to be an immaterial, immortal soul.

Christians have traditionally rejected the immortality of the soul in favor of the resurrection from the dead. Early Christians believed that death was followed (at some point) by a resurrection to a new and glorious life, a renewed bodily existence granted by *God. The resurrection of Christ served as the paradigm for the belief in the future resurrection of other persons (hence Christ was described as the "first fruits" of the resurrection). This affirmation of eternal embodiment follows from the belief in the *goodness of creation and thus the goodness of the body. This is a point of difference between Greek and Christian thought, though aspects of the Christian tradition, and much of popular Christianity, hold a more Greek than biblical view of life after death. (Oscar Cullmann contended that Christians should not believe in the immortality of the soul.) Orthodox Christian traditions affirm the goodness of the body on the basis of the resurrection. In contrast to Platonism, in these Christian traditions the body, though fallen, is not evil. God's care for the body after death suggests that we should care about the bodies of persons prior to death, as well as the physical world in which those bodies participate. The Christian valuing of the embodied existence reflects the incarnation of Christ at the center of Christian *faith. As a result, bodily existence cannot be intrinsically flawed or beyond redemption, but is rather an integral aspect of human identity.

Philosophers wonder how personal identity could be sustained through and beyond death. Several different positions are on offer, even among Christians. *Dualists assert that a person's essential identity is bound up with his or her soul. They believe that the disembodied soul exists in the intermediate state between a person's death and the general resurrection from the dead. Insofar as the soul survives the death of the body, a person's unique identity is protected. Christian materialists, who deny the existence of an immaterial soul, argue for a renewed embodied existence of the individual after the general resurrection. *Aquinas offers a third alternative: arguing that human identity is the essential union of body and soul, he concedes the indestructibility of the soul. So for Aquinas, during the intermediate state my soul survives, but since this is only "part" of my identity, it is not properly "me." Thus, insofar as "I" have been promised eternal life, it is necessary that my soul be reunited with my body in the resurrection.

The resurrection of Jesus formed the pivotal historical claim on the basis of which Christianity argued for a radical theological reorientation toward death. Further, the Apostles' Creed, echoing 1 Corinthians 15, confesses that the hope for every Christian is future resurrection of the body. Early Christian *apologists often focused on the historical resurrection of Jesus as the primary evidence for the *truth of the Christian message.

See also Aquinas, Dualism/Monism, Hell, Metaphysics/Ontology, Mind/Soul/Spirit, Naturalism/Materialism, Plato and Platonism.

Bibliography. John Cooper, *Body, Soul, and Life Everlasting;* Oscar Cullmann, *Immortality and Resurrection;* Kevin Corcoran, ed., *Soul, Body, and Survival.*

Schleiermacher, Friedrich (1768–1834)

German philosopher and theologian who is considered the founder of *modern theological liberalism as well as modern *hermeneutics. Influenced by *Kant but critical of the *Enlightenment, Schleiermacher developed an experiential understanding of religion and a Romantic theory of interpretation. He was important in the founding of the University of

Berlin, in which the diverse disciplines revolved around a philosophical center. At Berlin, Schleiermacher gave expression to the now common division of the theological disciplines into its fourfold structure: biblical, dogmatic, historical, and pastoral. The religious disciplines were to be governed by the universal principles intrinsic to all academic disciplines—those of critical historical inquiry. As a result, theology became religious studies under his influence.

According to Schleiermacher, religion has to do with a feeling or consciousness of absolute dependence as opposed to a belief in a divine being. Religious experience is the foundation of his claim that *God is not a personal deity "out there." The raw experience of being dependent upon reality may be conceptualized by different cultures in different ways, each of which mistakenly supposes that its conceptualization is absolutely *true. All of the conceptualizations of the primordial experience of dependence point to the inexpressible nature of God. So religion is not a form of knowing but a form of doing; it is primarily *ethical in orientation. The Christian *faith is less about specific doctrinal claims than it is about following the example of Jesus.

Schleiermacher also influenced the development of contemporary hermeneutics. He was one of the first thinkers to develop a general theory of interpretation, which applied not solely to one discipline but to all acts of human interpretation. Interpretation is an act of communication in which author and reader engage in a conversation with the goal that the reader understand the author's intention. Unlike Enlightenment hermeneutics, which attempted to apply dispassionate, objective interpretive principles to the explication of a text, Schleiermacher was aware of the unavoidably subjective elements brought to the conversation by both the author and the reader. The Romantic element involves the reader's empathetic entering into the life and world of the author in order to penetrate what the author intended to communicate through the words written on the page. The art of hermeneutics involves subjective, *aesthetic, and spiritual elements. As a result of Schleiermacher's work, later theorists paid greater attention to the role of the reader and their contexts in the act of interpretation. Schleiermacher also defended what came to be known as a hermeneutical circle: the parts (the writings) must be understood through the whole (the life and history of the author) and vice versa. He greatly influenced the major theorists of interpretation that followed in the nineteenth century, Max Weber (1864–1920) and Wilhelm Dilthey (1833–1911), and in the twentieth century, Hans-Georg Gadamer (1900–2002).

See also Enlightenment, Hermeneutics, Kant, Religious Language.

Bibliography. Keith W. Clements, *Friedrich Schleiermacher*; Brian A. Gerrish, *A Prince of the Church*; Catherine Kelsey, *Thinking about Christ with Schleiermacher*.

Scholasticism The philosophical and theological tradition of the medieval "schools," including Oxford and the University of Paris, of the twelfth and thirteenth centuries. Influenced by *Augustine and *Aristotle, the scholastics developed methods of inquiry that used precise definition (with many distinctions) and careful argument to develop Christian theology and its philosophical underpinnings. These methods, which were by no means universal, were taught in the medieval universities (schools) by the schoolmen or scholastics, most prominently by philosopher-theologians such as Bonaventure, Albertus Magnus, *Scotus, and especially *Aquinas. Whatever their subsequent differences, all scholastics were supremely confident of the power of *reason to pursue truth—but always understood as a project of *faith seeking understanding. Their work is rigorously comprehensive and systematic. Insofar as these characteristics were also true of post-Reformation theologians such as Francis Turretin, they are sometimes described as "Reformed scholastics."

Scholastic vocabulary centered around concepts such as matter/form and *substance/attribute. The scholastics were concerned, for instance, with the ontological status of people, angels, and *God. They considered whether angels were pure form (with no matter), matter (without body), or a form/matter composite, which led to the great scholastic caricature as concerned with idle curiosities: How many angels can dance on the head of a pin?

Scholasticism divided into two schools of thought: the Thomists, who emphasized intellect, and the Scotists, who emphasized will. *Ockham, Scholasticism's most potent critic, attacked the endless distinctions and overreaching rationalism of the scholastics, especially of Scotus. Scholasticism gradually declined until it was eclipsed in the fifteenth century by *Renaissance humanism. However, in 1880 Pope Leo XIII commended the study of Scholasticism and declared Aquinas the "official doctor" of the Catholic Church, which ushered in over a century of "neo-Scholasticism."

Today, the term *scholastic* is generally taken to be a derogatory label for thought that is abstruse, arcane, and highly speculative—though this is not a fair charge to the original scholastics.

See also Aquinas, Aristotle, Augustine, Faith and Reason, Metaphysics/Ontology, Ockham, Scotus.

Bibliography. Etienne Gilson, *The Spirit of Medieval Philosophy*; Richard Muller, *Post-Reformation Dogmatics*; Herman Dooyeweerd, *Reformation and Scholasticism in Philosophy*.

Scotus, John Duns (1266–1308)

Late medieval philosopher with a significant impact on early *modernity, including the Reformers. He was born in Scotland (John Duns of Scotland) and entered the Franciscan order at the age of twenty-five. Not much else is known of his early years. He taught at Cambridge, Oxford, and Paris and died in Cologne, where he was working on a commentary on Peter Lombard's *Sentences*. Commenting on Lombard's major work continued a scholastic tradition and was the standard form for theological disputations. Scotus's central contribution was his interpretation and critique of Augustinian as well as Thomistic traditions.

Scotus was an original thinker, especially skilled in the analysis of arguments. He is most known for his metaphysical reflections, arguing that "being" is a perfectly univocal or universal term, equally applicable to *God and to creatures in the same sense. From this he developed proofs of God's existence from the nature of creation, as well as the nature of being in general. Scotus's technically complex argument for God's existence derives from elements of Aquinas's *cosmological argument and *Anselm's ontological argument.

Scotus's enduring contribution in the area of *metaphysics was twofold. First, he argued that every individual thing is distinct from every other individual thing by virtue of possessing a "thisness" *(haecceity)* created by God. This principle of individuation is as fundamental to existence as the categories or kinds to which everything belonged. A particular horse was different from every other horse because each horse possesses a *haecceity*—an individual *essence. Second, Scotus argued that the categories (for example, "horseness") are actually real. There are not only individual horses, but also the universal property of horseness that all horses possess. Thus he was a realist when it came to *universals, in contrast to the later nominalism of *Ockham.

Scotus also affirmed that the will is genuinely free from causal determination and, further, that this freedom to act to the contrary is precisely that which made the will independent from the *mind. This freedom is also the safeguard of human rationality. Scotus believed that the will is naturally inclined toward the *good, though it does not always act according to this inclination. By analogy, God's freedom is of the same sort as human freedom. God's goodness, however, does not consist in following a moral law, as is the case with human goodness. Rather, God's goodness is ultimate. The "good" is what God commands, and it is good because God commands it. Divine command theories were largely rejected during the *Enlightenment but have been rehabilitated by several contemporary philosophers of religion.

See also Anselm; Anthropomorphic Language; Aquinas; Aristotle; Augustine; Ethics, Biblical; Euthyphro Problem; Free Will; Good/Goodness; Metaphysics/Ontology; Natural Theology; Religious Language; Theistic Arguments; Universals.

Bibliography. Thomas Williams, ed., The Cambridge Companion to Duns Scotus; Richard Cross, Duns Scotus; Alexander Broadie, The Shadow of Scotus; Allan Wolter and Marilyn McCord Adams, eds., The Philosophical Theology of Duns Scotus; John Hare, God's Call.

Self   The center of human identity, often thought identical to the person. The philosophical use of the term *self* is fairly recent and includes all of those aspects that are integral to one's identity. It does not refer simply to "consciousness" or the "*mind," but also to aspects of embodiment, one's past experiences, and one's sociocultural formation.

*Descartes, *Kant, and others are often accused of taking the "self" to be a relatively stable, abstract (and immaterial) entity—one's identity is generally defined by rationality. They tend to view the self as largely *a*historical: a rational, conscious entity, more or less bound up with a body (though not essentially). Thus the "self" is usually identified with the mind, ego, or consciousness, as Descartes asserted: "I am a thinking thing." But, on these matters, Descartes and others were simply trying to answer "What am I?" (what is my *essence), not "Who am I?" so they were simply not addressing issues of the self.

In the late nineteenth century, the more existential question, Who am I? came more to the fore as some Western philosophers attended to the *historical* nature of existence and the effects of history on our identity. Thus, beginning with figures such as *Kierkegaard and *Nietzsche through Dilthey and *Heidegger, philosophers began to note the ways in which the "self" is the product of historical and cultural forces, and linked to the vagaries of embodied existence. This same insight would later fuel *feminist conceptions of identity, linked to the specificities of gender, and particularly the social construction of gender. So while the *modern self was a given, these thinkers take the self to be a *construction,* albeit with some "given" raw materials.

Segments of *postmodernism have launched a radical critique of the very notion of a "self," particularly in the work of Gilles Deleuze and Michel Foucault, both of whom represent a radically Nietzschean account. According to Foucault, the very notion of a "self" was a modern invention that has met a postmodern demise; whereas for Deleuze there is no stable self, but only a pliable nexus of forces. The postmodern self is neither given nor constructed, but almost *dissolved.*

Two countertrends in postmodernity with respect to the self have developed, both of which resonate with theological accounts of selfhood. First, rather than seeing the self as a given or sheer construction, many (such as Paul Ricoeur) have begun to think of the self as *storied*—that our selfhood is a *narrative* construction. "I" am my *story.* Second, religious philosophers such as

Emmanuel Levinas and Jean-Luc Marion have emphasized that our identities as subjects are first and foremost subjects *of* responsibility: we are called to be subject by our obligations to the Other. Both of these themes can be found embodied in the project of *Augustine's *Confessions* and resonate with the New Testament notion that our identities are something to be "worked out" in "fear and trembling."

See also Augustine, Descartes, Dualism/Monism, Essence/Essentialism, Free Will, Heidegger, Human Nature, Kant, Kierkegaard, Mind/Soul/Spirit, Nietzsche.

Bibliography. Calvin Schrag, *The Self After Postmodernity;* Charles Taylor, *Sources of the Self;* Jean-Luc Marion, *Being Given;* Paul Ricoeur, *Oneself as Another;* LeRon Shults, *Reforming Theological Anthropology.*

Semiotics   The analysis of "signs," particularly with respect to language, from the Greek *semeion*, indicating a "mark" or a sign of something (as in smoke is a sign that there is fire). Just as a street sign can *point* the way to the park, so words can function as "pointers" or signs of things and ideas. Words, for instance, whether oral or written, are understood as "signs" of both thoughts and wishes of a speaker or author, as well as signs pointing to specific realities.

Classically, *Aristotle spoke of signs in terms of *symbols:* "Spoken words are the symbols of mental experience and written words are the symbols of spoken words" *(De interpretatione).* Further developed by the *Stoics, semiotics was advanced by *Augustine's discussion of signs in his *On Christian Teaching.* In the twentieth century, and in light of the "linguistic turn," Ferdinand de Saussure made semiotics central to the discourse of most disciplines. (Saussure's classical model was a primary target of Derrida's *deconstruction.) Of particular concern was how to understand the relationship between the "signifier" (a particular word or mark) and the "signified" (that to which the mark "pointed"). Saussure suggested that the relation between signifier and signified was entirely arbitrary.

Semiotics and the notion of "signs" has permeated theological discourse not just with respect to language and interpretation, but most importantly regarding the nature of the sacraments. As such, twentieth-century debates in semiotics tended to replay late medieval and Reformation debates about the nature of the Eucharist and how to understand the relationship between the signifier and the signified—the relationship between the bread as "sign" and the risen, ascended body of Christ. Catholic theology argues for an *identification* of the signifier and signified, whereas Reformed accounts, while arguing for a "real presence" of Christ in the Eucharist, nevertheless also emphasize the bread as a *pointer* to that which is not fully present. Zwinglian (or "memorialist") models of the sacraments tend to be "Saussurean" insofar as they see no real presence of the signified in the signifier, but *only* a pointer to remind us of that which is absent. In all cases, theological discussion of the Eucharist requires some facility with semiotics.

See also Hermeneutics, Religious Language.

Bibliography. Robert Corrington, *A Semiotic Theory of Theology and Philosophy;* David Power, *Sacrament;* Stephen Moore, *Poststructuralism and the New Testament;* Ferdinand de Saussure, *Course in General Linguistics.*

Simplicity   The focus of two different philosophical discussions, both stemming from the basic notion of something "without parts" or complexity: on the one hand, there is the simplicity of *theories,* and on the other, the simplicity of *God. The former concerns the *metaphysical virtue of a theory that posits fewer entities than its contraries. The latter concerns the interdependence of God's attributes on one another.

In evaluating diverse theories, all of which appear to account for the facts, philosophers often suppose (based on an axiom like *Ockham's razor) that *simpler theories* are preferable: "The simple is the sign of the *true." For example, theories of planetary motion are more simply explained by Copernicus's heliocentric system than the Ptolemaic geocentric system that required the postulation of extremely complex cycles for the planets to preserve the idea that the earth is the center of the universe and that the heavens move in circular (i.e., perfect) orbits (assuming both theories are *underdetermined by the data). As historians of science review cases like this, several questions emerge. What makes one theory simpler than another? More fundamentally, why should simplicity be thought preferable to complexity? A simple theory may be *aesthetically more pleasing to some, but it is not obviously more likely to be true than a complex theory.

The analogy is straightforward with theological theories. If certain religious *phenomena could be explained with reference to fewer ontological entities, it is apparently better. Liberal historians of religion throughout the twentieth century assumed that events like the *resurrection of Jesus could be explained by reference to the "feelings of new life" in the early disciples, or that the dreamlike prophecies of the Old Testament could be explained without reference to supernatural entities like angels or demons. Religious *naturalism is a simpler theory and therefore preferable. However, the same questions eventually emerged about this preference for simplicity in religious explanations. Why is a simpler theory more likely to be true than a complex one? Of course, simplicity is not the only factor in decision making; one must consider the theory's adequacy as well.

The *simplicity of God* is the claim that God's being, unlike created beings, is not composed of parts. In other words,

God's existence is identical with God's *essence (God's essence is existence). The medieval and Reformation theologians who affirmed this were trying to represent God's uniqueness in all of the created order. God alone is indivisible. So God is not a composite of matter-form, substance-attribute, essence and existence.

Critics of divine simplicity contend that it entails (a) that all attributes are identical. If God is love and God is omnipotent, then love is *omnipotence. But while these terms have the same reference, they have different senses. Intuitively, these different attributes of God appear to be different, which would be a denial of divine simplicity. And (b) if God is simple, all of God's attributes are *necessary. For example, God cannot be God and fail to be omnipotent; so God is necessarily omnipotent. But, if God is free, God might not have created Adam, in which case God is only contingently the creator of Adam. So if God acts freely, there seem to be properties God possesses only contingently while other properties God possesses necessarily. This would mean that God could have had different kinds of properties, another denial of divine simplicity.

The debate over divine simplicity also impinges on our description of God as trinitarian. Christian thought has long preferred to emphasize the unity of God as prior to the plurality of persons in God. Following Barth, many recent theologians have emphasized the plurality of persons in the Trinity as prior to the unity of God. To older theological traditions, divine simplicity seemed an obvious outworking of the priority of the unity of God (monotheism). By contrast, the Social Trinitarians' emphasis on the relational character of God has been wary of divine simplicity.

See also God, Nature of; Metaphysics/ Ontology; Ockham; Ontotheology; Reductionism; Underdetermination.

Bibliography. Christopher Hughes, *On a Complex Theory of a Simple God*; Gerald Hughes, *The Nature of God*;

Norman Kretzmann, *The Metaphysics of Theism*; Richard Swinburne, *Simplicity as Evidence of Truth*; idem, *The Christian God*.

Stoicism   A *philosophy that emphasizes the control of one's emotions and passions; very influential on early Christian thought, including Paul and *Augustine. Stoicism began about 300 B.C.E. and was influential for the next six or seven centuries. It received its name from the porch (Greek *stoa*) of the Athenian acropolis where its original members met for discussion. Stoicism developed during a time of political instability when people were anxious about their life prospects. Stoicism provided a means for maintaining tranquillity amid the struggles of life.

Stoicism is a rational approach to the vicissitudes of life. Stoics believed that the world is governed by an impersonal fate or providence. Everything is destined to happen as it happens, and there is nothing we can do about it. Things happen whether we want them to or not. Our task is simply to want whatever happens, then we will never be disappointed. The Stoics sought to liberate themselves from the disturbing passions such as hope or fear. If we hope for something and it does not happen, we will be disappointed. If we fear something and it happens, we will be disappointed. The Stoics willed to accept everything that occurs gladly, as part of the overall *good of the universe as a whole. They sought the development of self-control as the means to the attainment of tranquillity. If we can reform our attitudes, accepting what comes without emotional disturbance, we can be at peace.

The Stoic sage has rid her life of the *disturbing* passions (she is *apatheia*). The Stoics allowed that such a life includes the undisturbing passions of joy, wishfulness, and caution. The sage has seen the folly of letting his fulfillment depend on Fortune: what Fortune gives, Fortune can also take away. Instead, the sage has turned his attention to what he can control, namely, his own soul. He refuses to seek fulfillment from external comforts and instead finds it within. He is self-contained and has attained equanimity. He is freed from his attachments to this world and is fully reconciled to the way the world is: it can bring his neither grief nor excessive delight. He is serene.

Stoicism finds expression in Christian theology both in terms of *ethics and theology proper. Augustine, for example, applied the Stoic ideal both to *God and to human life. God, who focuses only on God (who is a source of fulfillment that cannot be lost), lives in a state of perpetual, undisturbed bliss; God has no upsetting emotions because God's eros is not directed toward things that can be lost (i.e., toward any earthly things). God is *impassible. Likewise, human beings should focus their eros on God and not on any earthly things (which can be lost). Perfected human beings will find their satisfaction completely in God and cannot be disappointed by anything that occurs in their earthly life. We should, like God, live in unperturbable bliss. Finally, the Stoic view of providence influenced Christian views.

See also Aquinas; Augustine; Ethics; Ethics, Biblical; Happiness.

Bibliography. F. H. Sandbach, *The Stoics*; John Rist, *The Stoics*; idem, *Augustine*.

Substance   The substrate or foundation of a thing; the stuff (Greek *ousia*) in which an individual thing's properties or attributes inhere (*ousia* was translated by the Latin *substantia*, "to stand under"). Substances individuate separate things: Donna and Amy share many of the same properties (e.g., being a person, being female), but are individuated from each other by having different substance. Individual things may undergo changes of color, shape, and size, but that which endures through these changes is the substance. *Ordinary language most often uses nouns to refer to substances and adjectives to refer to its properties or characteristics. Most philosophical schools assume some version of a "substance" *ontology.

The notion of substance was challenged in early *modern *philosophy as a result of the rise of the new science. Increasingly it seemed difficult to distinguish between the substance of a thing and its properties. Nothing could be perceived of an object other than its properties; no substantial "core" underneath the properties is accessible to sensory experience. Consider an apple: How does one know what is present other than the properties one perceives—red, round, tasty, and so forth? The notion of substance appeared to be merely an abstract philosophical idea or a prejudice without any real meaning or warrant. John Locke called the substance behind the appearances of a thing "the something we know not what." David *Hume, rejecting the notion of substance entirely, supposed that objects in the world are simply bundles of properties. But defenders of the notion have contended that "substance" is the only means to do justice to the prephilosophical intuition that something persists through changes of properties.

The Greek notion of substance, particularly that of *Aristotle, provided philosophical categories for thinking about the nature of *God, particularly in early discussions of the Trinity. The creeds of the early Christian church confessed that God was three in one—three persons *(hypostases)* and one substance *(ousia)*. It has proven notoriously difficult to comprehend how a being could be three (in persons) but one (in substance). How does one reconcile the twin Christian commitments to monotheism and trinitarianism? Most philosophical accounts of the Trinity typically lean toward either unity or *plurality. Classical theism has emphasized the unity of God's being/substance as ontologically prior to the plurality of persons. This is often referred to as the *ontological trinity.*

Much recent theology by contrast has defended *social trinitarianism*—emphasizing instead the genuine plurality in God, and accounting for the oneness of God in terms of unity of purpose rather than unity of substance. We should not find it surprising that Christians have more generally believed the Trinity to be a conceptual mystery.

See also Aristotle; Epistemology; Essence/Essentialism; God, Nature of; Hume; Idealism; Kant; Leibniz; Metaphysics/Ontology; Mind/Soul/Spirit; Naturalism/Materialism; Process Thought; Simplicity.

Bibliography. Michael Loux, *Metaphysics*; idem, *Substance and Attribute*; Roger Olson and Christopher Hall, *The Trinity*; Colin Gunton, *The Triune Creator*.

Teleology   From the Greek term *telos*, meaning "end, goal, or purpose"; thus, something is *teleological* if it is directed toward a specific purpose or goal. The term is often applied to the natural world but figures prominently in *ethics as well. With respect to the natural order, *Aristotle believed that every natural object had an intrinsic purpose that could be stated in terms of the goals toward which it tended. The purpose of an acorn, for example, is to grow into an oak tree. Events in the natural order could be explained in part by reference to the "final *cause": the goal that coaxed a thing from its present form (acorn) to its future form (oak tree). The telos of an object, part of its internal structure, "move" an object to action toward its goal.

Under the influence of *Augustine, early Christian thinkers argued that *God beneficently created the world for a purpose. The created order reflects God's purpose. God provided the world with a blueprint and it acts in accord with that divine plan and purpose. Teleology was used as evidence in support of God's existence. Relying on a form of the argument from *Aquinas, William Paley

(1743–1805) defended the claim that the world manifests abundant evidence of purpose and design—the web of a duck's foot, the hump of the camel, the structure of the eye—which cannot be accounted for other than by appeal to a Great Designer (God). By contrast, *Hume argued that the existence of *evil (the apparent lack of purpose) was evidence against the existence of a beneficent, *omnipotent being.

Charles Darwin (1809–1882) offered the central challenge to teleology as a natural phenomenon. Although deeply influenced by Paley as a young man, Darwin argued that the apparent design or purpose in the natural world could be explained nonpurposively by natural selection. Natural selection (as opposed to supernatural selection or guidance) operates blindly, with no thought to end or purpose. In fact, natural selection is little more than death: environmental changes (new predators, scarce resources, competitors for resources, natural calamities, etc.) cause the death of unfit creatures, while those suited to survive under the new conditions live to pass on their genes to subsequent generations. Although the Darwinian framework has become part of philosophical orthodoxy in the twentieth century, it has been challenged by some (including "intelligent design" theorists) who contend that some natural phenomena are so remarkably complex they could not have developed through a Darwinian step-by-step process of the accumulation of accidental variations.

With respect to the ethical and human realm, Aristotle argued that there is a specific telos toward which human beings are directed: *happiness (eudaimonia). The specificity of this telos then functions as a criterion for determining how one ought to be human, so as to achieve the stated telos. A similar teleological framework was adopted by *Aquinas, with the modification that the ultimate telos of human beings was "friendship with God."

Teleology is also a principal tool of Old Testament interpretation for Christian theologians. Since Augustine, the Old Testament has been read as prefiguring the Christ, so passages that seem literally irrelevant to Christian doctrine are assigned spiritual meanings.

See also Aristotle, Augustine, Ethics, Happiness, Hermeneutics, Theistic Arguments.

Bibliography. Kelly James Clark and Anne Poortenga, The Story of Ethics; Michael J. Behe, Science and Evidence for Design in the Universe; Alasdair MacIntyre, First Principles, Final Ends, and Contemporary Philosophical Issues; Del Ratzsch, Nature, Design, and Science.

Theistic Arguments Arguments aimed at proving the existence of *God. Theistic arguments come in two forms. A posteriori arguments rely on premises that are known or knowable through experience. A priori arguments are based on premises that are known or knowable independent of experience. The most significant a priori argument for the existence of God is the ontological argument: since God, by definition, has every perfection and existence is a perfection, God must exist. This beguiling but unpersuasive proof, first offered by *Anselm, has elicited a tremendous amount of criticism. Let us now consider the a posteriori arguments.

The *cosmological argument. *Aquinas's "Five Ways" include cosmological arguments that rely on the facts of motion and change and the claim that an infinite regress of movers or changers is impossible. So there must be a first and unmoved mover or changer. Most people believe that these arguments rely on an outdated Aristotelian science.

*Leibniz's version of the cosmological argument has supporters even today:

1. The universe exists.
2. There is a sufficient explanation of the existence of everything.
3. God is the sufficient explanation of the existence of the universe.

Leibniz's argument depends upon the *principle of sufficient reason*: for every fact, there is a sufficient reason for its existence. The universe is contingent and so requires an explanation outside itself while God's existence is self-explanatory (necessary). Objectors reject the principle of sufficient reason.

If the cosmological argument were sound, it would establish the existence of an immutable and necessarily existent something on which the world depends. This is "the God of the philosophers," as *Pascal wrote, not the God of Abraham, Isaac, and Jacob.

The argument from design. Many people, taken with the beauty of the world, contend that it could not have occurred by accident:

1. The world is designed.
2. Design implies a designer.
3. Hence, the world is designed.

William Paley's version of the argument compares the universe to a watch. As with watches, the watchlike character (i.e., purposive design) of the universe implies that the universe has a designer. *Hume's famous criticism of the argument is considered by some to be the definitive critique of all theistic arguments. Darwin offered natural selection as an alternative to design in the biological realm.

Recent versions of the argument from design have emerged. One argument rejects Darwinism, claiming that items in many biological phenomena, such as cells and kidneys, are beyond the reach of chance. The so-called Fine-Tuning argument notes the remarkable confluence of physical constants, such as the law of gravity and the initial explosive forces of the big bang, that are precisely fine-tuned for the existence of life and thereby suggest the existence of a being who intended to create a world with persons.

Moral arguments. Consider the following moral argument:

1. Right and wrong are objective properties.

2. The best explanation of the existence of objective moral properties is their agreement or disagreement with the will of God.
3. Hence, there is a God.

Recent defenders of divine command views of morality have offered ingenious attempts to avoid the *Euthyphro problem with which moral arguments are afflicted.

The balance of probabilities. Some defenders of theistic arguments take all the evidence—the existence of the universe, the alleged design of the universe, morality, and religious experience—conjointly rather than singly. Using probability theory, these arguments seek the best explanation of all of the relevant data taken together. Defenders of these so-called cumulative case arguments contend that the best explanation is God.

Long after Hume and his followers proclaimed the death of theistic arguments, they have found new life. The old arguments are being revived in new, more powerful versions. And new arguments are being developed based on, for example, big bang cosmology, beauty, the human ability to know, and the existence of colors and flavors.

See also Anselm; Apologetics; Aquinas; Aristotle; Augustine; Cosmology; Descartes; Enlightenment; Faith and Reason; God, Belief in; Hume; Kant; Kierkegaard; Leibniz; Metaphysics/Ontology; Modernity/Modernism; Natural Theology; Pascal; Reason and Belief in God; Teleology.

Bibliography. Steven Davis, *God and Theistic Proofs*; Kelly James Clark, *Return to Reason*; Basil Mitchell, *The Justification of Religious Belief*; Richard Swinburne, *The Existence of God*.

Theodicy   An attempt to justify *God given the fact of *evil. The so-called "problem of evil" is stated as follows: If God is perfectly *good and *omnipotent, how can it be that evil exists? If God is good, he should *want* to prevent evil. If God is omnipotent, he would be *able* to do so. If God is both of these things, then *why* is there evil? A theodicy attempts to answer these types of questions. Some theodicies, however, are not open to orthodox Christian theology. For instance, *process theology attempts to "solve" the problem of evil by denying God's omnipotence. Practitioners of Christian Science deny the reality of evil. But these are generally understood as inconsistent with orthodoxy. However, if unorthodox theodicies deny some of God's attributes, orthodox theodicies sometimes run the risk of denying the reality of evil.

The most influential theodicy is *Augustine's *free-will theodicy. Augustine claims that God created a good world and placed good persons in it. These perfect persons used their free will to rebel against God by eating the forbidden fruit. In so doing, they unleashed both moral and natural evil in the universe. So the one responsible for evil is not God but the free creatures who abused their freedom. Although humans are responsible, God foreknew that the fall with its horrific consequences would happen and failed to prevent it. If so, in what sense is God good? In *City of God*, Augustine contends that God is good in an *aesthetic sense: God is painting a maximally beautiful picture that would not be complete without dark spots (evil).

John Hick's soul-making theodicy unites the free-will explanation of moral evil with a view of *human nature and creation as less than perfect. In the traditional, Augustinian view of human nature, according to Hick, humans were created perfect (but with free will) and placed in paradise. Given these circumstances, how humans could fail is a mystery (or a contradiction). If human beings were less than perfect, however, and were not placed in paradise, then human failure seems almost inevitable. What could justify God's putting people like us in harm's way? According to Hick, God

could not accomplish the goal he set for human beings—to freely become children of God—without them facing real dangers and challenges. Hick's "soul-making theodicy" explains how natural evils assist in the development of such virtues as courage, patience, and generosity. Evil is justified because it is necessary for immature, incomplete people to grow to become heirs of *eternal life.

Recent discussions consider the problem of excessive, horrendous, or pointless suffering. Marilyn Adams defines horrendous evil as one that would give one reason to doubt whether one's life could be a great good to him or her on the whole (such as individual suffering in the Holocaust). Adams, eschewing classical theodicies, asks how God could be good to such people. She suggests that God integrates participation in horrendous evils into a person's relationship with God, such as by identification with the suffering Christ or a vision into the inner life of our suffering God.

Another alternative, as seen in Paul Ricoeur and biblical theologian Walter Brueggemann, is to reject the project of theodicy as logical "problem solving," and rather grapple with the problem of evil in terms of *lament*. Lament is the biblical response of protest that does not "make sense" of evil by giving it a place within the system of creation, but rather faithfully protests that these things "should not be" and hopes, eschatologically, for their undoing.

Theodicies have consequences for one's view of divine goodness. The good to which Augustine appeals does not benefit the individual sufferer (indeed, *God* is primarily benefited as we glorify God for God's beautiful creation). This view of divine goodness would make God a consequentialist—performing the action that maximizes goodness and minimizes badness in the universe as a whole. Others claim that God's goodness extends to individual persons. Jesus gave the blind man sight, brought Lazarus back from the dead, changed water into wine, and died for our salvation; this tends toward universalism. It is likely that any fully adequate theodicy must unite the two types of goodness.

See also Anthropomorphic Language; Augustine; Evil, Problem of; Free Will; God, Nature of; Hell; Omnipotence; Teleology.

Bibliography. John Hick, *Evil and the God of Love;* Steven Davis, *Encountering Evil;* Kelly James Clark, *When Faith Is Not Enough;* Marilyn McCord Adams, *Horrendous Evils and the Goodness of God;* Susan Neiman, *Evil in Modern Thought;* Paul Ricoeur, *Figuring the Sacred.*

Transcendence To be above or beyond a particular order or sphere. For *Plato, the "*Good" is transcendent insofar as it is "beyond being." *God is said to be "transcendent" insofar as God is outside or beyond the order of creation. This immediately leads to questions about just how God could be conceptualized, and thus the claim that God transcends the limits of human language and cognition leads to one of the central problems of *religious language. Some believe that it is impossible to speak meaningfully or to know anything at all about God, a belief that can be called *radical transcendence.* Some take transcendence more modestly: God is partially but not fully graspable by human concepts; this can be called *moderate transcendence.* God is moderately transcendent in the literal sense of going beyond whatever descriptive terms are predicated of God. The central theological problem is whether God is radically or moderately transcendent.

In the *modern era, radical transcendence finds inspiration in the work of the philosopher Immanuel *Kant, who drew a sharp distinction between reality as we humans experience it, shaped by our human conceptual framework, and reality as it is in itself. The boundaries of human thought are determined by empirical concepts—those that categorize what we can see, hear, touch, taste, or smell. Since God transcends empirical concepts, knowledge of God is impossible. One can thus locate quite disparate theologians such as Gordon Kaufman and Karl Barth within this broadly post-Kantian tradition. The theological consequences of radical transcendence seem to be disturbing. We cannot know if God is loving or hateful, righteous or wicked, concerned or unconcerned about human welfare or salvation, or even person or thing. Is God so "wholly other" that we are invariably reduced to uttering and thinking nonsense concerning God's true nature?

There are at least two ways that God might be moderately transcendent: first, if God has properties that are somewhat like but vastly exceed those possessed by humans; second, if God has some properties that humans cannot grasp at all. If we have been created in God's image, we share some divine properties, perhaps being free, rational, moral, creative, social, and knowers. So God has similar properties but also transcends any human grasp of them. Consider God's *causal powers: God is able to directly bring about vastly more states of affairs than human beings can and in ways that humans could not imagine (ex nihilo). Yet God and humans create in the sense that they intend for something to be that is not and then bring it about. God is also a holder of beliefs. Unlike humans, all of God's beliefs are *true, and the domain of divine beliefs is infinite. In addition, God is good. Yet God's superiorities of knowledge and power render the actions expressive of divine goodness vastly different from those required and permitted of human beings. Finally, God is social, suggesting that contained within God's nature is a multiplicity of persons who perfectly cooperate with one another; so we are also social. And so on. If we are made in the image of God, then some humanly available concepts apply to God (who vastly exceeds them).

Christian thinkers have generally embraced some version of moderate transcendence. *Augustine held that God is like a vast ocean: even the unlearned can paddle about in the shallows and the trained theologian can swim out a bit farther; but both are of such limited ability that they would be swallowed up in the depths. *Aquinas contended that because of the disproportion of our finite intellect and God's infinitude, our knowledge of God is "dark and mirrored and from afar." *Kierkegaard maintained that there is an "infinite qualitative difference" between humans and God, and that humans, due to their sinful nature, are tempted to domesticate God to make God serve them. Like Calvin, however, Kierkegaard offers an account of God's "accommodation" to finitude by condescending to our level. In this respect, the incarnation is taken as the paradigm of God's "condescension," bridging the gap between transcendence and immanence.

See also Anselm; Anthropomorphic Language; Aquinas; Augustine; God, Nature of; Good/Goodness; Heidegger; Kierkegaard; Metaphysics/Ontology; Ontotheology; Pseudo-Dionysius; Religious Language; Scotus.

Bibliography. Karl Barth, *Church Dogmatics;* William Placher, *The Domestication of Transcendence;* James K. A. Smith, *Speech and Theology.*

Truth   A property of statements or claims about reality; thus a claim is "true" (or "false"). *Aristotle claimed that truth is "to say of what is that it is, and of what is not that it is not." This notion of truth involves both a saying ("of something that it is") and reality ("what is or is not"). So there are two elements to truth: the *truth bearer* (a proposition, statement, or a sentence) and the *truth maker* (the world, a fact, or a state of affairs). In making a true statement, one asserts a proposition and reality makes that proposition true (or false). The dominant metaphor used to describe this relationship is the *correspondence theory of truth,* which holds that a claim is true insofar as it corresponds to the external or extramental world. So my claim "the chair is red" is true if, in fact, that particular chair has the property of redness.

Correspondence theories have been rejected for two reasons. First, there is the difficulty of specifying how sentences (linguistic reality) could correspond to facts (nonlinguistic reality). Second, the correspondence theory offers no suggestions as to how to ascertain the statement-fact relation, so it is not useful in the discovery of truth. For these reasons, other theories of truth have been offered. The *coherence* theory of truth argues that claims or propositions are true insofar as they are consistent within a system or "web" of belief. A *pragmatic* theory of truth suggests that claims and ideas are true insofar as they produce "fruitful" consequences and practices. Coherence and pragmatic theories are also offered because they make it easier to tell if one has a true belief. These theories are often rejected because of their tendentious relationship to reality (the truth makers).

Christian theology, because of its *realism, has tended to adopt some version of the correspondence theory of truth. With respect to central spiritual truths, it matters whether the sentences "Christ is God incarnate" and "Jesus rose from the dead" are made true by the facts that Christ is God incarnate and that Jesus rose from the dead. The biblical witness adds that people need to be related appropriately to Jesus, the Truth (John 14:8). This relational dimension suggests that grasping Christian truth involves a way of being-in-the-world and being-in-relation-to-God. Finally, the New Testament emphasizes a correlation between truth and love (1 Corinthians 8:2–3; 13:1–3).

See also Epistemology, Pragmatism, Realism.

Bibliography. Frederick Schmitt, *Truth;* Richard Kirkham, *Theories of*

Truth; Brian Hebblethwaite, *The Ocean of Truth;* Ian Markham, *Truth and the Reality of God.*

Underdetermination The belief that for some sets of data, there are many hypotheses that adequately explain the data but are mutually incompatible with one another. Most of our theories of the world—philosophical, commonsensical, or even scientific—are underdetermined by the evidence that supports them. They are consistent with the facts, but the facts are not so compelling that their competitors can be shown to be logically inconsistent with the facts. When two such theories are in competition, no appeal to the evidence, therefore, could determine the winner.

Biblical interpretations and theological statements are underdetermined by the biblical data. Scripture is a mixture of history, myth, poetry, moral instruction, praise, hyperbole, prophecy, and so forth. Sorting through this array of genres requires some sort of *hermeneutical method. The inerrancy or infallibility of Scripture are of themselves incapable of delivering *God's *truth. Without a hermeneutical method, the inerrant or infallible biblical data cannot communicate truth claims.

Even if the biblical text is God speaking (even if Scripture is inerrant), one must still make hermeneutical decisions about whether God's speaking is intended as a depiction of the nature of God. Suppose God intends to impart information about God's nature, is this information literal or metaphorical? Indeed, judgments must be made about how the Creator could possibly communicate information about God's self to God's creatures; how has God accommodated God's self to human cognitive limitations? How does one tell if there has been accommodation or not?

Underdetermination may account for the apparent intractability of theological disputes. Consider the standoffs between Catholics and Protestants, Catholics and Orthodox, Calvinists and Arminians, Baptists and Anabaptists, and classical and open theism. Theologians on both sides of these disputes believe their doctrines to be the only adequate explanation of the biblical data. However, if their competitors also adequately account for all of the biblical data, no appeal to the evidence could resolve the dispute.

See also Anthropomorphic Language; God, Nature of; Hermeneutics; Pragmatism; Reductionism; Religious Language; Simplicity.

Bibliography. Thomas Kuhn, *The Structure of Scientific Revolutions.*

Universals A general property or term that different individual objects can possess. There are many individual apples, all of which share the property of being an apple, some of which share the property of being red (which they also share with fire trucks and blood). The classic philosophical controversy about universals has to do with their *metaphysical status. Do universals actually exist or are they merely names given to similar objects? The former position is called *realism* (universals are real) and the latter is called *nominalism* (universals are simply names).

*Plato, the paradigmatic realist, argued that universals (the Forms) exist in a spiritual realm. So the Forms redness and appleness exist in that realm and individual apples participate in those Forms. For Plato, genuine knowledge involves grasping these eternal and unchanging Forms. *Augustine was a realist who believed that universals exist in the *mind of *God as a kind of blueprint of the world. *Aristotle was a realist who rejected the independence of universals from the objects that possess them. Universals do genuinely exist but only in the objects themselves. *Aquinas would follow Aristotle's view.

Realist theories of universals have been rejected for three reasons. First, it is difficult to specify the nature of the relationship between an abstract but real universal and the particular object(s) that has it. Second, how do we experience universals (as distinct from experiencing objects that possess them) if they exist in a *transcendent realm? Third, how do we know we are discovering a shared attribute and not just applying a property created by the human mind?

These criticisms prepared the way for the emergence of nominalism, most prominently defended by *Ockham. The nominalist holds that there are no real abstract objects (called universals) that exist over and above concrete particular objects. Universals are simply general terms or words that we apply to similar things. They are simply names we attach to different but similar objects. Nominalism is criticized because it does not permit genuine sharing of properties between objects. *Wittgenstein might be seen as a contemporary nominalist. He contended that it is impossible to specify precisely the conditions for membership in a class (of, say, apples or red things); at most such objects bear a *family resemblance* to one another. But use of such terms reflects linguistic conventions, not another reality.

Behind the debates about universals lay the issue of God's relationship to the world, in particular, the manner in which the natural world is "patterned" according to universals that perhaps exist in the mind of God.

See also Aquinas, Aristotle, Augustine, Metaphysics/Ontology, Neoplatonism, Ockham, Plato and Platonism, Realism/Anti-Realism, Scotus.

Bibliography.   James P. Moreland, *Universals*; Michael J. Loux, *Metaphysics*.

Wittgenstein, Ludwig (1889–1951)

One of the towering figures of twentieth-century *philosophy. Born in Vienna, Wittgenstein was educated at Manchester and Cambridge, taught for a time at Cambridge, and died in Cambridge. He was a meandering soul who felt restless and misunderstood. He was a genius of the first rank, whose work was continually misinterpreted. Wittgenstein repudiated his first book, *Tractatus Logicus-Philosophicus*, in his later work *The Philosophical Investigations*. His ideas are often discussed as the "early" Wittgenstein (of the *Tractatus*) and the "later" Wittgenstein (of the *Investigations*). His favorite thinkers were the deeply religious *Kierkegaard and Tolstoy.

The principal idea of the *Tractatus* is the "picture theory of language," which supposed that sentences (composed of terms arranged in a logical structure) are analogous to the way a picture depicts a scene (composed of objects in spatial relations). In other words, sentences are verbal pictures, and language grasps the world the way a picture represents the world. Terms name things and grammar arranges the terms in a sentence the way the things they name are arranged in the world. Only those statements that picture empirically verifiable states of affairs are meaningful. All other statements such as those in *ethics, theology, and *aesthetics were declared meaningless because there was no object or state of affair in the world being pictured in those statements. Although the *logical *positivist movement found inspiration in the *Tractatus,* Wittgenstein denounced their use of his theory to circumscribe the world. According to him, the book is important for what it does not, and cannot, say. Beyond the limits of meaningful language lies the inexpressibly mystical: *God, ethics, and the meaning of life. Wittgenstein, believing he had solved all of the problems of philosophy in this book, left philosophy for other pursuits.

Coming to view the *Tractatus* as a mistake, Wittgenstein returned to philosophy and rejected the picture theory of language. Wittgenstein argued that language is a living, unsystematic, and polymorphous array of human conventions for a large range of human activities. The meaning of a word is not the object that it pictures, but rather the use of a word within the context of a sentence in which it finds life. Put differently, words only have meaning within the context of human practices. Words are used variously to give directions, to share emotions, to promise, to pray, to play a game. . . ad infinitum. Grammar does not portray the logical structure of the world but is like the rules for a game. Wittgenstein referred to linguistic phenomena as "language games"—the set of rules, intentions, human practices, and sociohistorical contexts that give shape to the particular language in which people communicate.

Many of Wittgenstein's students are Christians who have used his later views on language to liberate religious beliefs from the positivist legacy that declared nonempirical propositions to be cognitively meaningless. After Wittgenstein, religion is no longer held hostage to the notion that it does not satisfy a theory of language that exalts the natural sciences. Two diverse extensions of Wittgenstein's thought can be found in recent Christian thought. Reformed *epistemologists Alvin Plantinga and Nicholas Wolterstorff have defended the claim that belief in God need not rest on classical foundations, but ought instead consider religious claims as meaningful as they are used in actual religious contexts such as worship and mission. William Alston, George Lindbeck, and Hans Frei have argued that Christian doctrine ought to be understood as rules by which the Christian language game is conducted, rather than as pictorial representations of the world. As a result of Wittgenstein, both movements have tried to pay much closer attention to the way Christians use words. Finally, Wittgenstein's followers have developed what has come to be called "Wittgenstein fideism," a defense of a groundless belief in God.

See also Ordinary Language Philosophy, Positivism, Reason and Belief in God, Religious Language.

Bibliography. A. C. Grayling, *Wittgenstein*; Fergus Kerr, *Theology After Wittgenstein*; D. Z. Phillips, *Wittgenstein and Religion*; George Lindbeck, *Nature of Doctrine*; Hans-Johann Glock, *Wittgenstein*.

Bibliography

Adams, Marilyn McCord. *Horrendous Evils and the Goodness of God*. Ithaca: Cornell University Press, 1999.

———. *William Ockham*. Notre Dame: University of Notre Dame Press, 1987.

Adams, Marilyn and Robert. *The Problem of Evil*. Oxford: Oxford University Press, 1990.

Adams, Robert Merrihew. *Finite and Infinite Goods*. New York: Oxford University Press, 1999.

———. *Leibniz: Determinist, Theist, Idealist*. New York: Oxford University Press, 1994.

———. *The Virtue of Faith and Other Essays in Philosophical Theology*. New York: Oxford University Press, 1987.

Alston, William. *Divine Nature and Human Language: Essays in Philosophical Theology*. Ithaca: Cornell University Press, 1989.

———. "Psychoanalytic Theory and Theistic Belief," in *Faith and the Philosophers*, edited by John Hick, 63–102. New York: St. Martin's Press, 1964.

———, ed. *Realism and Antirealism*. Ithaca: Cornell University Press, 2002.

Anglin, W. S. *Free Will and the Christian Faith*. New York: Oxford University Press, 1990.

Annas, Julia. *The Morality of Happiness*. New York: Oxford University Press, 1993.

———. *Plato: A Very Short Introduction*. New York: Oxford University Press, 2003.

Ashley, Benedict M. *Living the Truth in Love: A Biblical Introduction to Moral Theology*. New York: Alba House, 1996.

Atkinson, David John, ed. *New Dictionary of Christian Ethics and Pastoral Theology*. Downers Grove, Ill.: InterVarsity Press, 1995.

Audi, Robert. *Epistemology: A Contemporary Introduction*. New York: Routledge, 2003.

Augustine. *On the Free Choice of the Will*, translated by Thomas Williams. Indianapolis: Hackett, 1993.

Ayer, A. J. *Language, Truth, and Logic*. New York: Dover, 1952.

Baker, Gordon, and Katherine Morris. *Descartes' Dualism*. New York: Routledge, 1996.

Balthasar, Hans Urs von. *The Glory of the Lord*. T. & T. Clark, 1989.

Barbour, Ian. *Nature, Human Nature, and God*. Minneapolis: Fortress Press, 2002.

Barnes, Jonathan. *Aristotle: A Very Short Introduction*. Oxford: Oxford University Press, 2000.

———, ed. *The Cambridge Companion to Aristotle*. New York: Cambridge University Press, 1995.

Barrett, William. *Irrational Man: A Study in Existential Philosophy*. New York: Doubleday, 1958.

Barth, Karl. *Church Dogmatics*, edited by G. W. Bromiley and T. F. Torrance. 4 vols. in 13. New York: Scribner, 1936–1962.

———. *Protestant Theology in the Nineteenth Century: Its Background and History*. Reprint, Grand Rapids: Eerdmans, 2002.

Basinger, David. *Religious Diversity: A Philosophical Assessment*. Burlington, Vt.: Ashgate, 2002.

Beckwith, Francis, and Greg Koukl. *Relativism: Feet Firmly Planted in Mid-air*. Grand Rapids: Baker, 1998.

Begbie, Jeremy. *Beholding the Glory: Incarnation Through the Arts*. Grand Rapids: Baker, 2000.

———. *Voicing Creation's Praise: Towards a Theology of the Arts*. Edinburgh: T. & T. Clark, 1991.

Behe, Michael, William Dembski, and Stephen Meyer, eds. *Science and Evidence for Design in the Universe.* San Francisco: Ignatius Press, 2000.

Beilby, James. *Divine Foreknowledge: Four Views.* Downers Grove, Ill.: InterVarsity Press, 2001.

———, ed. *Naturalism Defeated? Essays on Plantinga's Evolutionary Argument Against Naturalism.* Ithaca: Cornell University Press, 2002.

Berger, Peter, and Thomas Luckmann. *The Social Construction of Reality: A Treatise in the Sociology of Knowledge.* Garden City, N.Y.: Doubleday, 1966.

Berman, David. *George Berkeley: Idealism and the Man.* New York: Oxford University Press, 1994.

Boethius. *The Consolation of Philosophy,* translated by P. G. Walsh. New York: Oxford University Press, 1999.

Bracken, Joseph. *The One in the Many: A Contemporary Reconstruction of the God-World Relationship.* Grand Rapids: Eerdmans, 2001.

Brand, Hilary, and Adrienne Chaplin. *Art and Soul: Signposts for Christians in the Arts.* Carlisle, Calif.: Piquant, 2001.

Broadie, Alexander. *The Shadow of Scotus: Philosophy and Faith in Pre-Reformation Scotland.* Edinburgh: T. & T. Clark, 1995.

Brockelman, Paul T. *Cosmology and Creation: The Spiritual Significance of Contemporary Cosmology.* New York: Oxford University Press, 1999.

Brom, Luco van den. *Divine Presence in the World: A Critical Analysis of the Notion of Divine Omnipresence.* Kampen: Kok Pharos, 1993.

Brown, Hunter. *William James on Radical Empiricism and Religion.* Toronto: University of Toronto Press, 2000.

———, ed. *Images of the Human: The Philosophy of the Human Person in a Religious Context.* Chicago: Loyola University Press, 1995.

Brown, Peter. *Augustine of Hippo: A Biography.* Berkeley: University of California Press, 1967.

Brown, Terrance, and Leslie Smith, eds. *Reductionism and the Development of Knowledge.* Mahwah, N.J.: Erlbaum, 2003.

Brown, Warren S. *Whatever Happened to the Soul? Scientific and Theological Portraits of Human Nature.* Minneapolis: Fortress Press, 1998.

Brueggemann, Walter, William C. Placher, and Brian K. Blount. *Struggling with Scripture.* Louisville: Westminster John Knox Press, 2002.

Buckley, Michael. *At the Origins of Modern Atheism.* New Haven: Yale University Press, 1987.

Bultmann, Rudolf, and Hans Bartsch. *Kerygma and Myth: A Theological Debate.* New York: Harper & Row, 1961.

Bunge, Mario. *Causality and Modern Science.* New York: Dover, 1979.

Byrne, James M. *Religion and the Enlightenment: From Descartes to Kant.* Louisville: Westminster John Knox Press, 1996.

Caputo, John. *Deconstruction in a Nutshell: A Conversation with Jacques Derrida.* New York: Fordham University Press, 1997.

———. *Heidegger and Aquinas: An Essay on Overcoming Metaphysics.* New York: Fordham University Press, 1982.

———. *The Prayers and Tears of Jacques Derrida: Religion Without Religion.* Bloomington: Indiana University Press, 1997.

———. *Radical Hermeneutics: Repetition, Deconstruction, and the Hermeneutic Project.* Bloomington: Indiana University Press, 1987.

———, and Michael J. Scanlon, eds. *God, the Gift, and Postmodernism.* Bloomington: Indiana University Press, 1999.

Caton, Charles E. *Philosophy and Ordinary Language.* Urbana: University of Illinois Press, 1963.

Charles, David, and Kathleen Lennon, eds. *Reduction, Explanation, and Realism.* Oxford: Oxford University Press, 1992.

Clark, Kelly James. *Philosophers Who Believe: The Spiritual Journeys of 11 Leading Thinkers.* Downers Grove, Ill.: InterVarsity Press, 1993.

———. *Return to Reason: A Critique of Enlightenment Evidentialism and a Defense of Reason and Belief in God.* Grand Rapids: Eerdmans, 1990.

———. *When Faith Is Not Enough.* Grand Rapids: Eerdmans, 1997.

———, and Anne Poortenga. *The Story of Ethics: Fulfilling Our Human Nature.* Upper Saddle River, N.J.: Prentice-Hall, 2003.

Clayton, Philip. *Explanation from Physics to Theology: An Essay in Rationality and Religion.* New Haven: Yale University Press, 1989.

———. *The Problem of God in Modern Thought.* Grand Rapids: Eerdmans, 2000.

Clements, Keith W. *Friedrich Schleiermacher: Pioneer of Modern Theology.* San Francisco: Collins, 1987.

Cobb, John, and David Griffin, *Process Theology: An Introductory Exposition*. Philadelphia: Westminster Press, 1976.

———, and Clark Pinnock, *Searching for an Adequate God: A Dialogue Between Process and Free Will Theists*. Grand Rapids: Eerdmans, 2000.

Coles, Peter. *Cosmology: A Very Short Introduction*. Oxford: Oxford University Press, 2001.

Cook, John W. *Wittgenstein, Empiricism, and Language*. New York: Oxford University Press, 2000.

Cooper, John. *Body, Soul, and Life Everlasting: Biblical Anthropology and the Monism-Dualism Debate*. Grand Rapids: Eerdmans, 1989.

Corcoran, Kevin, ed. *Soul, Body, and Survival: Essays on the Metaphysics of Human Persons*. Ithaca: Cornell University Press, 2001.

Corrigan, Kevin. *Reading Plotinus: A Practical Introduction to Neoplatonism*. London: Eurospan, 2002.

Corrington, Robert. *A Semiotic Theory of Theology and Philosophy*. Cambridge: Cambridge University Press, 2000.

Cottingham, John, ed. *The Cambridge Companion to Descartes*. Cambridge: Cambridge University Press, 1992.

Cowan, Steven, and William Lane Craig, eds. *Five Views on Apologetics*. Grand Rapids: Zondervan, 2000.

Craig, William Lane. *The Only Wise God: The Compatibility of Divine Foreknowledge and Human Freedom*. Grand Rapids: Baker, 1987.

———. *Reasonable Faith: Christian Truth and Apologetics*. Wheaton, Ill.: Crossway Books, 1994.

———, and Quentin Smith. *Theism, Atheism, and Big Bang Cosmology*. Oxford: Oxford University Press, 1993.

Creel, Richard. *Divine Impassibility: An Essay in Philosophical Theology*. Cambridge: Cambridge University Press, 1986.

Critchley, Simon. *Continental Philosophy: A Very Short Introduction*. Oxford: Oxford University Press, 2001.

Crockett, William, ed. *Four Views on Hell*. Grand Rapids: Zondervan, 1992.

Cross, Richard. *Duns Scotus*. New York: Oxford University Press, 1999.

Cullmann, Oscar. *Immortality of the Soul: Or, Resurrection of the Dead? The Witness of the New Testament*. New York: Macmillan, 1958.

Cunningham, Conor. *A Genealogy of Nihilism: Philosophies of Nothing and the Difference of Theology*. New York: Routledge, 2002.

Dancy, Jonathan. *Berkeley: An Introduction*. Oxford: Blackwell, 1987.

Davies, Brian. *The Thought of Thomas Aquinas*. Oxford: Oxford University Press, 1992.

Davis, Stephen. *God, Reason and Theistic Proofs*. Edinburgh: Edinburgh University Press, 1997.

———, and John Cobb. *Encountering Evil: Live Options in Theodicy*. Atlanta: John Knox Press, 1981.

De Bary, Philip. *Thomas Reid and Scepticism: His Reliabilist Response*. New York: Routledge, 2002.

Deleuze, Gilles. *Nietzsche and Philosophy*. New York: Columbia University Press, 1983.

Derrida, Jacques. *Acts of Religion*, translated by Gil Anidjar. New York: Routledge, 2002.

———. "Circumfession," in *Jacques Derrida*, ed. Geoffrey Basington and Jacques Derrida. Chicago: University of Chicago Press, 1993.

———. "Letter to a Japanese Friend," in *A Derrida Reader*, ed. Peggy Kamuf. New York: Columbia University Press, 1991.

Desmond, William. *Hegel's God: A Counterfeit Double?* Burlington, Vt.: Ashgate, 2003.

Despland, Michel. *The Education of Desire: Plato and the Philosophy of Religion*. Toronto: University of Toronto Press, 1985.

Dilman, Ilham. *Free Will: An Historical and Philosophical Introduction*. New York: Routledge, 1999.

Dooyeweerd, Herman. *Reformation and Scholasticism in Philosophy*. Collected Works. Lewiston, N.Y.: Edwin Mellen, 2004.

Dorner, Isaak August, and Robert Williams. *Divine Immutability: A Critical Reconsideration*. Minneapolis: Fortress Press, 1994.

Dulles, Avery. *A History of Apologetics*. New York: Corpus, 1971.

Earman, John. *Hume's Abject Failure: The Argument Against Miracles*. Oxford: Oxford University Press, 2000.

Edwards, Jonathan. *The Freedom of the Will*. 1754. Reprint, New Haven: Yale University Press, 1957.

———. *The True Believer*. Morgan, Pa.: Soli Deo Gloria, 2001.

Ekstrom, Laura. *Free Will: A Philosophical Study*. Boulder, Colo.: Westview Press, 1999.

Ellis, Brian D. *The Philosophy of Nature: A Guide to the New Essentialism*. Montreal: McGill-Queen's University Press, 2002.

Engel, Morris. *With Good Reason: An Introduction to Informal Fallacies*. New York: St. Martin's Press, 1976.

Evans, C. Stephen. *Faith Beyond Reason: A Kierkegaardian Account*. Grand Rapids: Eerdmans, 1998.

104   Bibliography

———. *Kierkegaard's "Fragments" and "Post-script": The Religious Philosophy of Johannes Climacus*. Atlantic Highlands, N.J.: Humanities Press, 1983.

———. *Passionate Reason: Making Sense of Kierkegaard's Philosophical Fragments*. Bloomington: Indiana University Press, 1992.

———. *Subjectivity and Religious Belief: An Historical, Critical Survey*. Grand Rapids: Christian University Press, 1978.

Evans, G. R. *Anselm*. London: Morehouse-Barlow, 1989.

———. *Anselm and Talking About God*. Oxford: Oxford University Press, 1978.

Farley, Edward. *Ecclesial Reflection: An Anatomy of Theological Method*. Philadelphia: Fortress Press, 1982.

Ferré, Frederick. *Language, Logic and God*. New York: Harper, 1961.

Fideler, David. *Jesus Christ, Sun of God: Ancient Cosmology and Early Christian Symbolism*. Wheaton, Ill.: Quest Books, 1993.

Fish, Stanley. *The Trouble with Principle*. Cambridge: Harvard University Press, 1999.

Flint, Thomas. *Divine Providence: The Molinist Account*. Ithaca: Cornell University Press, 1998.

Fogelin, Robert J. *Routledge Philosophy Guidebook to Berkeley and The Principles of Human Knowledge*. New York: Routledge, 2001.

Ford, Lewis. *Transforming Process Theism*. Albany: State University of New York Press, 2000.

Fox-Genovese, Elizabeth. *Feminism without Illusions: A Critique of Individualism*. Chapel Hill: University of North Carolina Press, 1991.

Frankena, William. *Ethics*. Englewood Cliffs, N.J.: Prentice-Hall, 1973.

Frei, Hans. *The Eclipse of Biblical Narrative: A Study in Eighteenth and Nineteenth Century Hermeneutics*. New Haven: Yale University Press, 1974.

French, Peter, and Theodore Uehling, eds. *Studies in Essentialism*. Minneapolis: University of Minnesota Press, 1986.

Fuchs, Stephan. *Against Essentialism: A Theory of Culture and Society*. Cambridge: Harvard University Press, 2001.

Fudge, Edward, and Robert Peterson. *Two Views of Hell: A Biblical and Theological Dialogue*. Downers Grove, Ill.: InterVarsity Press, 2000.

Furley, David. *From Aristotle to Augustine*. New York: Routledge, 1999.

Ganssle, Gregory E., and Paul Helm, eds. *God and Time: Four Views*. Downers Grove, Ill.: InterVarsity Press, 2001.

Gay, Peter. *The Enlightenment: An Interpretation*. 2 vols. New York: Knopf, 1966–1969.

Geach, P. T. *God and the Soul*. New York: Schocken, 1969.

———. *Truth and Hope*. Notre Dame: University of Notre Dame Press, 2001.

Geisler, Norman. *Miracles and the Modern Mind: A Defense of Biblical Miracles*. Grand Rapids: Baker, 1992.

Gergen, Kenneth. *Social Construction in Context*. Thousand Oaks, Calif.: SAGE, 2001.

Gerrish, Brian A. *A Prince of the Church: Schleiermacher and the Beginnings of Modern Theology*. Philadelphia: Fortress Press, 1984.

Gill, Robin, ed. *The Cambridge Companion to Christian Ethics*. Cambridge: Cambridge University Press, 2001.

Gillespie, Michael Allen. *Nihilism Before Nietzsche*. Chicago: University of Chicago Press, 1995.

Gilligan, Carol. *In a Different Voice: Psychological Theory and Women's Development*. Cambridge: Harvard University Press, 1982.

Gilson, Etienne. *Being and Some Philosophers*. Toronto: Pontifical Institute of Mediaeval Studies, 1952.

———. *The Christian Philosophy of St. Thomas Aquinas*. New York: Random House, 1956.

———. *The Spirit of Medieval Philosophy*. 1936. Reprint, Notre Dame: University of Notre Dame Press, 1991.

Glock, Hans-Johann. *Wittgenstein: A Critical Reader*. Malden, Mass.: Blackwell, 2001.

Grant, Edward. *God and Reason in the Middle Ages*. Cambridge: Cambridge University Press, 2001.

Grayling, A. C. *Wittgenstein: A Very Short Introduction*. Oxford: Oxford University Press, 2001.

Gregory, John. *The Neoplatonists: A Reader*. New York: Routledge, 1999.

Grenz, Stanley J., and John R. Franke. *Beyond Foundationalism: Shaping Theology in a Postmodern Context*. Louisville: Westminster John Knox Press, 2001.

Groenhout, Ruth, and Marya Bower, eds. *Philosophy, Feminism, and Faith*. Bloomington: Indiana University Press, 2003.

Grondin, Jean. *An Introduction to Philosophical Hermeneutics*. New Haven: Yale University Press, 1994.

Gunton, Colin. *The One, Three and the Many: God, Creation and the Culture of Modernity*.

Cambridge: Cambridge University Press, 1993.

———. *The Triune Creator: A Historical and Systematic Study.* Grand Rapids: Eerdmans, 1998.

Guthrie, W. K. C. *A History of Greek Philosophy.* 6 vols. Cambridge: Cambridge University Press, 1962–1981.

Gutiérrez, Gustavo. *Theology of Liberation: History, Politics, and Salvation.* Maryknoll, N.Y.: Orbis, 1973.

Hacking, Ian. *The Social Construction of What?* Cambridge: Harvard University Press, 1999.

Hadot, Pierre, and Arnold Davidson. *Philosophy as a Way of Life: Spiritual Exercises from Socrates to Foucault.* Oxford: Blackwell, 1995.

Haight, M. R. *The Snake and the Fox: An Introduction to Logic.* New York: Routledge, 1999.

Hanfling, Oswald. *Philosophy and Ordinary Language: The Bent and Genius of Our Tongue.* New York: Routledge, 2000.

Hare, John. *God's Call: Moral Realism, God's Commands, and Human Autonomy.* Grand Rapids: Eerdmans, 2001.

———. *The Moral Gap: Kantian Ethics, Human Limits, and God's Assistance.* Oxford: Oxford University Press, 1996.

———. *Why Bother Being Good? The Place of God in the Moral Life.* Downers Grove, Ill.: InterVarsity Press, 2002.

Harnack, Adolf von. *What Is Christianity?* New York: Harper, 1957.

Harrington, Daniel J., and James Keenan. *Jesus and Virtue Ethics: Building Bridges Between New Testament Studies and Moral Theology.* Lanham, Md.: Sheed & Ward, 2002.

Hart, Kevin. *The Trespass of the Sign: Deconstruction, Theology, and Philosophy.* Cambridge: Cambridge University Press, 1989.

Hartshorne, Charles. *Omnipotence and Other Theological Mistakes.* Albany: State University of New York Press, 1984.

Harvey, David. *The Condition of Postmodernity: An Enquiry into the Origins of Cultural Change.* Oxford: Blackwell, 1989.

Harvey, Van. *Feuerbach and the Interpretation of Religion.* Cambridge: Cambridge University Press, 1995.

Hasker, William. *The Emergent Self.* Ithaca: Cornell University Press, 1999.

———. *Metaphysics: Constructing a World View.* Downers Grove, Ill.: InterVarsity Press, 1983.

Hauerwas, Stanley. *The Peaceable Kingdom: A Primer in Christian Ethics.* Notre Dame: University of Notre Dame Press, 1983.

Healy, Nicholas. *Thomas Aquinas: Theologian of the Christian Life.* Burlington, Vt.: Ashgate, 2003.

Hebblethwaite, Brian. *The Ocean of Truth: A Defence of Objective Theism.* Cambridge: Cambridge University Press, 1988.

Heidegger, Martin. *Identity and Difference.* New York: Harper & Row, 1969.

Helm, Paul. *Eternal God: A Study of God Without Time.* Oxford: Oxford University Press, 1988.

———. *Faith and Understanding.* Edinburgh: Edinburgh University Press, 1997.

Hemming, Laurence. *Heidegger's Atheism: The Refusal of a Theological Voice.* Notre Dame: University of Notre Dame Press, 2002.

Hick, John. *Evil and the God of Love.* New York: Harper & Row, 1966.

———. *God Has Many Names.* Philadelphia: Westminster Press, 1982.

———, Dennis Okholm, and Timothy Phillips, eds. *Four Views on Salvation in a Pluralistic World.* Grand Rapids: Zondervan, 1996.

Howard-Snyder, Daniel. *The Evidential Argument from Evil.* Bloomington: Indiana University Press, 1996.

Hughes, Christopher. *On a Complex Theory of a Simple God: An Investigation in Aquinas' Philosophical Theology.* Ithaca: Cornell University Press, 1989.

Hughes, Gerald. *The Nature of God.* New York: Routledge, 1995.

Hume, David. *Dialogues Concerning Natural Religion.* New York: Routledge, 1991.

Husserl, Edmund. *Cartesian Meditations: An Introduction to Phenomenology.* The Hague: M. Nijhoff, 1960.

Huxley, T. H. *Agnosticism and Christianity, and Other Essays.* 1931. Reprint, Buffalo: Prometheus, 1992.

Hyman, Gavin. *The Predicament of Postmodern Theology: Radical Orthodoxy or Nihilist Textualism?* Louisville: Westminster John Knox Press, 2001.

Israel, Jonathan. *Radical Enlightenment: Philosophy and the Making of Modernity, 1650–1750.* Oxford: Oxford University Press, 2001.

Janik, Allan, and Stephen Toulmin. *Wittgenstein's Vienna.* New York: Simon & Schuster, 1973.

Johnson, Paul. *The Renaissance: A Short History.* New York: Modern Library, 2000.

Jones, L. Gregory, and Stephen E. Fowl, eds. *Rethinking Metaphysics.* Oxford: Blackwell, 1995.

Jones, Serene. *Feminist Theology: Cartographies of Grace.* Minneapolis: Fortress Press, 2000.

Jones, W. T., and Robert Fogelin. *A History of Western Philosophy: The Twentieth Century of Quine and Derrida*. Fort Worth: Harcourt Brace Jovanovich College Pub., 1980.

Jordan, Mark. *The Alleged Aristotelianism of Thomas Aquinas*. Toronto: Pontifical Institute of Medieval Studies, 1992.

Karnos, David, and Robert Shoemaker. *Falling in Love with Wisdom: American Philosophers Talk about Their Calling*. New York: Oxford University Press, 1993.

Kaufmann, Walter, ed. *Existentialism: From Dostoevsky to Sartre*. New York: Meridian, 1956.

Kelsey, Catherine. *Thinking about Christ with Schleiermacher*. Louisville: Westminster John Knox Press, 2003.

Kerr, Fergus. *Theology After Wittgenstein*. Oxford: Blackwell, 1986.

Kirkham, Richard. *Theories of Truth: A Critical Introduction*. Cambridge: MIT Press, 1992.

Kisiel, Theodore. *The Genesis of Heidegger's Being and Time*. Berkeley: University of California Press, 1993.

Kockelmans, J. *Phenomenology: The Philosophy of Edmund Husserl and Its Interpretation*. Garden City, N.Y.: Anchor, 1967.

Konyndyk, Kenneth. *Introductory Modal Logic*. Notre Dame: University of Notre Dame Press, 1986.

Koons, Robert. *Realism Regained: An Exact Theory of Causation, Teleology, and the Mind*. New York: Oxford University Press, 2000.

Kraye, Jill, ed. *The Cambridge Companion to Renaissance Humanism*. Cambridge: Cambridge University Press, 1996.

Kreeft, Peter, and Ronald Tacelli. *Handbook of Christian Apologetics: Hundreds of Answers to Crucial Questions*. Downers Grove, Ill.: InterVarsity Press, 1994.

Kretzmann, Norman. *The Metaphysics of Theism: Aquinas's Natural Theology in Summa Contra Gentiles I*. New York: Clarendon, 1997.

Kuehn, Manfred. *Kant: A Biography*. New York: Cambridge University Press, 2001.

Kuhn, Thomas. *The Structure of Scientific Revolutions*. Chicago: University of Chicago Press, 1970.

Kvanvig, Jonathan. *The Possibility of an All-Knowing God*. New York: St. Martin's Press, 1986.

Lehrer, Keith. *Thomas Reid*. New York: Routledge, 1989.

Le Poidevin, Robin. *Arguing for Atheism: An Introduction to the Philosophy of Religion*. New York: Routledge, 1996.

Levinas, Emmanuel. *Of God Who Comes to Mind*, translated by Bettina Bergo. Stanford: Stanford University Press, 1998.

Lewis, C. S. *Mere Christianity*. 1952. Reprint, New York: Touchstone, 1996.

———. *Miracles: A Preliminary Study*. New York: Macmillan, 1947.

Lindbeck, George. *The Nature of Doctrine: Religion and Theology in a Postliberal Age*. Philadelphia: Westminster Press, 1984.

———, et al. *The Nature of Confession: Evangelicals and Postliberals in Conversation*, edited by Timothy R. Phillips and Dennis L. Okholm. Downers Grove, Ill.: InterVarsity Press, 1996.

Lloyd, Genevieve. *The Man of Reason: "Male" and "Female" in Western Philosophy*. Minneapolis: University of Minnesota Press, 1984.

Loux, Michael J. *Metaphysics: A Contemporary Introduction*. New York: Routledge, 1998.

———. *Substance and Attribute: A Study in Ontology*. Boston: D. Reidel, 1978.

Lundin, Roger, Clarence Walhout, and Anthony Thiselton. *The Promise of Hermeneutics*. Grand Rapids: Eerdmans, 1999.

Lyotard, Jean-François. *The Postmodern Condition: A Report on Knowledge*. Minneapolis: University of Minnesota Press, 1984.

MacIntyre, Alasdair. *After Virtue: A Study in Moral Theory*. Notre Dame: University of Notre Dame Press, 1981.

———. *First Principles, Final Ends, and Contemporary Philosophical Issues*. Milwaukee: Marquette University Press, 1990.

———. *A Short History of Ethics*. New York: Macmillan, 1966.

Macquarrie, John. *Heidegger and Christianity*. London: SCM, 1994.

Marcuse, Herbert. *Eros and Civilization: A Philosophical Inquiry into Freud*. Boston: Beacon, 1966.

Marion, Jean-Luc. *Being Given: Toward a Phenomenology of Givenness*. Stanford: Stanford University Press, 2002.

———. *Cartesian Questions: Method and Metaphysics*. Chicago: University of Chicago Press, 1999.

———. *God Without Being: Hors-Texte*. Chicago: University of Chicago Press, 1991.

———. *Idol and Distance: Five Studies*. New York: Fordham University Press, 2001.

Markham, Ian. *Truth and the Reality of God: An Essay in Natural Theology*. Edinburgh: T. & T. Clark, 1998.

Marsh, James, John Caputo, and Merold Westphal. *Modernity and Its Discontents*. New York: Fordham University Press, 1992.

Martin, Francis. *The Feminist Question: Feminist Theology in the Light of Christian Tradition*. Grand Rapids: Eerdmans, 1994.

Martin, Glen. *From Nietzsche to Wittgenstein: The Problem of Truth and Nihilism in the Modern World*. New York: P. Lang, 1989.

McDonald, Paul. *History of the Concept of Mind: Speculations About Soul, Mind, and Spirit from Homer to Hume*. Burlington, Vt.: Ashgate, 2003.

McDonald, Scott. *Being and Goodness: The Concept of the Good in Metaphysics and Philosophical Theology*. Ithaca: Cornell University Press, 1991.

McFayden, Alistair. *The Call to Personhood: A Christian Theory of the Individual in Social Relationships*. New York: Cambridge University Press, 1990.

McInerny, Ralph. *St. Thomas Aquinas*. Boston: Twayne, 1977.

Mele, Alfred, ed. *The Oxford Handbook of Rationality*. New York: Oxford University Press, 2003.

Mellor, D. H. *The Facts of Causation*. New York: Routledge, 1995.

Menand, Louis. *The Metaphysical Club: A Story of Ideas in America*. London: Flamingo, 2001.

Middleton, Richard, and Brian Walsh. *Truth Is Stranger Than It Used to Be: Biblical Faith in a Postmodern Age*. Downers Grove, Ill.: InterVarsity Press, 1995.

Milbank, John. *Theology and Social Theory: Beyond Secular Reason*. Cambridge, Mass.: Blackwell, 1990.

Mitchell, Basil. *The Justification of Religious Belief*. New York: Oxford University Press, 1981.

Moltmann, Jürgen. *The Crucified God: The Cross of Christ as the Foundation and Criticism of Christian Theology*, translated by John Bowden and R. A. Wilson. New York: Harper & Row, 1974.

———. *Theology of Hope: On the Ground and the Implications of a Christian Eschatology*, translated by James W. Leitch. New York: Harper & Row, 1967.

Moore, Andrew. *Realism and Christian Faith: God, Grammar, and Meaning*. Cambridge: Cambridge University Press, 2003.

Moore, Stephen. *Poststructuralism and the New Testament: Derrida and Foucault at the Foot of the Cross*. Minneapolis: Fortress Press, 1994.

Moreland, James P. *Universals*. Montreal: McGill-Queen's University Press, 2001.

———, and William Lane Craig. *Philosophical Foundations for a Christian Worldview*. Downers Grove, Ill.: InterVarsity Press, 2003.

———, eds. *Naturalism: A Critical Analysis*. New York: Routledge, 2000.

Morris, Thomas. *Anselmian Explorations: Essays in Philosophical Theology*. Notre Dame: University of Notre Dame Press, 1987.

———. *Making Sense of It All: Pascal and the Meaning of Life*. Grand Rapids: Eerdmans, 1992.

———. *Our Idea of God: An Introduction to Philosophical Theology*. Downers Grove, Ill.: InterVarsity Press, 1991.

Mossner, Ernest. *The Life of David Hume*. Austin: University of Texas Press, 1954.

Mouw, Richard. *The God Who Commands*. Notre Dame: University of Notre Dame Press, 1990.

Mullen, John D. *Hard Thinking: The Reintroduction of Logic into Everyday Life*. Lanham, Md.: Rowman & Littlefield, 1995.

Muller, Richard. *Post-Reformation Reformed Dogmatics*. Grand Rapids: Baker, 1987.

Murray, Michael, ed. *Reason for the Hope Within*. Grand Rapids: Eerdmans, 1999.

Neiman, Susan. *Evil in Modern Thought: An Alternative History of Philosophy*. Princeton: Princeton University Press, 2002.

Neuhaus, Richard John. *Doing Well and Doing Good: The Challenge to the Christian Capitalist*. New York: Doubleday, 1992.

Ni, Peimin. *On Reid*. Belmont, Calif.: Wadsworth, 2002.

Nicholi, Armand. *The Question of God: C. S. Lewis and Sigmund Freud Debate God, Love, Sex, and the Meaning of Life*. New York: Free Press, 2002.

Noll, Mark. *The Princeton Theology, 1812–1921: Scripture, Science, and Theological Method from Archibald Alexander to Benjamin Breckinridge Warfield*. Grand Rapids: Baker, 2001.

Norton, David Fate, ed. *The Cambridge Companion to Hume*. Cambridge: Cambridge University Press, 1993.

Oberman, Heiko. *The Harvest of Medieval Theology: Gabriel Biel and Late Medieval Nominalism*. Cambridge: Harvard University Press, 1963.

O'Connell, Marvin R. *Blaise Pascal: Reasons of the Heart*. Grand Rapids: Eerdmans, 1997.

O'Connor, Timothy. *Persons and Causes: The Metaphysics of Free Will.* New York: Oxford University Press, 2000.

Olson, Alan. *Hegel and the Spirit: Philosophy as Pneumatology.* Princeton: Princeton University Press, 1992.

Olson, Roger, and Christopher Hall. *The Trinity.* Grand Rapids: Eerdmans, 2002.

O'Meara, Dominic J. *Neoplatonism and Christian Thought.* Norfolk, Va.: International Society for Neoplatonic Studies, 1981.

Ong, Walter J. *The Presence of the Word: Some Prolegomena for Cultural and Religious History.* New Haven: Yale University Press, 1967.

Ott, Hugo. *Martin Heidegger: A Political Life.* New York: HarperCollins, 1993.

Padgett, Alan G. *God, Eternity and the Nature of Time.* New York: St. Martin's Press, 1992.

Parsons, Susan, ed. *The Cambridge Companion to Feminist Theology.* New York: Cambridge University Press, 2002.

Paul, Ellen F., and Fred D. Miller. *Human Flourishing.* New York: Cambridge University Press, 1999.

Peacocke, Arthur. *Creation and the World of Science.* New York: Oxford University Press, 1979.

Pelikan, Jaroslav. *The Christian Tradition: A History of the Development of Doctrine.* Chicago: University of Chicago Press, 1974.

———. *Christianity and Classical Culture: The Metamorphosis of Natural Theology in the Christian Encounter with Hellenism.* New Haven: Yale University Press, 1993.

Peterson, Michael. *God and Evil: An Introduction to the Issues.* Boulder, Colo.: Westview, 1998.

Phillips, D. Z. *Wittgenstein and Religion.* New York: St. Martin's Press, 1993.

———, ed. *The Concept of Prayer.* New York: Schocken, 1966.

———, and Timothy Tessin, eds. *Religion without Transcendence?* New York: St. Martin's Press, 1997.

Pinckaers, Servais. *The Pursuit of Happiness—God's Way: Living the Beatitudes.* New York: Alba House, 1998.

Pinnock, Clark, et al. *The Openness of God: A Biblical Challenge to the Traditional Understanding of God.* Downers Grove, Ill.: InterVarsity Press, 1994.

Placher, William C. *The Domestication of Transcendence: How Modern Thinking About God Went Wrong.* Louisville: Westminster John Knox Press, 1996.

Plantinga, Alvin. *The Analytic Theist: An Alvin Plantinga Reader,* edited by James F. Sennett. Grand Rapids: Eerdmans, 1998.

———. *Essays in the Metaphysics of Modality,* edited by Matthew Davidson. New York: Oxford University Press, 2003.

———. *God, Freedom, and Evil.* 1974. Reprint, Grand Rapids: Eerdmans, 1977.

———. *The Nature of Necessity.* Oxford: Clarendon, 1974.

———. *Warrant: The Current Debate.* New York: Oxford University Press, 1993.

———. *Warranted Christian Belief.* New York: Oxford University Press, 2000.

———. *Warrant and Proper Function.* New York: Oxford University Press, 1993.

———, and Nicholas Wolterstorff, eds. *Faith and Rationality: Reason and Belief in God.* Notre Dame: University of Notre Dame Press, 1983.

Polkinghorne, John C. *The Faith of a Physicist: Reflections of a Bottom-Up Thinker.* Princeton: Princeton University Press, 1994.

Pope John Paul II. *Fides et Ratio.* Washington, D.C.: United States Catholic Conference, 1998.

Porter, Roy. *The Enlightenment.* New York: Palgrave, 2001.

Power, David. *Sacrament: The Language of God's Giving.* New York: Crossroad, 1999.

Prado, C. G. *A House Divided: Comparing Analytic and Continental Philosophy.* Amherst, N.Y.: Humanity Books, 2003.

Quinn, Philip. *Divine Commands and Moral Requirements.* Oxford: Clarendon, 1978.

———, ed. "Kant's Philosophy of Religion." Special issue, *Faith and Philosophy* 17, no. 4.

———, and Kevin Meeker, eds. *The Philosophical Challenge of Religious Diversity.* New York: Oxford University Press, 2000.

Quinton, Anthony. *Hume.* New York: Routledge, 1999.

Ratzsch, Del. *Nature, Design, and Science: The Status of Design in Natural Science.* Albany: State University of New York Press, 2001.

Rea, Michael. *World Without Design: The Ontological Consequence of Naturalism.* New York: Clarendon, 2002.

Ricoeur, Paul. *Figuring the Sacred: Religion, Narrative, and Imagination,* edited by Mark I. Wallace. Minneapolis: Fortress Press, 1995.

———. *Oneself as Another,* translated by Kathleen Blamey. Chicago: University of Chicago Press, 1992.

Ringe, Sharon. *Wisdom's Friends: Community and Christology in the Fourth Gospel.* Louisville: Westminster John Knox Press, 1999.

Rist, John. *Augustine: Ancient Thought Baptized.* New York: Cambridge University Press, 1994.

———. *Platonism and Its Christian Heritage.* London: Variorum Reprints, 1985.

———. *The Stoics.* Berkeley: University of California Press, 1978.

Rorem, Paul. *Pseudo-Dionysius: An Introduction to the Texts and Commentary on Their Influence.* New York: Oxford University Press, 1993.

Rorty, Richard. *Consequences of Pragmatism: Essays, 1972–1980.* Minneapolis: University of Minnesota Press, 1982.

———. *Objectivity, Relativism and Truth.* New York: Cambridge University Press, 1991.

———. *Philosophy and the Mirror of Nature.* Princeton: Princeton University Press, 1979.

Rouner, Leroy, ed. *Is There a Human Nature?* Notre Dame: University of Notre Dame Press, 1997.

Russell, Bertrand. *Why I Am Not a Christian, and Other Essays on Religion and Related Subjects.* New York: Simon & Schuster, 1957.

Russell, Letty M., ed. *Feminist Interpretation of the Bible.* Philadelphia: Westminster, 1985.

Rutherford, Donald. *Leibniz and the Rational Order of Nature.* New York: Cambridge University Press, 1995.

Sandbach, F. H. *The Stoics.* New York: Norton, 1975.

Sanders, John. *The God Who Risks: A Theology of Providence.* Downers Grove, Ill.: InterVarsity Press, 1998.

Saussure, Ferdinand de. *Course in General Linguistics*, translated by Wade Baskin. New York: Philosophical Library, 1959.

Schmitt, Frederick. *Truth: A Primer.* Boulder, Colo.: Westview Press, 1995.

Schor, Naomi, and Elizabeth Weed. *The Essential Difference.* Bloomington: Indiana University Press, 1994.

Scruton, Roger. *Kant: A Very Short Introduction.* New York: Oxford University Press, 2001.

Searle, John. *The Construction of Social Reality.* New York: Free Press, 1995.

Sessions, William Lad. *The Concept of Faith: A Philosophical Investigation.* Ithaca: Cornell University Press, 1994.

———. *Reading Hume's Dialogues: A Veneration for True Religion.* Bloomington: Indiana University Press, 2002.

Seymour, Charles Steven. *A Theodicy of Hell.* Boston: Kluwer Academic, 2000.

Shanks, Andrew. *Hegel's Political Theology.* New York: Cambridge University Press, 1991.

Shaw, Gregory. *Theurgy and the Soul: The Neoplatonism of Iamblichus.* University Park, Pa.: Pennsylvania State University Press, 1995.

Schrag, Calvin. *The Self After Postmodernity.* New Haven: Yale University Press, 1997.

Shults, LeRon. *Reforming Theological Anthropology: After the Philosophical Turn to Relationality.* Grand Rapids: Eerdmans, 2003.

Singer, Peter. *Hegel: A Very Short Introduction.* New York: Oxford University Press, 2001.

———. *Marx.* New York: Hill & Wang, 1980.

Smith, James K. A. *The Fall of Interpretation: Philosophical Foundations for a Creational Hermeneutic.* Downers Grove, Ill.: InterVarsity Press, 2000.

———. *Speech and Theology: Language and the Logic of Incarnation.* New York: Routledge, 2002.

Sobosan, Jeffrey. *Romancing the Universe: Theology, Cosmology, and Science.* Grand Rapids: Eerdmans, 1999.

Sokolowski, Robert. *Introduction to Phenomenology.* New York: Cambridge University Press, 2000.

Solomon, Robert C. *From Rationalism to Existentialism: The Existentialists and Their Nineteenth-Century Backgrounds.* New York: Harper & Row, 1972.

———. *A Passion for Wisdom: A Very Brief History of Philosophy.* New York: Oxford University Press, 1997.

Sorrell, Tom. *Descartes: A Very Short Introduction.* 1987. Reprint, New York: Oxford University Press, 2000.

Soskice, Janet Martin. *Metaphor and Religious Language.* New York: Clarendon, 1985.

Southern, R. W. *Saint Anselm: A Portrait in a Landscape.* New York: Cambridge University Press, 1990.

Spiegelberg, Herbert. *The Phenomenological Movement: A Historical Introduction.* The Hague: M. Nijhoff, 1982.

Springsted, Eric. *The Act of Faith: Christian Faith and the Moral Self.* Grand Rapids: Eerdmans, 2002.

Stevenson, Leslie, and David Haberman. *Ten Theories of Human Nature.* New York: Oxford University Press, 1998.

Stich, Stephen, and Ted Warfield, eds. *The Blackwell Guide to Philosophy of Mind.* Malden, Mass.: Blackwell, 2003.

Stiver, Dan R. *The Philosophy of Religious Language: Sign, Symbol, and Story.* Cambridge, Mass.: Blackwell, 1996.

Stock, Brian. *Augustine the Reader: Meditation, Self-Knowledge, and the Ethics of Interpretation.* Cambridge: Harvard University Press, 1996.

Stump, Eleonore. *Aquinas*. New York: Routledge, 2003.

———, and Norman Kretzmann, eds. *The Cambridge Companion to Augustine*. New York: Cambridge University Press, 2001.

Swinburne, Richard. *The Christian God*. New York: Clarendon, 1994.

———. *The Coherence of Theism*. Oxford: Clarendon, 1977.

———. *The Concept of Miracle*. New York: St Martin's Press, 1970.

———. *The Evolution of the Soul*. New York: Clarendon, 1986.

———. *The Existence of God*. New York: Clarendon, 1979.

———. *Miracles*. London: Macmillan, 1989.

———. *Revelation: From Metaphor to Analogy*. Oxford: Clarendon, 1992.

———. *Simplicity as Evidence of Truth*. Milwaukee: Marquette University Press, 1997.

Taliaferro, Charles. *Consciousness and the Mind of God*. New York: Cambridge University Press, 1994.

Tanner, Michael. *Nietzsche*. New York: Oxford University Press, 1994.

Taylor, C. C. W., and R. M. Hare, eds. *Greek Philosophers*. New York: Oxford University Press, 1999.

Taylor, Charles. *Sources of the Self: The Making of the Modern Identity*. Cambridge: Harvard University Press, 1989.

———. *Varieties of Religion Today: William James Revisited*. Cambridge: Harvard University Press, 2002.

Taylor, Mark C. *Erring: A Postmodern A/Theology*. Chicago: University of Chicago Press, 1984.

Thiselton, Anthony. *New Horizons in Hermeneutics*. Grand Rapids: Zondervan, 1992.

Torrance, Thomas F. *Divine and Contingent Order*. Edinburgh: T. & T. Clark, 1998.

Trible, Phyllis. *Texts of Terror: Literary-Feminist Readings of Biblical Narratives*. Philadelphia: Fortress Press, 1984.

Trigg, Roger. *Ideas of Human Nature: An Historical Introduction*. New York: Blackwell, 1988.

Turner, James. *Without God, Without Creed: The Origins of Unbelief in America*. Baltimore: Johns Hopkins University Press, 1985.

Twiss, Sumner, and Walter Conser, eds. *Experience of the Sacred: Readings in the Phenomenology of Religion*. Hanover, N.H.: University Press of New England, 1992.

Van Buren, John. *The Young Heidegger: Rumor of the Hidden King*. Bloomington: Indiana University Press, 1994.

Vanhoozer, Kevin. *Is There a Meaning in This Text? The Bible, the Reader, and the Morality of Literary Knowledge*. Grand Rapids: Zondervan, 1998.

Vanier, Jean. *Happiness: A Guide to a Good Life: Aristotle for the New Century*. New York: Arcade, 2001.

Van Inwagen, Peter, and Dean Zimmerman. *Metaphysics: The Big Questions*. Malden, Mass.: Blackwell, 1998.

Volf, Miroslav. *Exclusion and Embrace: A Theological Exploration of Identity, Otherness, and Reconciliation*. Nashville: Abingdon, 1996.

Wainwright, William. *Reason and the Heart: A Prolegomenon to a Critique of Passional Reason*. Ithaca: Cornell University Press, 1995.

Wallace, Mark. *Fragments of the Spirit: Nature, Violence, and the Renewal of Creation*. New York: Continuum, 1996.

Wallace, Stan, ed. *Does God Exist? The Craig-Flew Debate*. Burlington, Vt.: Ashgate, 2002.

Walls, Jerry. *Hell: The Logic of Damnation*. Notre Dame: University of Notre Dame Press, 1992.

Ward, Tim. *Word and Supplement: Speech Acts, Biblical Texts, and the Sufficiency of Scripture*. New York: Oxford University Press, 2002.

Warner, Richard, and Tadeusz Szubka, eds. *The Mind-Body Problem: A Guide to the Current Debate*. Oxford: Blackwell, 1994.

Watson, Natalie. *Feminist Theology*. Grand Rapids: Eerdmans, 2003.

Watson, Richard. *Cogito, Ergo Sum: The Life of René Descartes*. Boston: David R. Godine, 2002.

West, Cornel. *The Cornel West Reader*. New York: Basic Civitas Books, 2000.

Westphal, Merold. *Becoming a Self: A Reading of Kierkegaard's Concluding Unscientific Postscript*. West Lafayette, Ind.: Purdue University Press, 1996.

———. *Overcoming Onto-Theology: Toward a Postmodern Christian Faith*. New York: Fordham University Press, 2001.

———. *Suspicion and Faith: The Religious Uses of Modern Atheism*. Grand Rapids: Eerdmans, 1993.

———, ed. *Postmodern Philosophy and Christian Thought*. Bloomington: Indiana University Press, 1999.

Wierenga, Edward. *The Nature of God: An Inquiry into Divine Attributes*. Ithaca: Cornell University Press, 1989.

Wilcox, Donald J. *In Search of God and Self: Renaissance and Reformation Thought*. Boston: Houghton Mifflin, 1975.

Williams, Thomas, ed. *The Cambridge Companion to Duns Scotus.* New York: Cambridge University Press, 2003.

Wing, Adrien, ed. *Critical Race Feminism: A Reader.* New York: New York University Press, 1997.

Winston, David. *Logos and Mystical Theology in Philo of Alexandria.* Hoboken, N.J.: Hebrew Union College Press, 1985.

Wolter, Allan, and Marilyn McCord Adams, eds. *The Philosophical Theology of Duns Scotus.* Ithaca: Cornell University Press, 1990.

Wolterstorff, Nicholas. *Art in Action: Toward a Christian Aesthetic.* Grand Rapids: Eerdmans, 1980.

———. *Divine Discourse: Philosophical Reflections on the Claim That God Speaks.* New York: Cambridge University Press, 1995.

———. "God Everlasting," in *God and the Good,* ed. Clifton Orlebeke and Lewis Smedes. Grand Rapids: Eerdmans, 1975.

———. *Lament for a Son.* Grand Rapids: Eerdmans, 1987.

———. *Reason within the Bounds of Religion.* Grand Rapids: Eerdmans, 1976.

———. *Thomas Reid and the Story of Epistemology.* New York: Cambridge University Press, 2001.

———. *Until Justice and Peace Embrace.* Grand Rapids: Eerdmans, 1983.

Wood, Allan. *Kant's Rational Theology.* Ithaca: Cornell University Press, 1978.

Wood, W. Jay. *Epistemology: Becoming Intellectually Virtuous.* Downers Grove, Ill.: InterVarsity Press, 1998.

Woods, John. *Argument: Critical Thinking, Logic and the Fallacies.* Toronto: Prentice-Hall, 2000.

Yandell, Keith. *Hume's "Inexplicable Mystery": His Views on Religion.* Philadelphia: Temple University Press, 1990.

Yong, Amos. *Beyond the Impasse: Toward a Pneumatological Theology of Religions.* Grand Rapids: Baker Academic, 2003.

Zagzebski, Linda, ed. *Rational Faith: Catholic Responses to Reformed Epistemology.* Notre Dame: University of Notre Dame Press, 1993.

Cross-Reference Index